# PERSONS, BEHAVIOR, AND THE WORLD

## The Descriptive Psychology Approach

### Mary McDermott Shideler

UNIVERSITY
PRESS OF
AMERICA

LANHAM • NEW YORK • LONDON

Copyright © **1988** by

**University Press of America,® Inc.**

4720 Boston Way
Lanham, MD 20706

3 Henrietta Street
London WC2E 8LU England

British Cataloging in Publication Information Available

**Library of Congress Cataloging-in-Publication Data**

Shideler, Mary McDermott.
Persons, behavior, and the world.
Bibliography: p. Includes index.
1. Descriptive psychology. I. Title.
BF39.8.S53     1988     150     87–31463 CIP
ISBN 0–8191–6786–X (alk. paper)
ISBN 0–8191–6787–8 (pbk. : alk. paper)

Thank you, Peter

# Table of Contents

# ACKNOWLEDGEMENTS

Peter G. Ossorio has graciously given me permission to quote herein material from all books copyrighted by him or by the Linguistic Research Institute to date, charts and other material from transcripts of presentations at conferences of The Society for Descriptive Psychology, and material from our conversations.

Octave from "Sonnet to Gath" by Edna St. Vincent Millay. From *Collected Poems*, Harper & Row. Copyright © 1928, 1955 by Edna St. Vincent Millay and Norma Millay Ellis. Reprinted by permission.

# INTRODUCTION

The instruction of the King of Hearts to the White Rabbit, "Begin at the beginning and go on till you come to the end; then stop," is in general sound advice when it comes to reading books. But there are exceptions, and this book may be one of them. I wrote it as I would want to read it, beginning with the structure of the Descriptive Psychology conceptual system—the "Person Concept" (Parts I-III)—then going on to consider some of its major practical applications and extensions (Parts IV-VI). Yet there may be readers who will find it more satisfactory to start with the practical applications, go on to the end, and only after that turn to the beginning.

As encouragement to anyone who becomes bogged down by a sentence or section that seems unclear, it is not imperative to master each step before proceeding to the next. Initially, it is more important to develop a sense of the structure, as preparation for mastering the detail that must follow if the structure is to be not merely a shell.

The best way to achieve that overview is unabashedly to skim on the first reading, like standing away from a painting to get a general impression of it before attending

1

to its specific features. A particular reason for this procedure is that we shall be dealing not only with logical and
causal relations of a linear kind, but also with non-linear,
part-whole relations. We shall be working with a conceptual system, and we acquire concepts—*a fortiori* conceptual systems—by practice and experience in using them,
in contrast to the ways that we assimilate information by
observation and thinking. The practice comes in the second
half of the book; in the first half, I am introducing what we
shall be practising with.

---

According to its official definition, the Person Concept of Descriptive Psychology is "a set of systematically
related distinctions designed to provide formal access to all
the facts and possible facts about persons and behavior—and therefore about everything else as well."[1] As
such, it is deeply concerned with the great, perennial questions of why we do what we do, how we become what we
are, in what ways we differ and are alike, and what kind of
world we live in. Its emphasis, however, is not on providing unique answers. Instead, it is primarily directed toward
systematizing the possible answers and the possibilities of
answering. In using it, we shall cultivate our abilities to see
with our own eyes, hear with our own ears, and understand
with our own minds, thus becoming increasingly competent
in answering such questions for ourselves, rather than pas-
sively (or eagerly) subscribing to one of the ready-made answers that are being offered on every corner. It is more a
way of looking at the world than a specification of what to
see.

At various times, Descriptive Psychology has been
compared with a set of tools, a painter's palette, a
geometry, a bookkeeping system, and a language. A better

---

[1]Ossorio, "Cognition", p.2.

analogy is with a numerical system and its operations of addition, subtraction, multiplication, and division, which in combination give us access to the whole domain of arithmetic. Still better is the analogy with a game such as chess, with its rules for how that game is to be played if it is to be **that** game. For example, in chess, a bishop is defined as a piece that is eligible to move only in a certain way, but in no way is that definition to be taken as a proposition that could be verified or falsified. Similarly, the Descriptive Psychology definition of—let us say—"person" specifies how that term is used in the "game" of Descriptive Psychology, and to someone who objects, "But that's not what a person *is*," the reply must be, "Perhaps not, perhaps so. Either way, that is one of the rules of *this* game."

Learning a language, a numerical system, a game, can be important for practical purposes or undertaken for their own sakes. Equally important, however, are what they contribute to the sensitivity of our perceptions, the precision of our thinking, and the power and flexibility of our responses. So also with Descriptive Psychology. Its use clarifies our appreciation of persons and the world, and of the comprehensive and coherent relationships among them. It enables us to widen our horizons by opening new possibilities for approaching all that is. And the elegance with which its elements are interwoven offers a genuinely aesthetic pleasure.

The resources of Descriptive Psychology—its conceptual structure and methodologies—are not mastered overnight, nor does their mastery consist of absorbing information or memorizing formulas and diagrams. The rules and diagrams and schemas, formulas and outlines and maxims, are simply aids toward the development of competence in making distinctions and tracing relationships. What really matters is developing the skills.

Make no mistake: acquiring competence in these conceptual-notational skills is as laborious as acquiring competence in chess or a language, or in mathematical or carpentry skills. There is no standard way of talking about concepts or methods that will guarantee success in acquiring them. For the most part, however, mastering the Person Concept is not as arduous as mastering entirely new skills, because we are already competent in many of those which it requires. Often we shall find ourselves in the position of Molière's character who as an adult discovered, to his astonished delight, that for his whole life he had been speaking prose. At times, the Descriptive Psychology codifications will give new meaning to what we have been doing—and doing right—all along. At other times, we may discover how and why things have gone wrong in our thinking, or in our personal and social relationships from individual to international, and discover clues as to how we might amend them.

---

Descriptive Psychology is a conceptual system, and two examples may help to clarify what a conceptual system is and is not. The first is the parametric analysis of color into the parameters hue, saturation, and intensity. With these parameters, we can identify any color and differentiate any two or more colors with great precision; and any color, with no exceptions, can be so analyzed. But learning to use those concepts, i.e., to act on those distinctions, is a matter of developing competence by practice and experience, rather than of simply accumulating data as we do when we learn the dates of wars or the physical geography of a country. Historically, the color-cone method of analyzing colors has been extremely useful, but it is not and cannot be true or false. Nor is it the only possible way of differentiating colors.

A set of distinctions cannot have truth value. It can be true that this book is red and that book is blue, but merely distinguishing red from blue, and acting on that distinction, is something we do or do not do. It does not carry any truth claims, even though we can formulate statements, such as "Red is different from blue", that will be true or false. Making distinctions and making statements are not the same, and a creature that has no verbal language can yet act on distinctions. The distinctions we make may be useful or not useful for a given purpose, and may be used clumsily or skillfully, appropriately or inappropriately, but the distinctions themselves, the concepts, cannot be true or false.

For our second example, any language exhibits a conceptual structure. A language supplies us with a set of distinctions, as between "book" and "table", "abstract" and "concrete", "before" and "after". Once we have mastered a given language, we can say whatever we please within the limits of its conceptual resources, and even increase those resources as by inventing new words or phrases to identify new distinctions. (Physical scientists are noted for doing this, e.g., quark, random access, etc.)

A language as such, however, cannot have truth value. It is simply "a form of behavior in which we explicitly make certain distinctions; and we have those distinctions because we engage in forms of behavior which involve making those distinctions and acting accordingly".[2] With English and many other languages, we can generate technical reports, create fiction or poetry, issue commands or instructions, make statements and ask questions, warn and remind, and use it for a variety of other purposes, including the reflexive use of language to analyze itself. And we can use it frequently or seldom, to confuse or to clarify, to lie or speak honestly.

Learning a theory can be likened to learning a language from the phrase books that travellers sometimes carry. As long as we do not need to say or understand more than the book (or the theory) provides for, we are in fine

---

[2]Ossorio, transcript, 11 December 75, p.7.

shape, but we cannot go further. Thus some things can be said easily in Hopi but only with difficulty in English, if at all, and other things easily in English but not in Hopi. Or to take another example, in some of the mechanistic psychological theories, the concept "person" has no place. Other theories have no place for the concept "the unconscious"; still others exclude "spirituality", or "racial memory", or "secondary reinforcement". When we want or need to go beyond a particular theory, as in attempts to compare and contrast different theories or to generate new descriptions, we shall need another conceptual system, and hence language, one that will be suitable for such tasks, as the color cone is suitable for distinguishing and comparing colors, and geometry is suitable for calculating areas.

Back of Descriptive Psychology lies a profound dissatisfaction with current psychological theories, and an even more profound dissatisfaction with psychological methodologies of the past and present. In their place, Peter G. Ossorio and his associates have proposed making a fresh start. They have proceeded not with assumptions or statements of fact, but with conceptual formulations and systematically related methodologies.[3] One of the ways of expressing the bases for this approach is by slogans, and a slogan, it should be noted, is not a proposition or assumption but a statement of a procedure. It does not incorporate any truth claims or necessarily carry any metaphysical implications.

One of the fundamental procedural slogans in Descriptive Psychology is, "The world makes sense, and so do people."[4]—which is how most of us live most of the time,

---

[3]See Ossorio, *"What Actually Happens"*, pp. ix-xvii, and "An Overview of Descriptive Psychology".

[4]Ossorio, "An Overview of Descriptive Psychology," p. 26.

anyway. Indeed, how could we live as human beings if we did not live by that? *What* sense the world and people make, and *how* they make sense, are related questions that have engaged philosophers, scientists, and others for millenia, and are engaging Descriptive Psychologists as well. But we do not need to wait for philosophic and scientific questions to be definitively answered, or for a divine revelation of ultimate truth, to make sense out of what we are observing and doing now.

Another slogan is, "It's one world".5 That is, in Descriptive Psychology we take it that everything is related to everything else, and one of our crucial tasks is to present a conceptual formulation of how things can fit together. In order to do so, we must make distinctions, and if we make inappropriate ones, we shall be led into blind alleys, confusions, contradictions, fragmentations, nonsense. If we make appropriate ones, we can not only see how things fit together, but also be able to move easily from any one thing or domain to another. We shall have a coherent system that is both all-inclusive and elegant.

A third slogan is, "Things are what they are and not something else instead".6 For example, persons are persons, to be understood and explained in person terms, not reducing them to agglomerations of chemicals, or to organisms or bundles of conditioned reflexes or anything else. Human behavior can indeed be described in terms of physical movements in space and time, but in Descriptive Psychology, behavior is not merely a set of movements but—as we shall see—something more complex and meaningful. If we are to deal with what things are in themselves, however, we shall sometimes have to make new distinctions, or reorganize some which we already make, and we must be able to show how they are systematically related.

---

5Ibid., p. 27.
6Ibid., p. 28.

A fourth slogan is perhaps the most interesting: "Don't count on the world's being simpler than it has to be".[7] It is tempting to systematize our understanding of what is going on around and in us by appealing to a few general principles. It is quite possible that by so doing, we shall lose far more than we gain. Over-simplifying can impoverish our observation and thinking.

For a number of years, people have been using the Descriptive Psychology formulation of the Person Concept in a wide variety of areas, and have found that its application stretches from the esoteric reaches of computer science to the intricacies of social organizations and multicultural interactions, and to the profundities of spirituality, as well as to psychotherapy, education, criminal investigation, the nature of consciousness, and everyday life. Many if not most of us yearn to make some kind of sense out of the whole of our experience, past, present, and to come. With this resource, we can do so without limiting ourselves in advance to a theory, or crushing our individual experience out of shape to make it fit into a simplistic framework. At the same time, it does full justice to the incredible complexity and richness of persons, behavior, and the world.

---

I have not attempted to retain consistently Dr Ossorio's "canonical" formulation of Descriptive Psychology, although I have worked closely with him to ensure technical accuracy. He is not, however, responsible for anything herein except direct quotations, not even for how I have used them. Neither is this a final or definitive formulation of Descriptive Psychology. It cannot be, because the system is still being developed and refined. To take only one example, the maxims are currently being elaborated and substantially increased beyond the nine that were originally

---

[7]Ibid.

ever, will in general supplement rather than supplant my introduction.

---

**A Note on Style.** It is only within very recent years that the noun "man" and the pronoun "he" have been taken by anyone as exclusively masculine in their reference. Before that, through the whole development of the English language, "man" and "he" were universally understood either as inclusively generic, like the Latin **homo**, or as masculine (the Latin **vir**), and I do not know of any evidence that during those many centuries, people had difficulty distinguishing whether **homo** or **vir** was meant in any particular situation. "Woman" and "she", however, have always been exclusively feminine. I have discussed at length with a number of people the possibility of using one of the "he and/or she" forms that are presently fashionable, but awkward in whatever variation, and have decided to keep to the traditional generic "man" and "he", trusting to the intelligence and good will of my readers to take that usage as non-sexist. Therefore, every use of the generic "man" and "he" should be taken as followed by the parenthetical "or she or it or they".

**A Note on References.** All my conferences with Dr Ossorio were recorded and transcribed. Quotations taken from those transcripts are identified in the footnotes by their date and page number. In footnote references to *"What Actually Happens"*, *Clinical Topics*, and *Positive Health and Transcendental Theories*, the relevant materials are so numerous and often so scattered that I can only refer the reader to their indexes. *Personality and Personality Theories* is not indexed, so references are to the dates of the seminars.

Footnotes prefaced by "see" are inserted for persons who wish to follow the presentation here with more de-

who wish to follow the presentation here with more detailed discussions in other sources.

––––––––––––––––

This book began as a collaboration with Dan Popov, and an early draft for trial use of Parts I-III bore both our names as joint authors. When he became unable to continue with the enterprise, I asked the late Jan Vanderburgh to join me, and the draft for trial use of the entire book carries all our names. Unfortunately, she too was impelled by circumstances to abandon the project. The three of us agreed, therefore, that this extensive and radical revision of the earlier version should carry my name as the sole author, and that I should take sole responsibility for it. I am exceedingly grateful to both for their contributions to this study, and regret that they could not play a larger part in its preparation.

My deepest gratitude goes to Peter G. Ossorio of the University of Colorado at Boulder, the founder of Descriptive Psychology and my mentor and friend, who has given lavishly of his time to critiquing the manuscript through many stages. Next, I happily acknowledge my debt to those of his colleagues and former students whose use of the Person Concept in a wide range of fields has contributed materially to its development. I cannot name them all, but notable among them—in addition to Dan Popov and Jan Vanderburgh—are Raymond M. Bergner, Earlene K. Busch, Keith E. Davis, H. Joel Jeffrey, Jane Littmann, Thomas O. Mitchell, Anthony O. Putman, Carolyn A. Zeiger, and H. Paul Zeiger.

My heartfelt thanks go also to Shirley Michaels, who designed and computer-set the book, but who is not responsible for typographical or other errors that survived my copy-editing and proof-reading.

# PART I

# DESCRIBING BEHAVIOR

# CHAPTER 1

# THE BEHAVIOR FORMULA[1]

The classic way to begin a discussion of behavior is by defining what we are talking about. What do we include in the term "behavior" and what do we exclude? If we are timorous, typically our definition will be so vague and all-inclusive that it fails to communicate the concept of behavior. If we are bold, our definition may be specific and vigorous, but so narrow in its reference as to be misleading: whatever is being called "behavior" is not what most of us mean by that term, and particularly not "the behavior of persons". Between these lie so many other definitions, none generally satisfactory, that finally we begin to wonder whether behavior is so amorphous that it cannot be defined at all. Or we might conclude that concocting a definition is simply not a good way to identify what "behavior" is.

A similar problem arises in other connections. Take, for example, the difficulty of defining a chair. A dictionary[2] defines it as "a seat, usually movable, for one person.

---

[1]See Ossorio, "Conceptual-Notational Devices" and *Personality and Personality Theories*, 13-14 July 1977.

[2]Webster's New International Dictionary, unabridged, second edition.

It usually has four legs and a back, and may have arms."
"Usually", twice repeated? "May or may not"? What good
is this? What about bean-bag chairs? Or a section of a log
pushed against a boulder? Or a large, overstuffed seat that
will accommodate two people if they are closely embrac-
ing? Or a high bar stool with a low back? Are they, or are
they not, properly called "chairs"? Nothing in the definition
will tell us. As a definition, it is singularly unhelpful because it does not include all chairs without exception, or
unambiguously exclude all non-chairs.

Notice, however, that we do not need to be able to
construct an impeccable definition of a chair in order to
recognize one, buy one, sit in one, or differentiate a chair
from a sofa, a bench, or a pillow deposited on the floor.
Because we are competent in the use of the concept
"chair", we get along very nicely without an unambiguous
definition, and are no worse off for not having one. Almost
without thinking, we distinguish a big chair from a small
one, a brown chair from a blue one, one upheld with legs
from another with a pedestal, a wooden chair from an up-
holstered one, and so on. So doing, we are likely to be engaged in what is called parametric analysis, often doing it
with considerable skill even though we do not realize that
this is what we are doing.

What a **parametric analysis** is can best be introduced
in Dr Ossorio's own words:

> In formulating a parametric analysis, we
> formulate the possibilities of what a phenomenon
> could be and still be a thing of that kind—a color,
> a chair, a behavior. Similarly, when we include a
> given parameter in a parametric analysis, we are
> collecting a set of possibilities. For example, if
> we are including length as a parameter of "table",
> we are including all the possibilities that we dis-
> tinguish of what the length of a table could be.

Hence in giving a description of the length of a given table, we need only to specify which of the possible lengths is the case for that table—for example, thirty-one inches.

The set of possibilities collected together under a given parameter is conventionally designated as the "values" of that parameter. This usage parallels the notion of the values of a variable in mathematical and logical systems. Thus, specifying possibilities in the context of a parametric analysis has come to be known as "plugging in values" of parameters.[3]

The parametric analysis of "chair" would include, among other parameters, the number of legs and arms, the size and shape of the seat and back, and the materials of which it is made. The usual parametric analysis of color, as we noted earlier, is performed using the parameters hue, saturation, and intensity. Likewise, daily and unreflectively—although perhaps unsystematically—we use the method of parametric analysis in differentiating one behavior from another (e.g., running a race from running away from a sinister dog), and to check on whether we understand a particular episode of behavior, and if not, where we need to assign values (e.g., "I know what she did but I don't understand why she did it," or "What did he actually achieve by going there?").

We are likely to use a more or less explicit parametric analysis of behavior only when something about that behavior is problematic. When we do need it, however, we shall use it far more effectively if we are familiar with the method, and not only identify explicitly the parameters of behavior, but also grasp how those parameters are systematically related to one another.

---

[3]Peter G. Ossorio, transcript, 16 February 1984.

Descriptive Psychology uses the eight parameters of a **behavior formula**[4] to specify how one behavior as such is similar to or different from another: *Identity, Want, Know, Know-how, Performance, Achievement, Person Characteristics,* and *Significance.* Taking them one by one:

**Identity (I)** is the aspect of behavior having to do with the identity of the individual engaging in that behavior. Behavior does not occur in the abstract, no matter how often or how authoritatively we speak of "aggressive behavior" or "considerate behavior" or "fear behavior".

What we have instead are Jane behaving aggressively, or Jerry performing a considerate act, or Joe reacting fearfully. Indeed, even if Jane, Jerry, and Joe all were doing what might be called "the same thing", like adding up the same column of figures, in the Descriptive Psychology game, the behaviors would be significantly different in that they were performed by the three different persons. The first of the eight parameters of behavior, the identity of the behaver, is different in each case. We can identify who is behaving by name, or by a description, or by pointing, or by some other means: "Joe", or "the girl over there", or "our next-door neighbor", or "whoever painted the picture".

The **Want (W)** parameter is the aspect having to do with the state of affairs that the behavior is designed to achieve, that is, what the person wants. And wants, desires, purposes, intentions—all these are familiar terms that we use to designate what a person's behavior is directed toward. When we know what this person wants to achieve, we are well on our way to understanding his behavior, and to being able to describe that behavior as like or unlike any other behavior.

---

[4]Ossorio, "Outline of Descriptive Psychology".

Mere movement can be random or reflexive, but behavior is distinguished by being goal-directed, purposive, intentional. The behaver wants something, even when what he wants is not clear at first glance or after the fifth hard look.

If, in a crowded hotel lobby, we observe Judd singing an aria from *Rigoletto* while standing on his head and playing a tambourine, our immediate reaction is likely to be, "Why in heaven's name is he doing that here? What is his reason?" Is he crazy (although even crazies have their reasons)? Or is he craving attention, or advertising an entertainment, or paying off a bet? It will be a different behavior in each of these cases. We may never find out what he wants to achieve by going through this elaborately coordinated performance, but we do know that he must be wanting something. He is not doing it at random or reflexively.

The **Know (K)** parameter has to do with the distinctions the behaver is acting upon. Certainly Judd is distinguishing between this and other forms of behavior. If he is paying off a bet, he must be distinguishing between losing and winning a bet, and between betting and other forms of agreement. If he is showing off, he must be differentiating behavior that will attract attention from behavior that will be ignored. We cannot want something unless we can distinguish that something from other things. More generally, what we do not know—what we cannot distinguish—limits what we *can* want, what it is logically possible for us to want. Before the piano was conceived of, nobody could want to be a pianist. A plainsman who has never seen or heard or thought of mountains cannot intend to climb one.

Know, then is the third of the parameters of behavior, having to do with the distinctions that are being acted upon in the behavior in question. When the distinction that a person is acting upon is a state-of-affairs distinction, such as Judd's having lost a bet or his now paying a bet, these distinctions correspond to state-of-affairs descriptions (see Chapter 9) and to ordinary-language descriptions ("Judd has lost a bet", etc.).

The state-of-affairs description on which the person is acting may be true or false, accurate or inaccurate, correct or incorrect. Let us suppose that Judd has been assured by a friend of his, who has hitherto been dependable, that the crowd in the hotel lobby consists of a convention of clowns who will take for granted that he is demonstrating his skills in their profession. Judd *knows* this. We, on the other hand, have been told by the receptionist at the main desk that this is a national meeting of business executives, so we are not surprised when they call the police to carry him off. The distinction that Judd was acting upon did not reflect the reality of the situation. All the same, when he initiated that behavior, it was predicated on what he took, with good reason, to be the case. Thus we shall be grossly mistaken in understanding his behavior if we fail to take into account that he is acting on the distinctions *he* is making, not on the different distinctions that we or anybody else might make.

**Know-How (KH)** is the competence aspect of behavior. A person's behavior depends not only upon who he is, and upon what he wants and knows, but also upon what he has learned how to do, his competence, his skills, his sensitivities. Know-how is acquired in the course of our learning-history, and this dependence upon learning is one of the ways that we differentiate behavior in its paradigmatic sense from the case where something is accomplished by accident or luck or chance. Judd did not just happen to stand on his head and sing. He had trained himself assiduously in those arts; he meant to do what he was doing; and he could repeat his performance if he wanted to without depending upon luck to pull him through.

Many times, when we observe a person failing to act as we expect him to, it is because in his learning-history he has not acquired the know-how to act in that way. "Why don't you take the car to go down town?" "Because I never learned to drive." Or, "You mean you don't know how to use a knife and fork?" "Why should I? I've lived all my life in Japan and always ate with chopsticks." Not all of us have learned how to treat a sprained ankle or a child in a temper tantrum or an ailing automobile engine, and what we have not learned will limit not only what we do, but also what we deliberately undertake.

The competence acquired by virtue of our learning-history contributes in an essential way to making behaviors possible for us, and so giving us the option of doing or not doing them. We cannot seriously intend to do what we know we are incompetent to do, however badly we may wish, want, or hope to do it, or by coincidence, luck, chance, or accident might succeed in doing it. Conversely, if we are called upon to do something we cannot do, we shall respond by doing something we do know how to do, such as calling for help, if we do anything at all (Maxim 5, see Chap. 2).

**Performance (P).** Performance encompasses the process aspect of behavior, and a process is distinguished by having a beginning, a middle and a end; it occurs at a particular time and place; it has a duration, is interruptible, and divides into smaller processes (see Chap. 9).

The kinds of process that are ordinarily involved in behavior are postures (which includes facial expressions) and movements (which includes changes in facial expression). Postures and movements are those aspects of behavior that are most readily observed—seen, heard, touched—and that lend themselves to more or less incomplete recording by mechanical or electronic means such as audiovisual equipment. We move our bodies when we run a race. We make sounds when we talk with a friend. We maintain a position when we sit still at a concert. Associated with these are internal movements, the neurological and other bodily-organ processes that are not readily observable. These are all performances, the processes whereby we do whatever we are doing.

Because many aspects of bodily movement are easily observed, measured, and recorded, they have sometimes been taken as all there is to behavior. But equating behavior with movement not only runs counter to our commonly accepted use of the term "behavior", but impoverishes our understanding of that phenomenon. And this would continue to be the case even if Want, Know, Know-how, and so on, were reintroduced as causative factors into the concept of behavior as movement.

Performance is indeed essential to our concept of behavior, but no more essential than the other parameters. To take this as the key to behavior will lead us into trouble, if only because performances can be unrevealing or flagrantly misleading. A diplomat's formal act of courtesy can mask irritation, boredom, enthusiasm, curiosity, distaste, chicanery, or genuine admiration and affection. A student's heavy dialect can conceal from all but the most perceptive teacher his high intellectual ability.

**Achievement (A)** codifies what the behavior accomplishes, what difference the occurrence of the behavior makes. One of the possible outcomes that is generally of particular interest is whether the individual's behavior has brought about the state of affairs that he wanted. In principle, what we want is to achieve a particular state of affairs. We want to gain—whatever: to win applause, to own a diamond necklace, to be promoted, to have peace of mind or revenge. Or we want to lose—whatever: to be cured of illness, rid of debt, released from confinement, secure from danger, free from our anxieties. If our achievement includes what we want, it can be counted as a success. If it does not, it counts as a failure. If it includes only part of what we want, it can still count as partially successful.

Achievement means more than just this kind of success or failure, however, because any but the most trivial behavior will have further consequences foreseen and unforeseen, desired and undesired, not only for the person but for the world. All these are included in the concept of the achievement aspect of behavior.

Returning to Judd's performance in the hotel lobby: he succeeded in doing what he wanted to do, i.e., he presented a creditable acrobatic and musical act. But he also achieved a period in police custody, and who knows what effects his behavior may have had on the individual members of his startled audience, on his relations with the friend who had misinformed him, and on their circle of friends? How far we trace the effects of a behavior—what it achieved—will depend upon our purpose in tracing them and upon how far we *can* trace them.

**Person Characteristics (PC).** Obviously, each behaving individual differs in general from all other individuals in his person characteristics, and those ways will make a difference in what he wants, knows, and knows how to do, and in his performances. Full consideration of this parameter will come in the three chapters of Part II. Until then, it will be enough simply to keep in mind what all of us already know: that person characteristics make such a difference in behavior that we cannot comprehensively understand and describe what is going on without reference to the behaver's person characteristics. Which of the person's characteristics are being expressed by this particular behavior?

**Significance (S).** Significance is marked by simultaneity: what else we are doing by engaging in the particular behavior in question, i.e., what are we doing by doing X? And this parameter has to do as well with the meaning and importance of the behavior for the person and the world, in that what we are doing by doing X *is* its significance and meaning.

To illustrate, let us suppose that Julie, Jack, and Jenny are all running a six-mile race. Julie is a trained athlete.

Jack is a novice who is attempting his first run of that distance. Jenny is mentally retarded and has poor physical coordination. Julie wants—and achieves—pleasure in the running performance. Jack wants to impress his family and friends by going the whole distance. But for Jenny, even her entering the race is world-shaking. She is associating with "normals" in one of their "normal" activities, and when she does not finish last, she and her peers, as far as the news travels, stand taller for days.

Time and again we ask, "What was he doing by doing that?", tacitly recognizing that very often we do things not just for their own sakes (intrinsic action), but as a way of doing something else (instrumental action). For Julie, running in the race is an intrinsic action: she is running for the sheer fun of it with no further considerations in mind. For Jack and Jenny, there is more to it than simply running the race. Jack is improving his status with his associates; Jenny is affirming her community with "normals"; and these—not the running per se—are intrinsic actions in their cases. Any behavior can in principle be described or redescribed as a case of engaging in an intrinsic practice. As such, it is undertaken with no further end in view. It is self-justifying. But it is something else to propose that the same intrinsic practice is at stake for all persons at all times and places. Theoreticians commonly attempt to pin down one sort of action or achievement that has universal significance for everyone, everywhere, with no exceptions—for example, pleasure or self-interest, or to gain power, or to be sexually satisfied, or to fulfil instinctual urges.

By transforming such wants into ultimates, however, ("The *only* thing *anybody* ever *really* wants is —"), we are likely to blind ourselves to what is happening before our eyes, with the result that our descriptions become so remote from the real world as to leave us without guidance in dealing with real-world persons and situations, or they provide us with defective or destructive guidance. In any case, we do not need such a theory in order to carry out our immediate task, which is to trace the significance series as far as it makes sense to do so. We can stop with Julie's pleasure, Jack's status-raising, Jenny's associating with "normals" on their terms, without detriment to the adequacy of our observations and descriptions as far as they go.

---

These eight parameters identify the ways in which one behavior can differ from another, and therefore what we need to know in order to differentiate one from another, or to understand a given behavior, or to specify in what ways our descriptions are incomplete. The parametric analysis of behavior can be expressed in any of several ways. The first is straightforwardly verbal:

**Behavior is something that has the following aspects: an Identity, what that individual Wants, Knows, Knows How to do, Performs. and Achieves, what his Person Characteristics are. and what the Significance of that behavior is.**

The second is the **behavior formula**, using the standard notation for a parametric analysis in Descriptive Psychology, with each of the characters representing one of the parameters:

$$B = <I, W, K, KH, P, A, PC, S>$$

The third is a diagram that has proved to be extremely useful for many purposes, even though it leaves out three of the parameters (I, PC, and S) for the sake of representational simplicity. Among Descriptive Psychologists it is familiarly known as "the diamond". Variations of the basic diamond will be shown in Chapter 3.

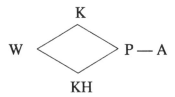

An intrinsic action can be shown with the basic diamond:

K =
<B> / <0> <0> <0> =
running the race contrasted with other behaviors

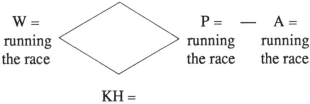

W =
running
the race

P = — A =
running    running
the race    the race

KH =
skills used in running the race

Given the behavior formula, we can generate **behavior descriptions** by assigning a content specification (value) to each of these parameters. A description can be generated as follows, beginning with the identity of the behaver:

Let us say that both Jim and Jeanne **(identities) want** some beer, Jim because he is thirsty and **knows** that beer will quench his thirst, Jeanne because she is throwing a party and **knows** that her guests will expect it. Both also **know** what beer is, and that it is for sale at a liquor store some distance away. Both **know how** to drive and Jeanne takes her car, but Jim does not have a car available so he rides a bus. Thus in getting to the store, each goes through a series of movements (**performance**): Jeanne walks to the car, opens the door, slides into the driver's seat, puts the key in the ignition, etc., and Jim steps on the bus, pays the fare, walks to a seat, sits down, etc. The postures and movements that are involved in those respective performances can be broadly sketched or finely detailed, as we choose.

In the end, Jim **achieves** what he wanted and set out to do, to buy and drink some beer, and Jeanne what she wanted, to obtain beer for her guests. Their **person characteristics** enter in because Jim is hedonistic and impulsive, while Jeanne is thoughtful and anxious about the success of her party. The **significance** of their behaviors is also different. Jim quenches his thirst, an intrinsic practice, and Jeanne pleases her guests. It should be noted that each time we give a Significance redescription of a behavior, we have a new set of Know, Want, etc., specifications that could be given, and each Significance redescription describes a different behavior.

Let us further stipulate that Jim is under the age for legally buying beer, while Jeanne is over that age, so that when Jim buys the beer, he is knowingly committing a crime. But for him, an added incentive is the prospect of getting away with that crime. His buying the beer, therefore, can be redescribed as two behaviors, with different wants, different achievements, and different significances in each case.

---

Several features of this form of behavior description deserve special mention. First, with respect to the Identity parameter, we can compare not only the behaviors of different persons, but also one person's behaviors at different times and in different circumstances—Jim's, for example, before and after the crucial birthday which determines when he can legally buy beer. And the person can be oneself, because the formula is reflexive. We can use it to understand and describe our own behavior just as well as other people's.

Second, in ordinary language, we are likely to use the same words, such as "buying beer", to describe the behavior (the set including all eight parameters), or merely what the person wants, or his performance, or his achievement. Often we do not need to separate them out. At other times, it is important to be clear which we are talking about, and the formula provides us resources by which we can do so.

Third, a person can have a number of wants at a given time, and sometimes they are incompatible. For example, the adventurous Want to break the law is incompatible with the prudential Want to play it safe, but Jim might want to do both. Questions having to do with choosing among possible behaviors must be left for another time. What is important at the moment is that in dealing with different wants (whether conflicting or not) in this way, we are not taking it that one is the *real* want, and the rest are illusory or trivial.

In principle, all these descriptions are equally to the point, equally realistic, equally accurate portrayals. "Jim, what do you want?" "To buy some beer ... to quench my thirst ... to see if I can get away with breaking the law ... ", just for a start. We do have some check on what else Jim may want by observing his circumstances, and his behaviors before and after the one we are concerned with. When he has come home with the beer, does he drink until he is no longer thirsty and then quit, or go on until he becomes incapable? Is he content with breaking the law on this occasion, or does he seek out other occasions which would have more serious consequences if he were caught?

For the time being, this should be enough to show the relation between the behavior formula and behavior descriptions, and how the descriptions can be developed in greater or less detail depending upon what we want or need to know. For most purposes, of course, we use names for behaviors: "Jim went to the liquor store and bought some beer"—and that name (or description) implies the parametric analysis, but we do not perform the full-fledged analysis unless there is something problematic about the behavior that calls for a more explicit, analytic approach.

In the behavior formula, we have what amounts to a check list to remind us of what we need to specify in describing a behavior. For the descriptions themselves, i.e., assigning values to the parameters in the formula, we must rely upon our competence in observation and discrimination.

# CHAPTER 2

# OBSERVING BEHAVIOR[1]

So far, our attention has been focussed on persons who are doing things like running races, standing on their heads, buying beer. They are the individuals (Identities) of the behavior formula in their status (performing their jobs) as **Actors (A)**. Throughout our descriptions of their behaviors, however, there have been persons lurking in the background and performing other jobs: ourselves, functioning as **Observer/Describers** and **Critic/Appraisers** of what was going on.

Observing a behavior is itself a behavior, of course, but because neither we nor anyone else can observe or critique a behavior unless that behavior occurs, logically the role of Actor is prior to the roles of Observer and Critic—and this whether the behavior we are observing is someone else's or our own. Behaving is the general case, and observing and critiquing behavior are special cases of behavior.

We were functioning as **Observer/Describers (O/D**

---

[1]See Ossorio, "Notes on Behavior Description," "Outline of Descriptive Psychology," and *Positive Health and Transcendental Theories.*

or simply O) in our examination of what Judd was doing when he behaved so peculiarly in the hotel lobby. We observed and described his behavior in a variety of ways, from the minimal account of his performance to alternative reasons why he may have been doing that at that time and place. When, as in this case, a behavior is puzzling or problematic, we shall try to give a description that suggests appropriate values for each of the eight parameters in the behavior formula (what Judd wanted, knew, knew how to do, performed, achieved, his person characteristics, and the significance of what he did). Where we lack information, as perhaps about Judd's person characteristics, probably we shall want to supply it if we can.

Mere observation is not enough, however. We need to evaluate our observations and descriptions. Are they lacking in important ways? Are they plausible, compatible with our other observations, and otherwise satisfactory? Here enters the **Critic/Appraiser** (**C/A** or simply **C**), a special case of Observer/Describer and therefore another special case of Actor. In general, his function is to appraise either the Observer's description (was it correct, accurate, sufficiently detailed, etc.?) or the Actor's behavior (was it appropriate, effective, rash, stupid, etc.?), or both the description and the behavior.

Actor, Observer, and Critic (**AOC**) are statuses, functions, jobs, and as persons, ordinarily we perform simultaneously the jobs of behaving, observing what we are doing, and evaluating the description and the behavior. Likewise, we guide our behavior toward other persons and things by our observation and appraisal of what they are doing. For the most part we do it intuitively, and often very efficiently, without any explicit description at all. For example, if we recognize something as a chair, we do not say to ourselves, "This is a chair"; we simply act on that discrimination. If we see something as dangerous, probably we shall not say or even think "Danger!", but simply engage in fear behavior, i.e., we try to escape. Nor do we think of ourselves ordinarily as functioning as Observer/Describers and Critic/Appraisers, or even as Actors. We are simply doing whatever we are doing.

The job of the Actor is to do what he feels like doing, and in this he is spontaneous and creative, assimilating the world to his behavior. The job of the Observer/Describer is to note what it is that is happening, what is the case, how it is that things are. Implicit in this are the norms of the culture in which the behavior takes place, for example, norms for what we call a chair and for what we take to be fear behavior.

The job of the Critic/Appraiser is fourfold: (1) to decide whether things are going satisfactorily, and if so, (2) to appreciate and enjoy that state of affairs and not to interfere with it. Since much of the time things are going right (cf. Maxim 9 below), often the Critic has very little more to do, if anything. If things are not going satisfactorily, however, his job is (3) to formulate what is going wrong (diagnosis), and (4) to prescribe ways to make it go better. Prescriptions constitute feedback to the Actor on how he might improve what he is doing.

Our continual monitoring of ourselves and of what is going on around us can be diagrammed as a negative (i.e., self-correcting) feedback loop, like a furnace (Actor) which is monitored by a sensor (Observer) which notes what the temperature is, and by the control setting (Critic) that decides (so to speak) that the temperature is just right, or too high or too low, and either does nothing, or turns the furnace off or on accordingly. Indeed, the furnace-control mechanism is a simplified version of how we ordinarily assess and adapt our behavior to our circumstances.

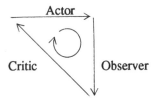

When everything is going satisfactorily, there is not much to be gained by concentrating on the different elements in the negative feedback loop and how they operate together. But when hitches or confusions arise, we can be immeasurably helped by being able to specify where the operation of the feedback loop has broken down. Is the Actor not responding to the Critic's evaluation of his behavior? Is the Observer/Describer incompetent to observe or biased in his description, led astray by his preconceptions (what he knows) or by person characteristics such as a trait of censoriousness? Is the Critic not appropriately monitoring the Actor, either because he is content to be no more than a Super-Observer, or because he has become a Super-Critic who, seeing danger of failure in anything that the Actor might do, makes no recommendation? In either of these last two cases, he will disrupt the functioning of the system. The directive, "Don't just stand there; do something," is as imperative as the complementary, "Don't just do something; stand there."

Answers to the above questions are not given by the AOC (Actor-Observer-Critic) construct. That, like the behavior formula and diagram, only provides us with resources that enable us to answer such questions ourselves with increased—and increasing—adequacy. As we become more proficient in thinking in these terms, we are likely to become more accurate in our assessment of situations, and swifter in our appraisals of what to do to correct whatever is going wrong. Thereby we are better able to keep the feedback loop functioning efficiently.

One person can function simultaneously as Actor, Observer, and Critic, or the different jobs can be performed by different people. At a concert, the soloist performs, the members of the audience observe, the music critic appraises. Of course the soloist is observing and appraising as well as acting. By listening the audience is acting and also appraising. And by appraising, the music critic is also acting and observing. But in every case, the person is functioning primarily in one or another job. Each has a special status within that social structure.

In other cases, one person can function primarily in any two of the roles, and another person in the third. And generally we speak of an Observer who is not directly involved in the outcome of a behavior as a **Spectator**.

---

It is already obvious that for any given behavior, we can have different descriptions, a fact that raises the question, "Which of those descriptions is the true one?" Neither here nor later shall we be concerned with truth as a philosophical issue, in the sense of seeking guarantees that we cannot possibly be wrong. Nor is the philosophical problem of relative versus absolute truth relevant here.[2] We are concerned instead with what we take to be adequate grounds for our behaviors.

Behaviorally, we act in terms of what we observe and how we appraise our observations. We take things to be as they seem unless we have reason enough to think otherwise (see Maxim 1, below). And if we do not know how things are, we can do something that does not depend upon how they are.[3] Thus we simply take it that the cup that we placed on the table a few minutes ago is still there and that

---

2See Ossorio, "Overview of Descriptive Psychology," and *Positive Health and Transcendental Theories*; and Shideler, "Creator and Discoverer" and "Science, Religion, and Religions".

3Peter G. Ossorio, transcript, 14 February 1985, p. 14.

the stuff in it has not changed from coffee to beer since the last time we drank from it. We take it that spring will follow winter even if belatedly. We are not certain whether we are able to do something, but we give it a try anyway. None of this should be taken as denying that there are indeed truth issues, because one of the things that we do when we are operating in this way is to try to establish what we shall take to be true.

If we do have reason enough to think that things may not be as they seem, as when we are faced with conflicting descriptions, we pull them together in such a way as to produce a version upon which we can act. What we act upon *is* we take to be true. Or as Critics we make a final-order, that is, a truth or reality, appraisal.

As an illustration, let us take our married friends, John and Jessie, who come to us separately with the tale of an argument they had had the evening before. The two accounts differ at so many points that they could almost be describing different incidents. All our experience with them has confirmed that both are intelligent, honest, and not malicious, unjust, or insensitive. Which account is true—or even more nearly true? Would that we had a videotape of the affair! Then we realize that even a videotape would be inadequate, because it could record only their performances—their postures, movements, words—leaving out the nature of their respective wants, the variance in what they know, the facts that he is more competent than she in verbal expression, and she more competent in reading "body language".

As Critics, we have no conceivable way of arriving at "the truth" in the merely philosophical sense, in this situation. If we undertake to calm the participants down so that later they can resolve their difficulties in a less heated atmosphere, the truth question is irrelevant for us. If we cannot avoid judging between their competing descriptions, what we do in fact is to look for untruths. We check each person's description against the other's to see if they are incompatible. If so, we separate the evaluations from the descriptions (is one or both falsifying or exaggerating, etc.?), because most apparent disagreements arise from the evaluations rather than from the descriptions as such. When we have taken out the evaluations, we ask if the descriptions are compatible, and if they could be, we take it that they are. Thus truth does enter in, although not as a philosophical absolute.

Any object, process, event, state of affairs, or relationship that can be described in one way can also be described in another way or in many ways, and even seemingly incongruent descriptions can indeed be congruent. A physicist once pointed out to me that the Ptolemaic astronomers were right when they described the sun as moving around the earth. It does—from the viewpoint of a person on the earth. That is, if I describe what I see when I look out my window toward the end of the day, I shall almost certainly speak of the sun as going down. In the same sense, Copernicus was also right that the earth moves around the sun. It does—from the viewpoint of an imaginary person who doesn't mind the heat and is standing on the sun. From a viewpoint outside the solar system, earth and sun move in relation to each other, but this description is no "truer" than the other two, and even today there is a point in using each of them for particular purposes. Moreover, if we take the different viewpoints into account, they are compatible. Each is a true story, but none is a complete story or the only story.

Long ago, by practice and experience we mastered the art of living in a three-dimensional world, so that we take into account that what we see—a chair, for example—depends upon our viewpoint. Photographs of it taken from different angles would be very different, yet when we move around it, we recognize that it is the same chair. Automatically we take our viewpoint (where we are) and our view (what we see from where we are) *as a pair*, along with others' viewpoints and their views *as pairs*.[4] In principle, we do the same when we observe and describe any state of affairs, such as the argument between John and Jessie, or a performance of *Hamlet* or whatever. In these cases, however, the viewpoint is identified not by the Observer's position in space but by his person characteristics. It requires practice and experience to acquire the ability to connect a personal viewpoint and view *as a pair*, just as it did for living in a three-dimensional world. But that we can learn to do so is why we can say, for example, "That was an excellent performance of *Hamlet* but I didn't like it."

In observing complex phenomena like solar systems and behavior, the practical benefits of generating different descriptions by adopting different viewpoints are unmistakable. All too often, however, that resource is overlooked because of a prevailing commitment to the philosophical postulate that there must be One Right Way to view the solar system (hence Galileo's condemnation) or behavior (hence exclusivist theories of behavior), and so on. But a God's-eye view, which presumably would be *the* one that is true in the absolute sense, is possible only for a god, and finite human beings do not qualify even as godlings.

Our own viewpoints are reflected in the descriptions we give, whether of the solar system or of the argument between John and Jessie. I want to comfort Jessie. You want to save John and Jessie's marriage. Their counsellor wants to bring into the open the unrecognized sources of tension that brought on the quarrel. I know Jessie intimately, John less so. You know both of them slightly and have a religiously-based abhorrence of divorce. The counsellor knows a great deal about them but keeps a carefully professional distance from them personally. I love; you

---

[4]See Ossorio, *Positive Health and Transcendental Theries.*

judge; the counsellor investigates; and the kind of differences between us are comparable to the kind of differences between Ptolemy, Copernicus, and Einstein.

Reconcilation of such descriptions requires that as Critics, we take the viewpoints of all the Observer/ Describers into account, as far as we have access to them. Always and always, as there is no behavior without a behaver, so there is no description (itself a behavioral achievement) without a describer, and frequently several describers, although different descriptions can also come from one person describing his own behavior or others' from several viewpoints. The Critic then can check their observations and descriptions for their consistency with one another and for their empirical validity—i.e., whether they are compatible with the observable facts on which, potentially, agreement could be reached.

---

A further way of checking is provided by the **Maxims for Behavior Description**[5] which are not truths, but rules: warnings and reminders by which we can distinguish logically applicable descriptions from logically inapplicable ones. They serve as logical constraints upon descriptions, in that a description must show the behavior to be an instance of one or more of the maxims. Or, to state it more strongly, a description must not violate any of the maxims, because if it does, there is almost certainly something wrong with that description. Most of the maxims are so obvious as to sound trivial, which may be one reason why they are so often unnoticed and so rarely applied systematically.

What the maxims imply is that under some descrip-

---

[5]See Ossorio, "Notes on Behavior Description," "Outline of Descriptive Psychology," *Place*, and *Personality and Personality Theories.*

tion, behaviors always make sense. If they do not, they are not *behaviors*. Further, they imply that any behavior will be in accordance with all the maxims simultaneously, and we can appeal to the different maxims to bring out whatever we want to bring out concerning the behavior.

**Maxim 1. A person takes it that things are as they seem, unless he has reason enough to think otherwise.** This maxim connects with the truth issue: we do not live by continually raising truth questions and making truth appraisals, and we could not. Truth is always a prerogative of statements, and we do not continually go around explicitly or implicitly making statements like "This is a chair" and "That food is good for you". Thus it follows that we are not constantly making truth appraisals. Instead, we make reality appraisals, and behaviorally, "reality takes precedence over truth".[6] We take it that this is a chair and that that food is nourishing, so we sit on the chair and eat the food. We can take Maxim 1 as the principle that governs reality appraisals: we appraise things as really being the way they seem, unless we have reason enough to think otherwise.

We may, indeed, have reason enough to think otherwise. We hear the first bars of a symphony and comment, "It's Beethoven's Fifth". Then with a lurch the music changes, and we recognize P. D. Q. Bach's master hand at work. Or returning to John and Jessie, John has come home from work to find that Jessie has moved his favorite chair from one side of the fireplace to the other without consulting him, and he takes it to mean that his opinion does not count in their household affairs. So reacting, he is exercising his competence (Know-how) to treat his wife's moving the chair (Performance) as being a case of degrading him, rather than a case of—let us say—her wanting to pleasantly surprise him or her expecting that he would not care one way or the other.

---

6Peter G. Ossorio, "Appraisal."

Jessie gives him several reasons for treating her performance as not having been a degradation, all of which he brushes off as attempts to cover up her indifference to his preferences, and even her immediately moving the chair back to its original position does not persuade him that in the first place she did not have a malicious intention. Exercising our function as Critics, we describe John's behavior as not violating Maxim 1, in that he took Jessie's behavior to be as it seemed to him—a provocation. Another person might have taken Jessie's explanation as reason enough to think otherwise, or to call John's judgement into question, but his person characteristics were such that Jessie's reasons were not, for him, reason enough to change his description of her behavior.

**Maxim 2. If a person recognizes an opportunity to get something he wants, he has a reason to try to get it.** What we have in this maxim is the logical form for answering the question, "Why did the person do that *then?*", which can be answered by noting what opportunities the situation provided, and that the person recognized as such. Moreover, this maxim reminds us of the necessary connection, in behavior description, between the Want (W) and the Know (K) parameters: we cannot want something unless we can distinguish it from other things.

For some time, John had wanted to have a greater voice in household matters, to be accredited as more important there, but no situation had arisen that provoked him sufficiently to protest what he took to be Jessie's excluding him from participation in those affairs. Now, therefore, he distinguished not only between being consulted and not being consulted, but also between the previous and present location of the chair, between Jessie's moving it and (conceivably) someone else's moving it, and so on. Further, he distinguished an opportunity to express his feelings about being disregarded (whether these were justified or not is beside the point). He had been waiting for an excuse to protest, and her moving his chair provided him with one.

**Maxim 3. If a person has a reason to do something, he will do it unless he has a stronger reason not to.** A few days earlier, John and Jessie had decided together what they would serve the friends who were coming to dinner that night. During the day, however, Jessie changed her mind and prepared something else, giving John an occasion to object that she did not take his opinions seriously. Therefore he was angry with her, and had a reason to act accordingly. However, since to act angrily at that time would have involved discourtesy to their guests, he had a stronger reason not to express his anger, and he did not.

This maxim is useful as a reminder of how priorities work in behavior, which is not as simply as we might think. We do not always give our highest values the priority in our choice of behaviors. Over the long run, John's relations with Jessie were far more important than his relations with their friends, but while they were entertaining guests was not a good opportunity to straighten things out with her, so he set aside the greater, long-run value for the sake of the lesser, short-run value.

**Maxim 4. If a person has two or more reasons for doing X, he has a stronger reason for doing X than if he had only one of those reasons.** Maxim 4 has been described as "a way of keeping Maxim 3 honest". Again we are dealing with priorities: Why, when we want most to do X, do we sometimes do Y instead? John had reason for behaving angrily toward Jessie, as well as reason for behaving courteously toward their guests, and he could perfectly well do both—but not at the same time. His confrontation with Jessie, however, could be postponed; the dinner party could not. Thus he had two reasons for acting on his lesser priority during the evening: he achieved the lesser goal (a pleasant evening) without sacrificing the opportunity to have it out with Jessie at a later time.

In this particular case, there was a further application

of Maxim 4. John did have two reasons for objecting strenuously to Jessie's unauthorized moving his chair. He wanted not only to be given more voice in their household arrangements, but also to punish Jessie for departing from the menu they had agreed upon for serving their guests. A third-party Critic might well conclude that the vehemence of John's behavior suggested that he was acting on additional reasons as well, and might recommend investigating those further reasons. If these were the last straws, what was the rest of the straw-stack made of?

**Maxim 5. If a situation calls for a person to do something he cannot do, he will do something he can do, if he does anything at all.** If I am called upon to provide a cake for a party but I do not have the ingredients to make it, I buy one instead or substitute something else. If, in a debate, a politician is asked a question that he cannot answer, he is likely to answer as if it were some other question. To continue with our illustration of John, Jessie, and the chair: a Critic might say that what their situation called for, almost from the outset, was for them to sit down quietly and discuss the matter: explain why they did what they did, describe what they felt and were feeling, and work out how to avoid future confrontations of this kind.

John's person characteristics, however, were such that from the first moment of seeing that his chair had been moved, he was outraged, and being outraged he *could* not discuss it quietly. What he could do, and did, was to explode verbally. As his anger escalated, that means of expression became inadequate, but some of the more adequate ones were—for various reasons—out of the question, like throttling Jessie or throwing the chair onto the fire in the fireplace. So he did what he could do, given his person characteristics and circumstances. He knocked over a lamp, stormed into their bedroom, locked the door, and did not come out until the next morning when he had to leave for work. Meanwhile, Jessie did what she could do, which included sleeping in the family room and not reappearing until John had left the house. The salient feature to which this maxim draws attention is the competence (Know-how) parameter of behavior: what John and Jessie separately and together can and cannot do.

These first five maxims provide for the Observer/ Describer a set of warnings and reminders by which he can test descriptions of a behavior for both their internal consistency and their empirical validity, which go together. Any two observations can be checked against each other, but we cannot make such checks without a framework such as the maxims provide, that specifies what is consistent with what. Only in special circumstances are the maxims used to evaluate the behavior itself for its appropriateness, ethical values, pleasurable quality, or effectiveness in achieving a goal. Primarily, we apply them to descriptions of behavior, rather than to appraisals.

In this connection, it may be salutary to look at what results if we violate the maxims. "He did it although he didn't have reason enough to do it." "He did it without having recognized any opportunity to do it." "He did it even though he had a stronger reason not to do it"—and so on through the whole set of nine maxims.

---

The next three maxims—six, seven, and eight—have to do with acquiring person characteristics, and the ninth and last with manifesting person characteristics.

**Maxim 6. A person acquires facts about the world primarily by observation, and secondarily by thought.** John discovered by observation that his chair had been moved. Jessie discovered by observation that John was angry, and when she moved the chair, that it was heavy. We discover by thought that $2 + 2 = 1 + 3 = 10 - 6 = 4$, and that A cannot be both A and not-A, but by observation that there are four people in the room, or that we are tired. In our behavior, we observe our circumstances and ourselves and act more or less accordingly, but our observation is limited in a way that is specified in the next maxim.

**Maxim 7. A person acquires concepts and skills by practice (participation) and experience in one or more of the social practices (customary pursuits, usages) which call for the use of that concept or exercise of that skill.** John could not have been angry at Jessie's moving his chair if he had not learned, at some stage in his history, to differentiate chairs from non-chairs and his chair from other chairs, not to mention Jessie from other persons, degradation from accreditation, and so on down the line. Competence in the use of concepts comes only by participation in social practices. Primarily, this participation occurs in normal living with other people. Secondarily, it takes place in special instructional situations, for example, in schools or apprenticeships.

A large part of socialization—not to mention education—consists of acquiring whatever concepts are necessary if we are to function in the society where we live. Such concepts might include redness, fair play, addition and multiplication, sister, potato, and policies such as "There are some things that people like us just don't do". What concepts are necessary will depend upon what community is in question: the Inuit of the Yukon, or a conclave of physicists, or an inner-city ghetto.

Think of so mastering the concept of number that we can put together the numerical symbol "4" and the word "four", of doing business with someone who has no notion at all of "mine" and "thine", of learning to communicate in a language that has no word for "no". We learn to make these distinctions in the same way that we learn the skills to cut down a tree or to play the harp or to dress ourselves: by participating in relevant social practices.

**Maxim 8. If a person has a given person charac- teristic, he acquired it in one of the ways it can be ac-**

**quired, i.e., by having the relevant prior capacity and intervening history.** This maxim differs from Maxim 7 in its greater range of application. Maxim 7 was limited to concepts and skills; Maxim 8 covers *all* person characteristics as they are detailed in Part II. A few examples will suggest how important this is. Let us say that John had the original capacity to become a relaxed and serene adult, or a tense and hostile one, or a gregarious or meditative one. In fact, he grew up among people who were strongly competitive but he never quite made it to the "outstanding" level among them, and so became somewhat insecure, with a tendency to feel that he had to press for the recognition which he felt was his due. Thus he acquired the trait of defensiveness, which was especially pronounced in his relations with his wife.

Jessie's original capacity for intellectual achievement was at least as great as John's, but she had left college in her second year to marry him. Since then she had concentrated on furthering his career, which called for manual and social rather than intellectual skills. She had a special gift for art which her parents had fostered, as did John, while he discouraged her from engaging in such intellectual pursuits as a university course in political science which she had considered taking.

Maxim 8 can be expressed in the **Developmental Formula: Capacity plus intervening history produces person characteristics (C + H —> PC).** The acquisition of new characteristics during the person's ongoing history implies the development of a new set of capacities, which with further history lead to further person characteristics and therefore capacities, and so on from birth until death. An individual can acquire new interests and powers. Or he can lose them. Following a history of discouragement or illness, person characteristics can change as from alertness to lethargy, or precision to clumsiness, or caring to indifference.

The intervening history can be of many kinds in addition to those in the illustrations: surgical intervention, for example, or drug administration, deliberate behavior modification, psychotherapy, religious instruction. What is normally an original capacity can be absent, as when a person is born blind or armless or with brain damage, or it can be present to an extraordinary degree, as in the case of genius. Thus the Observer would consider both capacity and history in his investigation into how an individual's person characteristics were acquired, and into why a particular individual does not have characteristics that would normally be expected.

**Maxim 9. Given the relevant competence, behavior goes right if it does not go wrong in one of the ways that it can go wrong.** This is the counterpart to Maxim 1, "A person takes it that things are as they seem, unless he has reason to think otherwise", with Maxim 1 in the context of knowledge, Maxim 9 in the context of behavior. Indeed, Maxim 1 is a special case of Maxim 9, in that both reflect the fact that we act with some awareness of our own abilities, skills, and sensitivities. Generally speaking, there is not much point in choosing behaviors that we do not have the know-how to execute, or that call for sensitivities we are lacking. As a matter of course, we take it that if we see something in a certain way, that is the way it is, unless — , and if we have the competence to do something, it will succeed, unless — . More simply, in normal circumstances we do not need reasons to take it that what we take to be the case is in fact the case, and that what we do will be successful, *unless* something goes or has gone wrong with respect to our knowledge (K), motivation (W), competence (KH), or performance or achievement (P-A), or cognition. (For more on the "unless-clauses", see Chapter 11.)

---

As the behavior formula provides us with a way to describe systematically what we are doing (or what he or she or they are doing), so the maxims provide us with a way to answer systematically such questions as "Why is this person doing this *now*?", and "Why did he do it *then*?", and "Why did he *not* do it?"—as well as "How did I or he or she or they get this way?" To anticipate, the formula and the maxims are applicable as well to groups of people acting in concert—a club, a political party, a nation.

The maxims serve as standards, to remind us that behavior has the aspects—the parameters—designated in the behavior formula, and that the values of those parameters must be those that the behavior in question calls for. We cannot describe a behavior as being a certain behavior, and then leave out of our consideration the appropriate values for those parameters. These are not arbitrary fiats. They are matters of coherence and internal consistency. For example, it would be inconsistent on the face of it to distinguish something as beautiful, want it, and be able to possess it, and then deliberately smash it in bits, "unless — ". Such a performance in such circumstances would cry out for an explanation, and the explanation would refer to other wants, discriminations, and so on.

We cannot achieve the ideal of "an absolutely complete description" of any phenomenon, in part because there is no way by which we could recognize one if we had it, and in part because we do not yet have the concepts that would be needed for many of the specifications. We can, however, identify what an incomplete description would be: one that specifies values for some parameters of a behavior, but does not specify others. We can describe why John was angry—Jessie had provoked him—and this is a complete and total description. Why he expressed his anger in the way that he did calls for another description. Yet even if, for example, we could describe all the facts that are involved in John's angry behavior—assign values to all eight parameters—that would not provide a complete characterization of everything that was involved in John's behavior as such. The phenomenon is richer than any particular set of facts or any description.

As Observer/Describers and Critics, we can go wrong even though we are using the formulas or the maxims, if we assign values that are not confirmed by observation or that are incompatible, or if we give too much or too little weight to some value, or omit one or more important elements because of our ignorance or carelessness. We can also go wrong by forgetting that even in observing and describing, and in appraising, our observations, descriptions, and critiques are themselves eligible for observation, description, and criticism by others—or ourselves.

The maxims can be compared with the rules of a game—in this case, the "game" of describing behavior. The rules of football and chess do not reveal how to win a game, and following them to the letter will not guarantee victory. All they do is to prescribe what the player must not violate if he is to play *that* game, and play it right.

# CHAPTER 3

# FORMS OF BEHAVIOR DESCRIPTION[1]

As Observer/Describers of behavior—others' and our own—we have as resources thus far the behavior formula, the maxims, and the forms of behavior description. By assigning values (content) to the content-free parameters of behavior, we can generate systematically differentiated descriptions of behaviors.

A good deal of the time, of course, we cannot give complex or comprehensive descriptions because we do not have the relevant concepts or information. At other times, a simple, discursive description is enough. Or we may need to know nothing more about a behavior than whether the achievement was of a certain kind; we have no interest in who did it, or why, or how—for example, was the letter mailed or was it not? Did the victim die or did he not? Or we may be called upon to specify what a particular person actually attempted, without regard to its success: Julie did

---

[1]See Peter G. Ossorio, "Notes on Behavior Description," "Outline of Descriptive Psychology," and *Personality and Personality Theories*, 14 July 1977.

run the race; Judd did put on his act. Or we may want to trace how one behavior is related to other behaviors—its place in a social practice. Or our task may be to describe a pattern of behaviors in general terms: fear behavior as such, for example, or playing chess or washing dishes or mailing a letter.

The value of having available different forms of behavior description is most clearly apparent in situations where Observers disagree in their description of a behavior, as John and Jessie disagreed about the significance of Jessie's moving John's chair. Jessie, disconcerted by John's violent reaction, gave a Performative form of behavior description (see below) of what she had done. John gave first an Achievement and then a Significance form of description (again, see below). Neither John nor Jessie had any idea of how these three forms of behavior description are related to one another, so is not surprising that they could neither reconcile their descriptions nor reach a consensus on what the fundamental issues were.

An Observer/Describer who is presenting a description will use one or more of the forms of behavior description in a given case, depending upon the empirical facts available to him, his purpose, his mastery of the logic of behavior description, and his competence in discerning what forms of description are both possible and appropriate for his needs. With practice and experience, an Observer/Describer can handle more and more complex behaviors with simple observation. An experienced teacher can tell from a few verbal or behavioral clues that "Karen's up to her old tricks", or a football coach from a glance at the field, "That's an off-tackle slant".

In mastering the logic of behavior description, it is convenient to differentiate two types of concepts. Mastering a concept like "red" or "tree" is like labelling. It has to do with a simple contrast between "red" and "not-red", "tree" and "not-tree". Mastering a concept like "addition", however, involves acquiring a skill. Once we have mastered it, there is something we know how to do. Mastering the concept of "behavior" is more like acquiring a skill than like labelling, in that when we have mastered it, there is something we know how to do, and the forms of behavior description illustrate the complexity and systematic character of what we can do with the concept of behavior, by means of the behavior formula.

---

We can start with **Intentional Action (IA) Description** as represented in the behavior formula, in which for Behavior, read Intentional Action. As we have already seen, Intentional Action is something that has the following aspects: Identity, Want, Knowledge, Know-how, Performance, Achievement, Person Characteristics, and Significance. What we have here, therefore, is a set of ingredients, and as we shall see shortly, a set of possible moves.

$$<B> = <IA> = <I, W, K, KH, P, A, PC, S>$$

Given that acquiring the concept of behavior is like acquiring a skill, the skill aspect can be illustrated by a calculational system. There are several ways of explaining what a calculational system is, one of which is the Element-Operation-Product model. In using that model, we begin with a finite set of Elements and Operations, and perform Operations on Elements to generate Products. Those products, in turn, are eligible to be further Elements.

A simple form of the EOP model is that in which there is only one Element and one Operation: as an example, the Element "zero" and the Operation "plus 1" gives us "1" as the Product. That Product constitutes a new Element (1) on which the same Operation (plus 1) can be performed, thereby giving us a new Product (2), and this can be continued indefinitely. To express it notationally: $0 + 1 = 1$;

$1 + 1 = 2; 2 + 1 = 3; 3 + 1 = 4$; etc., ad inf.

In dealing with behavior calculationally we shall take Intentional Action as our single initial Element, and perform three Operations upon it: Substitution, Deletion, and Reduction. The Products will be other, more or less elaborate, forms of behavior description.

---

**Cognizant Action Description.** First, we shall perform the Substitution operation on the Intentional Action representation in the behavior formula, by specifying that the value of the K (Know) parameter includes B (a behavior, i.e., an intentional action). That is, we substitute B in K. The primary use of this form of description is the case where the person knows what behavior he is engaging in. Another is to describe a case where a person is responding to someone else's behavior, which he is distinguishing from other behaviors.

To illustrate: Joan, who is preparing dinner for her kitten Juju, knows what she is doing, and not only distinguishes the cat's dinner from her own, and Juju's food dish from his water dish, but also distinguishes fixing his dinner from fixing her dinner, and both of those from sitting down to read the paper or getting dressed to go out or playing her guitar or telephoning a friend. In the formula for the Cognizant Action description, therefore, K is specified by $B_1$, which is the behavior that Joan knows she is engaging in.

$$\langle I,\ W, \begin{vmatrix} \langle B_1 \rangle \\ K, \end{vmatrix} KH,\ P,\ A,\ PC,\ S \rangle$$

Graphically, this can be represented by the diamond, with the $\langle B_1 \rangle$ representing what she knows she is doing, and $\langle B_{2\text{-}4} \rangle$ the behaviors which for Joan, then and there, contrast with $\langle B_1 \rangle$.

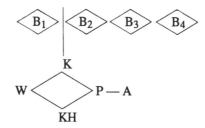

**Deliberate Action Description.** Deliberate action is normative for human behavior. Hence it is the archetype of behavior. The person not only knows what he is doing, but chooses to do that rather than something else. He does it on purpose. Joan indeed knew that she was preparing Juju's dinner; moreover, she wanted to do it at that time rather than at any other time, and rather than do any of the other things she might have been doing. Since she *wants* to engage in this particular behavior, W as well as K is specified by <B$_1$>, with <B$_{2-4}$> to represent what she chose not to do at that time

$$<I, \quad \begin{vmatrix} <B_1> \\ W, \end{vmatrix} \quad \begin{vmatrix} <B_1> \\ K, \end{vmatrix} \quad KH, P, A, PC, S>$$

—and graphically:

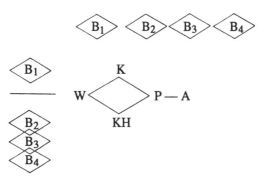

**Social Practice Description.** A social practice is a pattern of actions engaged in by one or more persons, a pattern that can be taught, learned, and done, and that is done. Joan's feeding Juju his dinner is a social practice; so are playing chess, cutting a slice of bread, performing a scientific experiment. A social practice has to be learned, and what we learn is to do it right according to the given standards for that practice. Therefore, when a person who has mastered a particular social practice is doing it, his success is attributable to his competence (KH) rather than to luck, coincidence, or accident. And his doing it at all is attributable to his knowledge (K) and motivation (W). A social practice can be diagrammed by specifying <B> as the value of the Achievement parameter, indicating that the occurrence of the second behavior is a partial specification of the achievement parameter of the first behavior, and so on recursively. Note that the occurrence of the second behavior is part of the achievement of the first behavior, and the occurrence of the third behavior is part of the achievement of the second behavior, and so on. Thus the whole second diamond represents the achievement of the first behavior, and so on.

$$<\text{I, W, K, KH, P,} \left| \begin{array}{c} <\text{B}> \\ \text{A} \end{array} \right| \text{PC, S}>$$

$$W \diamondsuit^{K}_{KH} P - W \diamondsuit^{K}_{KH} P - W \diamondsuit^{K}_{KH} P -$$

Such a sequence of diamonds can be of any length, and involve one person or a number of persons. The behaviors can be consecutive, simultaneous, or overlapping. In many social practices, the outcome of a given behavior will have more than one component, as in a football game, when the center snaps the ball, all the members of both teams surge into action. Or several behaviors can have a single outcome, as when the members of one team collaborate in interceptions to enable the ball-carrier to make a touchdown. The pattern may be as simple as Joan's rolling a ball and Juju's chasing it and bringing it back to her for her to roll again until one of them tires of the game, or as intricate as the complexities of international relations, although for representing complex cases, a better notation would be a Process or State of Affairs Description (see Chapter 9).

An important variant on the Social Practice Description is that which delineates a **Course of Action**. In normal circumstances, a person engaging in a social practice can expect to complete it successfully (Maxim 9). Joan knows how to open a can of cat food, and more generally, how to feed Juju. Most of us can write a letter and mail it without anticipating failure at any stage of the process. A professional writer can expect to be successful in the social practice of writing a book.

To write a successful book, however, is something else again, a course of action. Its success depends upon all sorts of factors over which the author has no control: the personal predilections of editors, the marketing policies of publishers, the current state of public taste, and a host of other factors. Almost anyone can succeed in the social practice of running for office, but to succeed in that course of action—to win the election—is another matter. When Joan and her friends play bridge, they are engaging in a social practice and can expect to succeed in playing the game. Winning, however, depends not only upon the interlocking competence of the players, but also upon the cards they happen to be dealt.

In a Course of Action, some competence (KH) that would be needed to ensure success is lacking at some place or places in the Social Practice pattern, so that success reflects in part the element of luck, chance, accident, coincidence, or (some would say) divine providence or miracle. The diagram for a Course of Action description, therefore, is the same as for a Social Practice, but with one or more of the KH parameters deleted to indicate that the behavior has all the characteristics of the corresponding deliberate action except some of the relevant competence.

Of crucial importance is the identity between participating in social practices or courses of action on the one hand, and on the other, engaging in deliberate actions. Specific deliberate actions are elements of social practices. For convenience, at times we focus upon a single element in a chain or web, and although this is legitimate, we should keep in mind that it has a place in that chain or web. No behavior is isolated from other behaviors, any more than a word can be a word apart from other words, or the number 5 without a numerical system that includes other numbers and the operations performed upon them. And any social practice can be articulated into constituent behaviors.

Generally speaking, those individual behaviors are smaller than most of us have in mind when we speak of "behaviors". Strictly speaking, a behavior is a single action such as unlocking a door, as distinguished both from the performance (movement) of turning the key, and from the social practice of getting into the house when we return home. Because in some cases it is important to distinguish these three, we need to know that there is a difference and what the difference is. Ordinarily, however, neither in this book nor elsewhere is it crucial to distinguish between a behavior and a social practice, just as in many cases it is not crucial to distinguish between crimson and scarlet.

---

**Significance (or Symbolic Behavior) Description.**
As the Social Practice and Course of Action descriptions provide a way to formulate sequences or networks of be-

haviors, the Significance Description gives us a way to formulate simultaneous behaviors. It is what the Observer/Describer will use to describe what the Actor is doing by doing whatever he is doing, and is generated by a substitution operation on the performance parameter.

By feeding her kitten (1), Joan is doing other things as well. She is caring for its needs (2); by caring for its needs, she is doing what a person ought to do for a pet (3), and for her, as for many other people, participating in a person-pet relation is an intrinsic action (4), i.e., self-justifying, something done for its own sake, so that she does not need an ulterior motive to engage in it.

Thus Joan's one performance of feeding Juju his dinner is an aspect of several behaviors simultaneously. By doing (1) she is doing (2). By doing (2) she is doing (3). By doing (3), she is doing (4)—an intrinsic action. Occasionally, but not often, we shall need to go further, into doing (5).

Because the term "symbolic" may be misleading, it needs to be pointed out that here it does not mean that any of these performances is *merely* a symbol, a sign pointing to something else. Instead, it is in general an implementation relationship. Sometimes it is also a part-whole relationship, specifically in the case where one is engaging in a social practice by engaging in one of its constituent behaviors. In such a part-whole or implementation relationship, (1) is a part of or an implementation of (2), (2) of (3), and so on. Each part of the whole has a place within the more comprehensive context of the whole. In the formula, then, <P> is specified by <B> and reads:

$$\left\langle I, W, K, KH, \left| \begin{array}{c} <B> \\ P \end{array} \right| A, PC, S \right\rangle$$

In the diagram, the B is specified by the diamonds themselves:

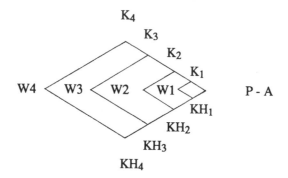

Whenever we do something by doing something else—when we do (2) by doing (1)—then (2) is the significance of (1), and (1) is the way that we do or did (2). Further, participating in a social practice is always a case of doing (2) by doing (1), because we are engaging in that social practice by engaging in one of its constituent behaviors.

---

In the Substitution operation, we specified a value ("plugged in content") for a parameter or parameters. This produced four forms of description, in each of which "behavior" substituted in one or more of the parameters of behavior: Cognizant Action (K), Deliberate Action (K and W), Social Practice (A), and Significance (P) Descriptions. Formally, all these are special cases of Intentional Action Description.

In the next operation, **Deletion**, values for certain parameters are deleted, so that the descriptions are explicitly noncommittal with respect to the values of those parameters.

There are many reasons why an Observer/Describer might want to give such incomplete descriptions. He may not have access to the information that would enable him to assign a value to that parameter (e.g., the detective does not know the identity of the criminal, so the I parameter is deleted). Or the detective knows who committed the crime but does not know why (delete W). Or the Observer/ Describer may simply wish not to commit himself as to what the Actor knows, or wants, or is competent to do, or performs, or achieves. Or he may not need a complete description: when Joan's veterinarian asks what Juju has been eating, he is not interested in who feeds him, or why, or what Joan knows about nutrition, that is, in Joan's behavior. His only concern is with what Juju himelf (Identity) has actually eaten (Achievement). Other uses for incomplete or noncommittal descriptions are suggested in the course of discussing the following forms of behavior description, which were chosen for their general usefulness.

---

**Agency** (or **General Behavior**) **Description.** This is the form of behavior description depicted in the basic diamond. It is what we use for representing a behavior as instrumental or purposive without regard for who does it, or what the individual's person characteristics are, or what is the significance of the behavior, i.e., what else is being done by doing this. Anyone who is interested in formulating general "laws of behavior", or in setting up behavioral experiments, will employ this form of description precisely because it does not require, or even allow for, an historical context or individual variation. Even more important is its use in delineating patterns of an individual's behavior, where the I and PC are constant, or the PC is in free variation, and therefore they need not be continually referred to. (The standard notation is to replace the deleted parameters with thetas. I have used strikeovers for heuristic reasons.)

<I, W̶, K, KH, P, A, P̶C̶, S̶>

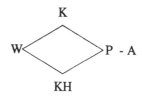

---

**Activity Description.** When the Observer/Describer cannot or does not want to identify the motivational aspects of the behavior, or needs only to specify those behavior patterns where motivation is not at issue, he can give an Activity Description, which is the same as the Agency Description except for the deletion of the W parameter. "Joan got a kitten, but I don't know why." Further, we give Activity Descriptions when we suspect or know that the behavior is being engaged in for an ulterior motive, or to deceive someone. "Julie is cleaning the house but her heart isn't in it," or "He's just marking time at his job." In such cases, we cannot give a Deliberate Action Description because the value of the Want parameter is missing. The description is correct only as an Activity Description, i.e., in the deleted form.

<I, W̶, K, KH, P, A, P̶C̶, S̶>                          K

P - A

KH

---

**Performance Description.** In a Performance Description, all the parameters are deleted except P and A. The Observer/Describer presents the description as the description of a behavior, but a description which is incomplete for some reason. In particular circumstances it may make no difference whether "his hand moved" or "he moved his hand". In other circumstances, the Observer may be uncertain which of these possibilities is the case. But where the Observer is giving a Performance Description, he is not denying that the behavior can in principle be described by assigning values to all eight parameters, even though in this situation he chooses to limit his description to these two, or must limit it because he does not have the information necessary to assign values to the other parameters.

This form of description is of special interest because historically behavior has so often been defined as consisting only of performance and achievement, thereby reducing behavior to movement-outcome, and presenting it in a way that makes it indistinguishable from mere movement. It is helpful to have this form of description available for when we need it, but not to restrict ourselves, a priori, to this form.

<I, W, K, KH, P, A, PC, S>

Achievement Description specifies the value of only the one parameter, achievement, and is explicitly noncommittal about all the rest. "The kitten has already been fed." "The letter was mailed on Monday." For some purposes, all we need to know is what was accomplished, or whether a particular something was accomplished—whether the job did or did not get done. We do not know or are not interested in who did it, or why, or what the person's competence was, or how it was done. For other purposes, the Identity of the achiever becomes important. In "They have passed the examination" or "the gambler squared his accounts," it is only the Identity and Achievement that matter; we do not assign values to the other parameters. And it may not matter whether the person had intended that particular achievement. For example, "They didn't accomplish what they set out to do, those princes of Serendip, but they did accomplish something." Again, it is essential to an Achievement Description that the Observer/Describer knows that he is describing a behavior and not merely a happening. He recognizes that it is an incomplete description and in what respects it is incomplete.

<I, W, K, KH, P, A, PC, S>

- A

An **Achievement-anchored Description** includes a reference to something more than the achievement itself, usually to performance but without saying anything about that performance. The key is that any performance which brings about the achievement will qualify, so that we are not committing ourselves to the particular way by which it is done. Any behavior which results in picking up a pencil will count as the behavior of picking up that pencil. To succeed in the achievement, there must be a process, but for an achievement-anchored description, it makes no difference what that process is as long as it succeeds.

---

**Performative Description.** The Performative Description is in a sense a complement of the Achievement Description, in that it specifies everything except the achievement. It differs from the Agency Description (the basic diamond) in that the content of the Achievement parameter is not specified, making it possible to to describe the behavior without referring to its outcome, whether because the outcome was unsuccessful, or because the behavior is still in progress, or because we do not want to commit ourselves with respect to the achievement. We use this form of description where we are not certain whether the given achievement was actually brought about, or where that aspect is not relevant. We are calling for this form of description when we ask of somebody, "What is he up to? What is he trying to do?", without regard to whether he succeeds.

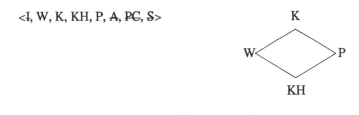

<I, W, K, KH, P, A, PC, S>

**Stimulus-Response Description.** The logic of deletion can be carried to an even finer degree if instead of deleting a parameter, we delete certain possible values of that parameter. If, for example, the value of the K parameter be limited to what is actually present here and now to the Actor in his circumstances, this will come very close to the traditional notion of "stimulus". If the values of either or both of the P and A parameters be limited to what is actually present here and now to the Observer/Describer, that will come very close to the traditional notion of "response" or "operant". And the variant, Stimulus-Organism-Response, needs only that values be assigned also to I and/or PC. What saves this description, in its terms of K plus P and/or A, from the mechanistic implications of the classic S-R and S-0-R is—yet again—that the Observer/ Describer recognizes it as being an incomplete or non-committal description of a behavior, in which the stimulus (K) and response (P, A, or P-A) occur within a context that is not for the moment spelled out, but is nevertheless understood to be there.

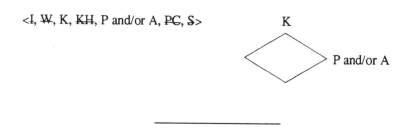

A third operation performed on the Intentional Action formula is **Reduction**, in which certain of the parameters are not differentiated one from the other. These descriptions are not incomplete, but degenerate. One of the possible results of using the operation of reduction is what amounts to cause-effect descriptions.

**Cause-Effect Description.** The W, K, and KH parameters, which have to do with what is the case, are collapsed into "cause". The P and A parameters, which have to do with what happens, are collapsed into "effect". What this comes to is that when certain things are the case, certain things happen, or in traditional language, this cause produces this effect.

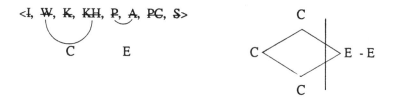

**Purposive Description.** In Purposive Description, the performance is dealt with as one of the causal elements, and the effect is limited to the achievement, which is to say that this cause will result in this condition. This form of cause-effect description corresponds to the experience of agency: on the one side, the achievement that we want to bring about, and on the other, all that we have which accounts for its coming about: our wants, knowledge, competence, and performance.

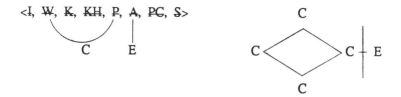

It is instructive to compare the Purposive Description with the Achievement and the Performative Descriptions. In both the Purposive and the Achievement Descriptions, the one parameter for which the value is precisely designated is the outcome of the behavior, the achievement. In the Achievement Description, however, the other parameters are merely not assigned values. Their identity as parameters is not lost. In the Purposive Description, W, K, KH, and P are reduced to a single parameter, Cause. Conversely, the Performative Description differentiates W, K, KH, and P, while the Purposive Description treats them as one. Consequently, whatever facts can be represented by a Purposive Description can be represented by the Achievement Description together with the Performative Description.

The forms of behavior description presented here do not by any means exhaust the possibilities of what could be generated by performing the operations of Substitution, Deletion, and Reduction upon the behavior formula. Indeed, they only hint at what can be done with these resources. To take one example, there is the undirected behavior of the person who does not know what he is doing, or does not know what he wants, or knows neither what he wants nor what he is doing. To take another: as we shall see later, Significance Descriptions give formal access to the facts of human behavior that traditionally have been talked about by reference to "the unconscious", which is why the alternative name for Significance Description is Symbolic

Behavior Description. And there is at least one other operation that can be performed, that of Identity, i.e., Intentional Action = Intentional Action, which there are systematic reasons for including, but are not relevant to our concerns here.

Finally, because these formulas and operations can be used in combination, and reflexively and recursively, they constitute a calculational system rather than merely a list, and the set of products that can be used to describe behavior is endless. In this way, the calculational system provides a conceptual framework that enables us to relate all the different forms of behavior description to one another. The experimental psychologist, for example, emphasizes Performance Descriptions, whereas the psychodynamic psychologist emphasizes Significance Descriptions, and so on. With a framework such as is being presented here, we can easily see that there are connections among them, what those connections are, and wherein they are similar and different.

# CHAPTER 4

# APPRAISING BEHAVIOR[1]

To generate the behavior formula, we needed only one protagonist, the Actor. To generate the forms of description, we needed two, the Actor and the Observer/Describer. To complete the feedback loop, we must have a third, the Critic or Appraiser, who stretches out one hand—so to speak—to the Observer/Describer and the other to the Actor. He appraises the Observer's description and the Actor's behavior.

It is not unlikely that the Critic will appraise a behavior as going all right—recall Maxim 9, "Given the relevant competence, behavior goes right if it does not go wrong in one of the ways that it can go wrong." Given this situation, the Critic has only to appreciate it, and appreciating, not interfere with it, or, where some things are going right and others wrong, enjoy the parts that are right and not interfere with those.

A telling sign of a good Critic is in his judgements when not to interfere with an Actor's behavior, except per-

---

[1]See Ossorio, "A Multicultural Psychology."

haps by giving it his blessing and encouragement. Often enough for it to be significant, persons are not sufficiently confident of their powers and achievements to persist in a course of action or even a social practice that is going well, without being reassured that it *is* going well. They do not trust their own critical abilities, or have never developed their critical capacities, or by the nature of the case are not eligible to make a definitive critical judgement on their achievement—a student does not grade his own examination paper, or a saint elevate himself to that status. On the other hand, a Critic may be less competent than the person whose behavior he is appraising, as in the famous question on one of the early IQ tests, "What should you do if you become lost?" The "correct" answer was, "Go back to where you were before you became lost". But if we could do that, we would not be *really* lost.

If, however, things are not going all right, or if there is something problematic about it that calls for diagnosis and prescription, as Critics we have a number of resources for appraising the circumstances, the Observer's description, and the Actor's behavior. Among them are the forms of behavior description and the maxims, and as well, four further resources that are discussed in this chapter: the Perspectives, the Judgement Diagram, Negotiation, and the Justification Ladder. Since all these are in everyday use, primarily what we shall be doing here will be to articulate systematically and in some detail certain of our ordinary procedures.

----

In Descriptive Psychology, we define appraisal as "a description that logically carries a motivational significance".[2] A standard example is the evaluation of a set of circumstances as dangerous, which tautologically carries

----

[2]See Ossorio, "Appraisal".

with it the motivation to escape the danger. Our standard illustration is that of a lion coming into the room where we are, so we jump out the window to escape it.[3] For us to evaluate the lion—or anything else—as dangerous to us *is* for us to be motivated to try to escape it. Similarly, for us to evaluate information as "good news" for us *is* for us to be motivated to celebrate; and for us to appraise something as a provocation to us *is* for us to be motivated to counter-attack or resist. More generally, being motivated in the relevant way is an aspect of making the appraisal.

In contrast, many of our descriptions are not appraisals. Simply to describe the wall as cream-colored, or to identify the animal as a kitten, does not in itself carry any motivational component.

As Critics appraising a description of a behavior, we can use terms like "right" and "wrong", "complete" and "incomplete", "rigorous" and "careless", "adequate" and "inadequate for the purpose", "misleading" and "illuminating". And the Maxims for Behavior Description can guide us in making those judgements. They warn and remind us of the logical constraints on the completeness and coherence of the description. Further, we shall want to know if the description conforms to what is empirically observable. For example, if Jessie accuses John of breaking the lamp but the lamp is still intact, Jessie's description of John's behavior can be faulted at that point.

When the Critic is appraising either a circumstance or a description, among the special kinds of questions that he can ask are, "Is it true?" and "Is it real?" Was it a real lion that came into the room or a prankster in lion costume, or were we hallucinating? If the lion was real, was it tame or under the control of its keeper, and therefore not actually a danger? Or: does the good news have a myriad of strings attached? Was the apparent provocation actually a way of

---

[3]For a full development of the lion illustration, see Chapter 15.

defending us—the violent shove a way of moving us out of the path of a speeding car, the severe critique a way of saving us from a major blunder? These reality judgements, or **final-order appraisals**,[4] are what we finally appraise as being the case and so are prepared to act upon.

Descriptions that we are called upon to appraise may be of many kinds, for example, a newspaper report on a political rally, gossip about a neighbor's activities, or a scientific report on an experiment. The reporter, tale-bearer, scientist, are all Observer/Describers, and the Critic who is appraising any of their descriptions can ask such questions as "What has this description left out?" and "Is that characterization clearly reasonable or atrociously far-fetched?" He can inquire whether irrelevant matters have been brought in, or relevant ones given wrong weights. If the description is of a behavior, what form of behavior description is our informant using, and is it an appropriate one in this situation?

A case in point is where we read several reviews of a book that some reviewers regard as very good and others as very bad. We shall probably appraise the critiques themselves in terms of how, in the review, the various reviewers handle any material that we ourselves are familiar and competent with. Having done so, we are motivated to act: we buy the book, or borrow it from a library, or pay no further attention to it.

───────────

When we appraise behaviors, our function as Critic is related to somebody's function as Actor. When the Actor is ourselves or someone else, this kind of appraisal affects the operation of our Actor-Observer-Critic negative feedback loop, making it more effective or, if our critique is inept,

───────────

[4]See Ossorio, *Clinical Topics* and *Positive Health and Transcendental Theories.*

less effective. Our appraisal constitutes a diagnosis of what has gone or is going wrong or right, and a prescription for correcting it or for not interfering. The primary value of the diagnosis is that it suggests a course of action, or several possible courses of action—recall that an appraisal is a description that logically carries a motivational significance.

As we have seen earlier, we can interfere with the operation of the loop by contenting ourselves with an unassailable diagnosis without following through on its relevance to the Actor. If the director of a play tells his cast, "Put on a perfect performance", he gives them nothing to work on or with as, for example, the direction in Actor's language, "Slow down in that scene," would. Or we can frustrate the operation of the loop in another way by criticizing every description and every possible course of action so stringently that we paralyze the system. Such a Super-Critic, however, represents a perversion of the Critic function.

We can appraise a behavior as being ethically wrong; or as going wrong by failing to achieve its purpose because some circumstance prevents or deflects it; or as reflecting some deficit or defect in what the person Wants, Knows, Knows How to do, or in his Performance, or Person Characteristics. We have already dealt with the appraisal of circumstances; the appraisal of Person Characteristics must wait.

For the appraisal of behavior as such, we can return to the behavior formula. Is the person acting on inappropriate or inadequate distinctions (K)? Does he want what is unattainable or unsuitable (W)? Does he lack the relevant competence (KH)? Is his performance ineffective (P)? Does he believe—mistakenly—that he is doing it right (K again)? As in all other appraisals, what is crucial is the Critic's competence, and competence is always within a given conceptual domain.

Whether the Critic is appraising circumstances, a

description, or a behavior, he is functioning within a domain—the butcher's, the baker's, the candlestick maker's, or any of an indefinitely large number of others. Paradigmatically, a domain corresponds to a self-contained conceptual system—and a given person may be more or less competent in that domain. To see things in terms of a domain is to operate from its perspective. To have such a perspective, then, corresponds to seeing things in terms of that domain. "He is a baker and this is how a baker sees things, and seeing things this way, and acting accordingly, is what it is to be a baker." Or a housewife or farmer or scholar.

The perspectives of the butcher, baker, and candlestick maker reflect social statuses, cultural patterns of activity which can change over time, and can differ from one time and place to another. In contrast, certain perspectives have universal relevance, notably the Hedonic, Prudential, Ethical, and Esthetic.[5] They cut across all domains. Indeed, they are so fundamental that there appears to be an almost universal agreement that mastery of these four perspectives is essential for being a normal adult person.

---

**Hedonic Perspective.** When we choose a behavior because it is, or promises to be, pleasurable, we are operating with the hedonic perspective, and this irrespective of what may please a given person. It may be playing a musical instrument, or listening to music, or among kinds of music: Bach or Bartok or Bacharach or Boogie. It may be playing football or chess, skiing or skating or sailing. We can take pleasure in observing with a jaundiced eye and describing with a vicious tongue, or with a compassionate eye and gentle tongue.

---

[5]See Ossorio, *Positive Health and Transcendental Theories, Personality and Personality Theories*, 20 July 1977, *Clinical Topics*, and Shideler, "The Lover and the Logician".

Hedonic reasons are predominant whenever we do something for the sheer pleasure in doing it, or avoid doing something because it is unpleasant, painful, or disgusting, and the variations among persons are extreme. What you do for fun, I do only if I am compelled to. Play is the most obvious form of pleasurable behavior, but by no means the only one. There are people who pity scientists or ballet dancers for what appears to be the years of drudgery required by their professions, never grasping that of all the things in the world they might do, this is what they enjoy most.

So intelligible is the pleasure motivation, and so widely recognized as a reason for behaving as we do, that "I'm doing it because I like to" calls for no further explanation. That is the kind of reason we give when there is nothing more to be said, even though from the point of view of the other perspectives, the behavior in question may call for justification. "I like it" is so often associated with selfish and anti-social attitudes that even Winston Churchill, in his delightful "Painting as a Pastime",[6] spends a considerable portion of the essay in pointing out the practical benefits of the pastime of painting. It is a significant commentary on Churchill's personal perspectives that, on the evidence of the essay itself, his primary reason for painting was straightforwardly hedonic. His appeal to prudential reasons, such as the need for relaxation, looks very much like a defense against real or imagined criticism of him as wasting his time by indulging in a pleasurable activity for its own sake.

---

**Prudential Perspective.** Prudence, or self-interest, is one of the general kinds of reasons that we accept unhesitatingly as a answer to the question "Why did you do what

---

[6]In Churchill, *Amid These Storms.*

you did?" In general, prudential concerns are concerns about safety, security, and stability (although it can be prudent sometimes to take risks), and ambition, self-aggrandizement, and so on.

An Actor's behavior can be self-serving or serving a special group with which he identifies himself. Or it can be self-defeating from the prudential perspective, even to the point of being stupid. In his own self-interest, a person may present himself or describe a situation to show himself in a favorable light. John and Jessie, our couple battling over the chair, each had prudential reasons to describe the argument in a way that tended to exonerate them respectively, and we—their friends and counsellors who are appraising the two descriptions—have every reason to take that possibility into consideration.

---

**Ethical Perspective.** "It's painful, and it's not going to benefit me, but it's the right thing to do." "There's nothing that would give me greater pleasure, and it would mean a long leap ahead professionally, but I won't do it. It's wrong." Such examples clearly set off the ethical perspective from the hedonic and prudential perspectives, although conflict between or among them is not inevitable and not necessarily frequent. What is good can be pleasurable, and what is pleasurable, good, just as what is prudent can be right and what is right can be prudent.

Both our descriptions and our behavior are likely to reflect our ethical judgements, but the fact that they are ethical does not guarantee that they are free from any possibility of error or distortion. No more than the judgements from the hedonic and prudential perspectives are they guaranteed to be impeccable. Think of the evil that has been perpetrated in the name of good—genocide, torture, treachery—as well as of the corruptions that have resulted from the pursuit of pleasure and self-interest.

The Critic will fail in his job if he does not attend to the possibility that the Observer's description may reflect, wittingly or unwittingly, his personal ethical judgements on the behavior he is describing, or on the Actor whose behavior it is. Or the Critic may note that the Observer is failing to recognize that an Actor's reasons are genuinely ethical, or is ascribing to the Actor ethical motives that are alien to him.

More generally, ethical judgements tend to be associated with communities in such a way that membership in a particular community is conditional upon adherence to its ethical (as well as other) norms. Thus an ethical violation, whether real or presumed, may carry the threat of expulsion, and ethical conformity carry assurance of belonging within that community.

------

**Esthetic Perspective.** The word that most accurately characterizes this perspective is "fittingness", with "appropriate" as a possible alternative. We can distinguish at least three varieties of fittingness: the artistic, the social, and the intellectual. In the arts of whatever kind—painting, poetry, dance, music, needlework, and all the others—the ultimate standard is whether the parts fit together to create a whole in a way that is *artistically* appropriate. "Why this dissonance?" "Because the whole passage—the whole sonata—needs that particular kind of accent just there." Or, "Couldn't you use some other word in that sentence?" "No. This is the only one that has the right rhythm and sound, as well as meaning."

As what is artistically fitting depends upon the artistic circumstances, so what is *socially* fitting depends upon the social circumstances. For example, eating with one's fingers is socially acceptable in India, and in America appropriate at a picnic although not at a formal dinner. Every society has its common courtesies, and its members generally agree on what is and is not appropriate behavior for a wide variety of situations, e.g., how one comports oneself at a business meeting, a funeral, a football game, a concert, and in a supermarket, on the street, in a crowded bus, at a remote camping site, in a hospital.

Almost anyone can learn such conventions, but there are many circumstances where the conventions do not apply or are not adequate guides. Take, for example, the tense committee meeting where somebody cleared the air by telling a joke. That move worked in this situation, but might not in others; either way, there is no convention governing such a choice among behaviors. Sensitivity to what is going on, a feeling for the fitness of things in the social milieu, an acute sense of timing, go beyond the conventions, and it is in such characteristics that mastery of the social perspective is most clearly manifested.

A judgement in terms of accuracy, precision, coherence, rigor, objectivity, can serve to illustrate concern for *intellectual* fittingness: Does it fit the facts? Is it logically sound? When the Critic uses the maxims to check on the completeness and coherence of an Observer's description of an Actor's behavior, he is functioning with this aspect of the esthetic perspective. When he tests that description for its empirical validity, this is the perspective he is taking, as well as when he recognizes that in order to fill in gaps, he may want to resort to the psychodiagnostic, literary, or situational formula (see Chapter 5). And, of course, when the Critic asks, "Is this real?", or "Is that a fact?", he is appealing to the intellectual-fittingness perspective.

It is possible, although not standard practice, to include a fourth category within the esthetic perspective: the *spiritual*, which has to do with whatever is transcendent, holy, timeless, and ultimate. How do the mundane world and its activities look under the aspect of eternity? What is ultimately significant? Spiritual fittingness can be subsumed under one of the other varieties, or treated separately.

The esthetic perspective—whether artistic, intellectual, social, or spiritual—is focussed upon the relation of the parts within the whole so that their interrelationships produce or maintain not only the integrity of the whole, but also the integrity of the parts into which it can be articulated. Persons as such have their very being as members of communities, yet no community can exist except by the participation of a number of individuals. And no person or community can exist apart from the real world, in isolation from the air we breathe and the food we eat, the nurturing we received as newborns, and the associates through whom we come to be who and what we are.

---

Together, the hedonic, prudential, ethical, and esthetic perspectives provide grounds (reasons, justifications) for choosing what we shall do now (cf. Maxim 2) in the absence of any definite assurance concerning the further outcome of what we do.

Frequently we are told that we ought to choose our behaviors in the light of their consequences. Such advice is blatantly impractical, however, because it is impossible to foresee, calculate, or predict the consequences of any behavior in sufficient detail to make such advice practicable. What we need, therefore, is a way of deciding among behaviors that does not depend upon the full range of their actual consequences, but does reflect our knowledge of their foreseeable consequences. The perspectives provide us with such a way. By giving us reasons upon which we can act, they make action possible.

In principle, in deliberate action we do not operate with only one of the perspectives, but with all four, and those reasons carry differentiated weights corresponding to our person characteristics and present circumstances. In some of our behaviors, of course, one reason will carry so much weight that we talk and act as if that were the only one. Even so, we are still operating with all four because by having them, we are enabled to recognize that in this case, certain perspectives are not applicable, or certain reasons carry very little weight.

To take as an example the beer-buying episode described in Chapter 2, Jim had a strong hedonic reason for going out to buy beer: he liked beer and wanted some at that moment. He had a fairly strong prudential reason not to: he was under the legal age for buying beer and might be caught and fined, jailed, or otherwise discommoded. His ethical reason against it was weak: he did not believe that it was ethically wrong to buy and drink beer even though it was illegal. And he had a strong social (esthetic) reason to buy the beer despite its being (in his case) illegal: he and his peers took it to be not only fitting and proper but even commendable to disobey laws that they considered unduly restrictive. Thus his reasons for doing it were stronger than his reasons for not doing it. His decision, to be sure, was accomplished intuitively, not by any such elaborate analysis. He was not reflective enough as a Critic to work things out thus systematically, but even if he had been, in this case he had no reason to.

Again, the parallel with speaking one's native language can be instructive. People can speak it grammatically and even beautifully without ever having studied grammar, because they have learned to do so. But from their use of the language, we can reconstruct a grammar, thus achieving a systematic reconstruction of what they are doing intuitively. And for certain purposes, such a reconstruction can be invaluable.

Normally it is only in the hard, major decisions that we sit down—or pace the floor—while we work out what our separate reasons are and how we are weighting them. Even then, however, the choice is not made by adding up figures, so to speak. If anything, the figures reflect the choice.

These four perspectives represent basic dimensions of our human world. They correspond to an empirical classification of reasons why people do what they do—empirical in that it is a reconstruction of actual behaviors. It is straightforwardly a matter of fact that when we push someone (including ourselves) to explain or justify what he is (or we are) doing, it is apparently impossible to give a satisfactory answer that does not reflect one or more of the perspectives. But of this, more will come later in connection with the Justification Ladder.

Again a diagram may be useful in summarizing where we have been so far. It is called the **Judgement Diagram**:7

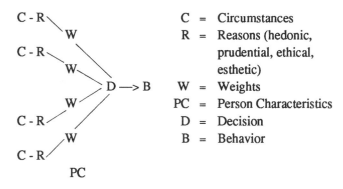

| | |
|---|---|
| C | = Circumstances |
| R | = Reasons (hedonic, prudential, ethical, esthetic) |
| W | = Weights |
| PC | = Person Characteristics |
| D | = Decision |
| B | = Behavior |

Our circumstances provide us with reasons for our behavior, reasons which may be hedonic, prudential, ethical, or esthetic. The different reasons carry different weights with us, and those weights reflect our person characteristics. In the light of our reasons and weights, we reach a decision and act on it.

---

Decision-making is not always easy and never fool-

---

7See Ossorio, *Clinical Topics*, "Appraisal", and *Personality and Personality Theories*, 20 July 1977.

proof. When difficulties arise, one of the resources available to us is **negotiation**, which is to be distinguished from bargaining, and from argument or debate. Bargaining is a way for reaching an accommodation: who is willing to do what, for what? Argument and debate are ways for defeating an opponent. In contrast, negotiation is a way of arriving at a good answer to the question at issue, and the question at issue divides into two main categories: what is true, and what to do.

To illustrate the process of negotiating, let us suppose that we have on hand two or more descriptions and/or appraisals of a person's behavior, and we must decide between them. It may be that different Observers are reporting their different versions of the same episode. Or the Actor, Observer, and Critic may be all the same person, and that person is describing and explaining his behavior in more than one way. Or an Actor is describing what he did in one way ("I was just kidding!"), but the Observer and/or Critic sees him as having done something else entirely ("In that tone of voice? With your fists clenched?")

Assuming that in such cases we—as Critics—do not summarily discard all except one of the conflicting descriptions, we can initiate the process of negotiation, which almost undoubtedly is as old as humankind, and is central to what philosophers have called the Court of Reason—the final appeal for settling questions. The **Negotiation Paradigm** that is relatively distinctive to Descriptive Psychology[8] represents it as a social practice having four stages: (1) taking positions; (2) criticizing and defending those positions; (3) adjusting positions if necessary, i.e., formulating new positions; and (4) drawing conclusions.

In Stage 1, both participants state their positions, and which are apparently in conflict. Just as two objects cannot be at a certain distance from each other unless they occupy

---

[8]See Ossorio, *Personality and Personality Theories*, 22 July 1977.

the same spatial framework, so two descriptions cannot be either compatible or incompatible unless they share a frame of reference. Thus a legal negotiation must take place within the framework of the relevant legal system, a personal negotiation within the framework of a personal relationship.

Stage 2 involves criticizing and defending positions. Often it entails, as well, requests for justification that are not criticisms, as when one participant asks the other merely to explain or clarify some aspect of his position. Justification involves giving reasons, and reasons are potentially justifications. In this connection, one of our important conceptual resources is the **Justification Ladder**.[9] The ladder is given this form to emphasize that we justify our behavior, or someone else's, by appealing to a higher "rung" on the ladder, sometimes the adjacent one, sometimes skipping over intermediate rungs.

Perspectives, Competence

Principle
Theory
Custom
Judgement

The bottom rung of the ladder is *judgement*. It is the level of our moment-to-moment appraisals of what is going on around us and what we are doing. If we are called upon to justify a judgement, we can appeal to *custom*: "This is what people customarily do, and this is the way it is customarily done". The child asks, "Why do I have to go to school?" We reply, "Because that's part of growing up in our society." He asks, "Why do you call this a street and

---

9See Ossorio, *Clinical Topics* and "Religion without Doctrine".

that an alley?" "Because those are the customary names we give to these different sorts of roadways."

If the custom be challenged—"But why do I have to grow up in this society?"—we take the next step up the ladder to a *theory* or *principle*; these differ mainly in scope and need not be precisely differentiated. "Because growing up means, among other things, being a member of a community, and this is your community." Or if the child challenges our nomenclature, saying, "But the distinction between ˌ street and alley is arbitrary," we can reply, "Originally it may have been, but now that it's established, it's no longer merely arbitrary, and using the terms correctly is one of the marks of membership in this community."

The next rung requires a long step, and of a different kind. As has wisely been said, "There are times when it is necessary to rise above principle." The appeal from theories or principles such as community values or procedures, or philosophical or religious doctrines, is to the perspectives—hedonic, prudential, ethical, and esthetic—and to our competence in the relevant conceptual domains. The final appeal is to the competence of the other person: "But *can't you see* that the proportions of this room are all wrong?" "*Isn't it obvious* that these two statements are contradictory?" An essential aspect of our competence in the relevant domain is that we understand the questions pertaining to that domain, and are therefore in a position to appraise the answers which are implicit in the appeal to judgement, custom, theory, and principle.

Another of our major resources in negotiating is the trading of facts. When we justify our own behaviors, we take certain facts as given. When we negotiate with another person, however, much of the process will have to do with trading facts: appealing to them, challenging them, bringing in new ones, construing them in different ways. We may argue over which facts are relevant, how much weight we shall assign to this or that, and what they severally imply.

Throughout this second stage of negotiation, a good-faith condition obtains. The participants must neither omit nor gloss over any important features of his position, and the criticisms they raise must represent objections that the participants actually have, not merely logically possible criticisms that somebody, sometime, might raise. In conjunction with this, all the significant objections must be raised. To reserve any would be a breach of good faith.

If criticisms have been raised which either participant cannot rebut, negotiation will proceed to Stage 3, in which he (or they) revise the original positions so that they will withstand the criticisms that have been presented. Such reformulations return the participants to Stage 2, including the possibility that new disagreements may arise on the basis of the adjusted positions, calling for further secondary or derivative negotiations.

Drawing a conclusion is Stage 4, and in this negotiation paradigm, a resolution is always available after all the apparently legitimate criticisms have been brought into the open. Initially, the problem was straightforwardly one of the subject-matter about which the participants disagreed. If agreement on that is reached, this constitutes a resolution, a good answer. But what if each comes out with a position that survives all criticism from the other, and those positions are still in opposition? Now there is a second kind of problem: how can there be two good answers, both of which withstand criticism by these two people at this time, in good faith?

A resolution of this second type of question is provided by a person-characteristic description, which typically will be of one of three kinds. Supposing the issue to have been the appropriateness of John's behavior relative to the moving of the chair, and the negotiators to be two Observer/Describers of that situation, the first resolution might take the form, "You're a friend of John's and I'm not, so it makes sense for you to view John's behavior differently from the way I do,"—and a position of this kind is legitimate. In the second form, we disqualify the other person: "You haven't responded to my criticisms of what John did, even though you think you have." The third form consists of disqualifying ourselves: "Well, you are more intimately acquainted with both John and Jessie than I am, so you see things in that situation that I don't see at all. You appreciate complications there that are beyond me."

The reason why such person-descriptions constitute a resolution, even without agreement, is that it answers all our questions about why we do not agree.

To anticipate the discussion of paradigm case methodology in the following chapter: two-person negotiation is a paradigm case, and other cases may be considered as cases of negotiation because of their resemblance to the two-person form. To specify only two of the possibilities: negotiation can be carried on by one person disputing with himself, taking different positions, criticizing and defending each, adjusting them, and achieving a resolution. Or there may be many participants, as in a dispute where each (or every) side is represented by a committee.

The key to negotiation is competence (KH). At the outset, the participants must take it (at least provisionally) that all of them are competent to make the necessary judgements, but during the process, the participants may exhibit various degrees of competence, and one of the aspects of negotiation can consist in making judgements about others' competence. Competence will be exhibited primarily in handling the subject-matter of the disagreement, and secondarily in using the forms of behavior description, the maxims, the perspectives, the behavior explanation formulas, and whatever else they are jointly appealing to. With a person who does not share the relevant competence and concepts, there can be no negotiation on that matter at all, but only incomprehension: "He may be hostile, but he cannot be critical: he does not know what is being discussed."[10]

Negotiation follows the logic of "two heads are better than one", because two people with the relevant competence are not likely to make the same mistake at the same time. In its logical form, negotiation is designed to bring out the nature of the disagreement by giving the participants an opportunity to raise the questions that express their disagreement. In practice, the way that individuals actually negotiate will be affected by their person characteristics: their values and interests, the facts each has available, and so on. They may not share all the relevant concepts (although this can be negotiated), or are of unequal competence in using them in this situation, or they can be giving priority to the different standards and perspectives which generate the different descriptions.

---

It will help us to become in general more competent Critics if we have some idea of what customs, theories, principles, and perspectives constitute our own basis for appraising others—and, reflexively, for appraising ourselves. We are not exempt from the requirements that we lay on other Actors, Observer/Describers, and Critics: our own descriptions and appraisals are open to various descriptions and appraisals.

We should ask: Is the description we are giving complete or incomplete, misleading or illuminating? Are we being unfair by giving too much or too little weight to this or that element? Moreover, what we are up to as Actor/Critics, is also subject to appraisal. Are we simply amusing ourselves (hedonic), or out for what we can get for ourselves (prudential), or doing our duty (ethical), or

---

[10]Lewis, "The Abolition of Man", p. 31.

working toward an artistic or social or intellectual adjustment (esthetic)? Do we want to convert the person whose behavior we are appraising to our point of view, or to impose our standards on him? Or do we want only to provide him with a listening ear while he works things out for himself? And are our conceptual resources and skills adequate to describe and appraise behavior (and persons and the world) in all its richness and complexity, without remainder or paradox or contradiction or confusion?

---

Before turning to the task of describing persons and the world, two general comments are in order. First, thus far little has been said about predicting behaviors, and little more will be said specifically about that in what follows. The reason for this omission is that this presentation of Descriptive Psychology is deliberately limited to its systematic conceptual basis, although given its resources, we can in principle predict behaviors at least as well as with any other set of resources.

The problem with all prediction of behaviors, however, is that from very general descriptions, we can predict with very high accuracy, but those predictions are likely to be uninteresting—for example, that if two persons are engaging in a conversation, they will continue to do so until there is some reason for stopping. The more specific the description, the less accurate and precise the prediction, because so much depends upon circumstances. Much of the time, however, we do not need to be able to predict what will happen next. For example, we can respond satisfactorily in a particular conversation without being able to predict what turn it will take in the next interchange.

What we need for nearly all our everyday, practical living is not the ability to predict, but simply competence in acting, observing, describing, and appraising; and to develop such competence we have available—among other resources—this set of systematically related concepts and procedures.

Second, although it has required many pages to analyze what goes on in describing and appraising behavior, actual description and appraisal can be done in the twinkling of an eye, and almost always are. What we have here is not some strange and esoteric achievement, but a detailed and orderly presentation of a natural, universal form of behavior which people engage in spontaneously, easily, intuitively, and without reflection. It is when we face problematic descriptions and difficult decisions that we need these explicit procedures of reflection and analysis.

# PART II

# DESCRIBING PERSONS

# CHAPTER 5

# PERSON CHARACTERISTICS[1]

The explanation of behavior leads us to the concepts of person characteristics (the PC aspect of behavior) and of circumstances (the K aspect of behavior). The conceptual relations among these, as shown in the behavior formula, are such that if we know any two of them, we may be able to derive the third, as in geometry, if we are given two angles of a triangle, we can calculate the third. The cases are only roughly parallel, because in the following **Behavior Explanation Formulas**, the connections are less strong than in the illustration from geometry. Knowledge of any two of the elements, however, will often enable us to reach a conclusion about the third that will be adequate for our purposes.

**The Psychodiagnostic Formula.** In *these* circumstances, it would take *that* kind of person to engage in *this* behavior. Circumstances and behavior are given; from

---

[1]See Ossorio, *Personality and Personality Theories*, 15 and 18 July 1977, *Clinical Topics* (indexed under "individual difference characteristics"), "Outline of Descriptive Psychology," and "A Multicultural Psychology".

these we draw conclusions about person characteristics.

**The Literary Formula.** In *these* circumstances, *this* kind of person *would* behave in that way. Circumstances and person characteristics are given, and from these we draw conclusions about behavior.

**The Situational Formula.** *This* kind of person would not behave in *this* way unless the circumstances were of *that* kind. Person characteristics and behavior are given; from these we draw conclusions about the circumstances—although this is the weakest of the formulas.

———————

Outstanding among the characteristics of persons is that we differ from one another in a great number of ways, while still being recognizably persons. There is no end to our differences or to our complexities. Yet observing ourselves and others, we also find similarities. Our problem in describing persons, therefore, is how to describe our similarities systematically in such a way as not to obscure our uniqueness, or more generally, to map out an order within a realm of incredible diversity without sacrificing any of its richness. And we need to do this in a way that will allow us to check our observations and analyses with those of other observers.

In Descriptive Psychology, we define a **person** as **an individual whose history is, paradigmatically, a history of deliberate actions**.[2] Because the definition involves the concept of paradigm case, we shall need to make a brief excursion into paradigm case formulation.

At times we need to define a term—and "person" is only one of many examples—but we cannot do so because although the things we want to talk about fit what the term designates, they have nothing else in common. There is no second thing that they share which we could refer to if we

———————

[2]See Ossorio, *"Persons"*.

wanted to construct a definition. In such a situation, we have the option of giving a **paradigm case formulation**,[3] a procedure in which we formulate a logical domain by picking out all the possible instances of the phenomenon in question, and nothing else. In this respect it is functionally equivalent to a definition.

The first move in a paradigm case formulation is to specify a **paradigm case** which identifies a sub-group of elements within the domain. To take a simple illustration: a paradigm case of "family" might be a father, a mother, and two children born to them, a girl and a boy—a description which picks out a sub-group of families. The next step is to introduce **transformations** of that paradigm case by changing one or more of its aspects, such as the number of children, and/or their ages, and/or their sex, and if they are adopted or foster children, their status. The father and/or mother may be a step-parent, or the parental function may be performed by foster parents who may or may not be blood-relatives of the children. For some purposes, we may include grandparents, aunts and uncles, cousins, and other degrees of consanguinity. Each of these (and any other) transformations constitutes a further sub-group, and this process is continued until all the sub-groups that we desire have been identified.

Using paradigm case methodology, we do not start by accumulating instances of actual families and then look for whatever they may have in common. Instead, we take a clear-cut case and relate all other cases to that paradigm by varying one or more aspects of the paradigm case. So doing, for specific purposes such as sociological studies, advertising, or taking a census, we can restrict or expand what we shall take as a family, without confusion or ambiguities.

A word of warning: thinking in terms of paradigm case formulation will be needed throughout this book in

---

[3]See Ossorio, "Conceptual-Notational Devices".

many more places than will be explicitly designated. Over and over we shall be confronting complexities that can be readily disentangled if we are thinking in these terms, but if not, are likely to remain obdurate. That is, frequently we shall present statements—whether labelled as paradigm cases or not—for which there are exceptions, so that they cannot be taken literally as having universal application. The exceptions, however, can be handled straightforwardly as transformations of the paradigm case. By taking account of the apparent exceptions—the transformations—in this way, we do not become mired down in details. And neither for the first nor the last time, what we are explicating is not some esoteric procedure, but something that we do normally and naturally, although often without being aware that we are doing it.

We are so used to working with the concept "family" that we do not often need to go through specific paradigm case formulation in discussing families. In practice, we make our judgements on what constitutes a family independently of any explicit reference to a paradigm case. With the concept of "person", however, there is more controversy over whether "person" does or does not apply to a given individual or class of individuals, and therefore a greater need for paradigm case formulation—a procedure that allows us to specify the grounds on which, on any given occasion, we do or do not extend the term to cover, e.g., foetuses, "human vegetables", and canine, feline, simian, delphine, and at least hypothetically, angelic individuals or types.

Let us go back to the definition of a person as an individual whose history is paradigmatically a history of deliberate actions. Deliberate action is a case where the individual knows what he is doing and chooses among possible behaviors. This definition implies a paradigm case formulation, and we need such a formulation because there are no actual, documented cases that fit the specification of a person whose history is composed of nothing except deliberate actions. All the actual cases we know or know of fit one or another of the transformations. For example, everybody sleeps (except, conceivably, angels. Remember that in paradigm case formulation, we are concerned with possible as well as actual instances of the range of phenomena), and while we are sleeping, we are not engaging in deliberate actions. Some persons, at times, are unconscious for various reasons. Or they may be dead drunk or in a coma or a drug-induced oblivion.

Thus a substantial part of a normal person's life-history does not consist of engaging in deliberate action—a fact which brings out that what is conceptually necessary may not be historically universal. Deliberate action is essential to the concept of person, even though persons are not engaging in deliberate actions all the time. What makes an individual a *person* is that his history consists essentially of deliberate actions.

---

Taking the notion of a person as an individual with a history of deliberate actions, we can articulate by a parametric analysis how any one of these individuals can be the same as, or different from, any other such individual by specifying types of behavior and patterns of their occurrence. We shall group the types and patterns into three categories: Dispositions, Powers, and Derivatives.

**Dispositions** are divisible into traits, attitudes, interests, and styles. These are paradigmatically expressed by a type of behavior with a high-frequency or low-frequency pattern of occurrence within a life-history. Let us take as our illustration a child, Jill, whom we have known since she was a baby, and who is always getting into cabinets, crawling under beds, taking toys apart, and asking Why? Why? Why? Like Kipling's Elephant's Child, she is blessed—or cursed—with an insatiable curiosity. So pervasive is this behavior, so frequent in its occurrence throughout a wide variety of situations, that we can say that she has the *trait* of being a curious person.

Thus there are as many traits as there are types of behavior: generous, aggressive, hostile, modest, excitable, suspicious, serene, and so on—anything like a complete list would have to be indefinitely long in order to do justice to the richness and complexity of human differences. We can give a *trait description* if we observe that an individual engages in that type of behavior more than we would expect, and enough more to be worth commenting on. Thus we may note that so-and-so is "very" or "somewhat" or "extremely" generous or ungenerous, modest or immodest. For example, Jill's life-history is characterized by curiosity behavior on almost every occasion except when she has strong reasons to refrain from that type of behavior.

Again, what is conceptually necessary may not be historically universal: the conditions may be such that a person does not display a particular trait which he has. Thus we can further differentiate *conditional* or *circumstantial traits*: recurring patterns of behavior that occur only when conditions that support them are present, as when Jill's father tells her teacher, "Jill is as good as gold as long as you keep an eye on her, but as soon as you turn your back, her inquisitiveness will get her into trouble."

As Jill grows older, she develops a particular affection for animals. In such cases we speak of *attitudes*, types of behavior and patterns of occurrence that are context-specific, in that they are directed toward an object or activity or institution or practice or other more narrowly defined focus of attention. The concept of attitude appears in the values of the Know parameter of behavior.

Traits and attitudes may contrast with each other. A person with the trait of loving-kindness may have a hostile attitude toward spiders. One who is generally calm may be excited by circuses. One who is stingy toward the rest of the world may be generous with his children. One who is characteristically trusting may be suspicious of public officials or very small dogs.

Formally speaking, any type of behavior can be used to generate a trait description, and any type of behavior in conjunction with any type of object can be used to generate an attitude description. Both traits and attitudes tend to be exhibited frequently in the person's behavior under normal conditions. When we give a trait or attitude description of a person, we are saying in effect that we expect from that person more (or less) of a certain kind of behavior than we would expect of just anybody, or alternatively, more or less than just what the situation calls for. How much more or less? Enough to be worth commenting on, and different Observer/Describers or Critics may decide differently depending upon their own purposes, values, sensitivities, or other person characteristics.

An *interest*, like an attitude, is characterized by having an object, but whereas with an attitude we have a single type of behavior, an interest generally involves several or even many types of behavior. Paradigmatically, an interest involves also an intrinsic action and a strong motivational priority. It is expressed in intrinsic behavior, i.e., behavior without an ulterior motive, without a further end in view, although some of those intrinsic behaviors may be accomplished by engaging in instrumental behaviors—recall the Significance Description of behavior.

Jill's interest in animals leads her to accumulate pets, to read about them, to take courses in zoology, to talk with veterinarians and wild-life specialists and zoo-keepers, to associate with other students who share that interest, and finally to make a career in that field. Such a wide range of behaviors reflects a strong motivational priority with respect to the object of her interest, and might be shown in such instances as her giving up a chance to attend a football game in order to help with an extracurricular experiment on animal behavior. Or she slights a history assignment in favor of studying biochemistry. She stops taking music lessons because practising takes time that she would rather spend in the laboratory.

In the fourth of the dispositions, *style*, what is specified about the behavior is values of the Performance parameter, that is, with how we do what we do: gracefully, vigorously, deviously, cautiously. "He's got class." "Whatever she does has a certain spark to it." Or the style description can be relative to a particular activity: "He speaks with a Southern accent." "She moves awkwardly." "He goes about his work enthusiastically." A chart may help to summarize the relationships among the Dispositions:

| Disposition: | Trait | Attitude | Interest | Style |
|---|---|---|---|---|
| Type of behavior | any | any | various (intrinsic) | all or most |
| Object? | no | yes | yes | no |
| Pattern of Occurrence | high or low frequency | high or low frequency | high or low frequency | high or low frequency |

What this chart obscures is that we do not have a type of behavior on the one hand, and an object on the other. Instead, what marks the type of behavior *is* the object.

Traits, attitudes, interests, and styles are grouped together as Dispositions because the person is disposed to behave in those ways, and he will normally display those characteristics in ordinary circumstances, that is, unless something prevents him from doing so. We expect those behaviors from him, basing our expectation on his known characteristics. If he behaves in ways that are contrary to what we know of his traits, attitudes, interests, and styles, we are surprised, and may want to seek an explanation for why, on this occasion, he is acting contrary to what we would expect. What we expect of him may indeed change, even radically, but in general Dispositions are acquired slowly and change slowly, so that we are likely to attribute a strong or swift change to a change of state (see below). Dispositions tend to be persistent even in the case where a person has the trait of being fickle or indecisive and thus is "constant in inconstancy".

---

A second group of person characteristics, **Powers**, differs from the Dispositions in that the criterion is the possibility or non-possibility of the occurrence of a behavior within a life-history, rather than the frequency of occurrence. Taking examples from each of the three Powers, abilities, knowledge, and values: if we do not have the ability to ride a bicycle, we cannot engage in the deliberate action of riding a bicycle, even though we might succeed in doing so by chance or luck. If we do not know where Barton-on-the-Beans is located, we cannot engage in any behavior which requires that knowledge. If we do not value punctuality, we cannot make any behavioral choices which require that priority.

An *ability* is the potentiality to accomplish something, and the type of behavior in question is defined by reference to the Achievement parameter of behavior. If a person has the ability to do something, under normal circumstances he can be expected to succeed in doing it if he tries. Like Know-how in the behavior formula, it is a competence concept, but whereas Know-how refers only to whatever skill is required for the successful performance of the given behavior, reference to an ability identifies a range of achievements which a person can be expected to accomplish under normal circumstances if he tries. Thus "has the ability to" means that normally, the person who attempts the specified achievement can be expected to succeed non-accidentally. His success can be attributed to that person characteristic rather than merely to chance or luck or exceptionally favorable circumstances. The qualification "under normal circumstances" acknowledges that unfavorable circumstances can preclude success even for a person of high ability. The most competent bicyclist cannot be expected to ride through a trackless forest, or if he is suffering from a broken leg, or if his vehicle is disabled.

In ordinary language, we have ways of dealing with gradations that fall below the level of ability. These have to do with the extent to which we explain a successful behavior by the person's competence, and the extent to which we attribute it to circumstances. We speak of someone's being "liable to succeed in doing X", or "capable of doing X", or "merely able": in other words, success depends to an important degree upon something other than the individual's person characteristics, i.e., his circumstances. If a person is merely liable to do X, or merely capable of doing X, his failure to succeed in doing X does not call strongly for an explanation, and the kind of explanation is relatively trivial, e.g., he wasn't lucky. In contrast, if the person has the ability, we attribute his success principally to that person characteristic, and less to circumstances—always with the qualification "under normal circumstances".

The other Power categories can be defined in terms of ability. A person's *knowledge* is the set of facts that he has the ability to act on. A person's set of *values* is the set of priorities among motivations that he has the ability to act on.

Our knowledge is what we have to draw on in generating our behaviors. Thus if any behavior (deliberate action) requires knowledge that we do not have, we cannot engage in that behavior—recall Maxim 5, "If a situation calls for a person to do something he cannot do, he will do something he can do, if he does anything at all." Our values are what we have to draw on in choosing among behaviors—recall the Perspectives: hedonic, prudential, ethical, and esthetic. We are unable to act unless we value states of affairs differently, so that we have corresponding priorities among our motivations, and therefore in any given situation are motivated to do one thing rather than another. These negative forms of description display clearly why the Powers are possible-impossible, yes-no categories: we cannot use what we do not have.

Abilities, knowledge, and values, like Dispositions, are concepts of relatively persistent person characteristics. In general they change slowly, although they may be acquired more rapidly, and they are retained unless something happens to bring it about that we lose them. We may have lost our knowledge of French verb-forms because we had never had occasion to use that information during the years after we took a course in French. We would lose our competence in gymnastics if we did not practise enough and appropriately. A particular value may be lost or significantly reduced when we acquire a new value. If a person's Dispositions and Powers change, we take it that they do not change without a reason.

We can do only what we can do, but the Powers we have, we do have; and in every behavior we are using some of our abilities, knowledge, and values. If we did not have those Powers, we would not be engaging in these behaviors, and if we want to engage in behaviors that are now impossible for us, we shall have to increase our Powers before we can do so.

---

The **Derivatives**, as we have already seen, are person characteristics that affect behavior by making a difference in the Dispositions and/or Powers. Those which we shall distinguish here are embodiment, capacity, and state. Capacity and state are explicitly defined in terms of the

Dispositions and Powers. Embodiment is independently defined, but it has "the difference it makes" as its most important concomitant.

The *embodiment*[4] person characteristic needs particular consideration because of the long philosophical history that attends it, a history in which human bodies have often been given special status as definitive of persons. This is a reductionist move that is neither necessary nor useful. Embodiment is directly linked to the Performance parameter which codifies the process aspect of behavior. Paradigmatically, performances require some sort of body, whether human or canine or mechanical or crystalline or nebulous, but performances by themselves no more determine what a behavior is than bodies by themselves determine who we are.

Embodiment is only one of the person characteristics, as Performance is only one of the aspects of behavior, and both persons and behavior have other, equally essential aspects. It is notable that we can lose or replace a fair number of our bodily parts (e.g., lose wisdom teeth or replace a hip joint) while remaining the same persons, although a considerable change in a trait, attitude, interest, or style, or in our abilities or knowledge or values, can elicit, "I'm a different person from what I was a year ago!" or "You've changed so much since you left home that I hardly know you any more."

We no more *are* our bodies than we *are* our Dispositions or Powers, but we have bodily—i.e., object—characteristics that can be described and compared in the same way that other objects can be described and compared (cf. the Basic Object Unit, Chap. 9). The kind of body we have—*homo sapiens*, electronic, arboreal, amoeboid, gaseous—will conspicuously affect not only our Performances ("We can do only what we can"), but also our

---

[4]See Ossorio, "Embodiment".

Style, the manner in which we do it. A person with two legs will propel himself along the ground in a manner very different from a robotic person on wheels.

In case the notion that a person might have a robotic or amoeboid or gaseous body seems far-fetched, we need to define three terms as they are used in Descriptive Psychology. *Homo sapiens* is a species of organism; it is a biological concept. A *person* is an individual whose history is paradigmatically a history of deliberate actions. And a *human being* is a person with a *homo sapiens* biological organism.

If we were to limit "person" to individuals with *homo sapiens* bodies, we would be arbitrarily limiting our range of observation and investigation, a move that would be methodologically unsound. Already we have at least two non-human candidates for the status of "person", the great apes and the dolphins, and none of us knows what else the universe may hold in the way of individuals whose history is paradigmatically a history of deliberate actions, but whose embodiment is other than that of *homo sapiens*.[5] It is interesting to consider the possibility that our being able to recognize and treat extraterrestrial persons with non-human bodies as persons may be a condition of the survival of our species.

The concept of *capacity* codifies the possibilities and impossibilities for acquiring person characteristics, a potential that will be actualized only as a result of an appropriate history. Remember Maxim 8 and the formula that can be used to express it: Capacity plus the relevant intervening history produces person characteristics (C + H —> PC). People cannot learn to ride bicycles unless bicycles are available for them to ride, the circumstances are such as to provide them with the motivation to master that skill,

---

[5]Schwartz, "The Problem of Other Possible Persons: Dolphins, Primates, and Aliens".

and the opportunity to do so is present.

Before the invention of the bicycle, doubtless a huge proportion of the human race had the capacity to acquire the ability to ride bicycles, but none of them could develop that capacity into that ability because the appropriate history was lacking. In fact, there would have been no way of knowing if they did have that capacity. Moreover, the kind of history and circumstances that are appropriate (i.e., effective for acquiring a given ability) need not be the same for every individual. One person may have the money to buy a bicycle whereas another does not; if he does not, he may or may not have a friend who will lend him one to learn on (history, circumstances). A person with a good sense of balance and physical coordination may acquire that ability rapidly, while a person with poor balance and coordination may require much help and encouragement before being able to do it at all (person characteristic).

To acquire an ability or knowledge or value increases our **behavior potential**,[6] the type and range of behaviors that are possible for us. Not to have a given ability (or knowledge or value), or to have a given disability, or to lose an ability, are all states of affairs that correspond to limitations on our behavior potential. If we succeed in some enterprise requiring an ability, knowledge, or value that we do not have, it will be by accident or luck, as when someone who does not know how to work an arithmetic problem answers it correctly by guessing. Our behavior potential embraces all that we are capable of doing, given our Dispositions and Powers, as our personal potential embraces all that we are capable of being.

A full discussion of capacity must wait for the following chapter on personal development. Meanwhile, we must consider one more type of person characteristic, *states*, in which there is a change in one's Dispositions

---

[6]See Ossorio, *Positive Health and Transcendental Theories.*

and/or Powers. States, like capacities, make a difference in behavior only indirectly, because changes in one's behaviors come about only by virtue of a change in his Dispositions and/or Powers. It is characteristic of states to be nonpersistent and reversible, and paradigmatically, the changes in question are relative to the person's own norm—his baseline, so to speak.

We commonly differentiate many states, such as tired, happy, asleep, excited, sick, depressed, elated, unconscious, stoned, confident, angry, when these are departures from that particular individual's norm rather than expressions of a trait. No single behavior or set of behaviors is necessarily associated with particular states—let us say, with being tired. Instead, when we are tired, we may well do whatever we normally do, but less easily and probably less quickly and less accurately. We pursue our interests less eagerly, and are less interested in what is going on around us. Or when we are especially confident, our Dispositions and/or Powers may be heightened and perhaps sharpened. How those changes in Dispositions and Powers are manifested in our behavior will depend upon what our circumstances are, what those Dispositions and Powers are, and what our normal behavior is; and the pattern of changes is specific to each state. In happy excitement, for example, we may perform a given task more quickly but less accurately. In unhappiness, we may find that our Powers are not diminished but that our attitudes and interests undergo alteration.

A given state does not imply a given behavior, but neither does a given behavior imply any given state. Let us take as an example a person who, being very tired, is engaged in the behavior of sitting or lying still for a considerable time. A person in great pain, however, or depression or terror or mystical ecstasy or profound meditation may also sit or lie unmoving for an extended period. In all these cases, the Performance is essentially the same, while the values of the Want, Know, Know-how, and Achievement parameters are quite different. An Observer/Describer could have access to what is going on if he had prior knowledge of the person and the circumstances, but he would need that knowledge.

The relation of our states to our embodiments calls for a clarification that cannot be complete until we have discussed the relations between objects and processes (cf. Chap. 9). States may have systematic relations to how our bodies function, but not as a rule to the color of our eyes, or our height, or the number of our fingers and toes. With a change of state, our hearts may beat faster or slower and our posture become more or less erect, yet we would give the same object-description of our bodies, just as we would describe an automobile as the same object whether it be parked or moving down the road.

*Pathological states*[7] may or may not be temporary and reversible, but they imply systematic changes in our Dispositions and/or Powers. **When a person is in a pathological state, he is significantly restricted in his ability to engage in Deliberate Action, or equivalently, is significantly restricted in his ability to participate in the social practices of the community.** Closely associated with this definition of pathology is the definition of **need** as a **condition or requirement which, if not met, results in a pathological state.** It is important to remember, in this connection, the identity between engaging in deliberate action and participating in social practices. Thus "pathological state" refers to a condition that can be described in two equivalent ways. It is also important to remember that states are related to behavior not directly, but indirectly through the person's Dispositions and/or Powers.

Two points need special attention here. First, these definitions of pathology and need are content-free and culture-free, making it possible for us to deal adequately with

---

[7]See also Chapter 18.

persons whose characteristics constitute disabilities in one community or culture, thereby restricting their participation, yet who in other cultures would not be under such restrictions. In ancient Greece, for example, no sanctions were imposed against those who had a homosexual orientation. In modern America, homosexuality significantly limits participation in some communities but not in others. Anger may be a pathological state for some persons in some situations, but not for other persons or in other situations. Or more vividly, as in Edna St. Vincent Millay's "Sonnet to Gath":[8]

> Country of hunchbacks!—where the strong,
>     straight spine
> Jeered at by crooked children, makes his way
> Through by-streets at the kindest hour of day,
> Till he deplore his stature, and incline
> To measure manhood by a gibbous line;
> Till out of loneliness, being flawed with clay,
> He stoop into his neighbor's house and say,
> "Your roof is low for me—the fault is mine."

Second, this definition of pathology is equally applicable to so-called "physical illness" and to "mental" or "emotional illness". Again, embodiment is not assigned a peculiarly important or unimportant status as against the Dispositions and Powers.

To see how this works, let us take the case (which is not at all uncommon) of a person who has died in an accident after a long life in which he was active physically and mentally until his death. An autopsy reveals that several of his organs were in a gravely debilitated condition, although nobody had suspected that this was the case. A physiological anomaly? Yes. A pathological state? Yes, in the sense

---

[8]Millay, *Collected Poems*. Reprinted by permission.

that there is present an ongoing process that is leading to a disability, even though neither signs nor symptoms are present. But No, in the sense that his bodily conditions had had no significant effect upon his abilities or behavior. Those chronic conditions were not associated with any changes in his person characteristics, so that we may indeed say that he was not ill, even though he would have become so if he had lived much longer and the conditions had not been corrected.

This is not to say that illness causes a deficiency of Powers, but rather that being in a pathological state implies having some deficit in Powers. Sometimes this reflects a loss of owers; sometimes it reflects a lack of development of Powers.

We may give different sorts of explanation for a pathological state, e.g., physical (such as a broken leg or an ulcer) or mental (such as the trait or attitude of paranoia), or our explanation may include components of both. In any case, this definition of pathology enables us to construct explanations without resorting to such reductionisms as "All illnesses are really only mental" or "really only physical—or nutritional or neurological or whatever". With this definition, we can bring in all the factors we know of without either ignoring or forcing the evidence, and without imposing a particular diagnosis that limits our observations and investigations.

The foregoing presentation of person characteristics can be displayed as follows:

| *Dispositions* (frequency) | *Powers* (yes-no) | *Derivatives* (indirect) |
|---|---|---|
| trait | ability | embodiment |
| attitude | knowledge | capacity |
| interest | value | state |
| style | | |

When we know these fundamental aspects of a person, we have guide-lines as to what to expect from him, how it is appropriate for us to treat him, and what is likely to be effective in dealing with him. Further, they provide us with a systematic way to make the adjustments we shall need in order to understand how another person sees the world and how we can expect him to behave—in short, to put ourselves in his place.[9]

---

Thus far in our analysis of person characteristics, we have been concerned almost entirely with persons as such, not their relations with other persons and the world, i.e., their place, their status. Neither have we dealt with what might be called their linear progress, their histories. Both these aspects are essential for our understanding of persons—others and ourselves—and in the following two chapters, we shall consider them.

---

[9]See Ossorio, "A Multicultural Psychology," and *Personality and Personality Theories*, 18 July 1977.

# CHAPTER 6

# THE STATUS OF PERSONS[1]

Because deliberate actions always take place within a context, we can elaborate on the basic definition of "person" by adding a final clause: "and a person's life history of deliberate actions has a place within a world history." This makes explicit the part-whole relation between deliberate actions and social practices, and the ongoing, historical nature of both. Moreover, the elaboration portrays more clearly than the simple definition that persons are who and what they are in great part by virtue of the place they have within a world, i.e., by the totality of their relationships. Thus what it is possible for them to do (behavior potential) and what they are eligible to do depend not only upon their person characteristics but also upon their place, their status, in the world.

In Descriptive Psychology, "status" does not refer primarily to social class or rank, which are taken to be special cases of the general notion of place-in-the-world, and a status may have nothing to do with class or rank, such as the status of "newborn". Instead, "status" is a way of talk-

---

[1]See Ossorio, *Place, Clinical Topics,* and "Appraisal".

ing about "a set of relations", and having a given status is the same as having a certain set of relations. One has *relationships* with other elements in a world or domain, and *status* within a whole domain. To specify a person's place or status in the world corresponds to specifying his relationships to that world, and implicitly involves the relations among other elements in that world—just as our place in a room corresponds to our relations to each of the other things in that room, and implicitly involves their relations to one another.

Roughly speaking, there is no way to specify a person's status in the world other than by specifying his relations to other things. To illustrate, we locate our place in a room by our relation to some particular part of the room such as "beside the window" or "two feet in front of the desk". In such descriptions, relations are explicitly stated, whereas status is implied.

The worlds or domains may be of home and family, of "the marketplace", of science or art or sports, of a given society or culture, or any of innumerable others. Commonly, a given person will have a different place in different domains (e.g., parent in the family, employee on the job, officer of the club), and the fact that he has those places is important for understanding him. Likewise, our having the places we do is important for understanding ourselves. The limiting-case domain is the real world (cf. Chapter 8), that which includes all other domains, and in relation to that we can speak of "a person's place" pure and simple.

No information about a person's Dispositions, Powers, Derivatives, or Behaviors directly implies his status—his place or position—in any domain, any more than an object-description of a particular table will tell us where it is in the room. Neither does it follow from the object-description of a piece of jewelry that we will know its market value. That a person has a particular status such as "child" or "foreigner" is a fact about him, just as his place in the room is a fact, but we can know a person's place without knowing his person characteristics, or his person characteristics without knowing his place. And generally speaking, his place need not be immovably fixed. He moves from his desk to the window; he grows up and acquires the status of grandparent; becoming a citizen, he loses the status of foreigner.

The writer of a book I have just read has the status "authority in that field". What I am now doing has the status "real", whereas what I remember experiencing last night has the status "dream". The experiment that the physicist is running has the status "scientific", and the information that this is a particular day, month, and year has the status "fact". And so on and on and on. Routinely, we make status assignments without recognizing that we have done so, or thinking about what status assignments we have made. Simply by treating something in one way rather than another, we reveal what status we have given it.

As Actors, we have a place in our activities for whatever it is we are interacting with. Conversely, our activities and we ourselves have a place in that "whatever". The world and all that is therein has a place for us, and we have a place for it. We may or may not discriminate the status that we have assigned to it or them: rarely do we think that our noting "Today is Tuesday" is a status assignment, although thereby we are recognizing its place explicitly within this week, and implicitly within a longer stretch of time.

We may or may not critique our status-assignments ("I've always supposed that my job is the most important thing in my life, but now I'm beginning to wonder if it really is"), but a Critic's appraisal is also a status-assignment. Thus however and whenever we critique anything—an object, process, event, or state of affairs, we give it a particular place in the world. Status-assigning, like sentence-constructing, is something that ordinarily we do without thinking about what we are doing. When we are talking, we are not deliberately "constructing sentences"; from our point of view, we are just talking. Or in the case of status-assigning, we are just living and acting.

Status pertains not merely to what place other things have in the world, but to the place we ourselves have. That place and part may be more or less ready-made: as infants, we had little or no choice about the place "baby" that we were given by those closest around us, a place that may have implied "therefore to be cherished" or "therefore to be victimized", or anything in between.

Some of those early statuses we do not ordinarily change or (most of us) want to change throughout our lives, e.g., human ("a homo sapiens who is also a person"), male/female, belonging to this family, being a citizen of our native country. Others we expect to change, e.g., immature to mature, dependent to independent. These examples are so culturally established (although differently, perhaps, in different cultures) that for nearly all practical purposes we accept them without question as definitive. They provide the setting within which we originally make our self-status-assignments, later refining and developing them.

Innumerable changes can be rung on what it means in detail to be a human being, or male or female, young or old, dependent or independent, and so on. How do we, individually, implement them? In doing so, what place—status—do we give to, e.g., literacy, a doctoral degree, manual or artistic achievement, conformity or nonconformity to a norm of "respectability", or to norms of "masculine" or "feminine"?

---

Our **self concept**[2] is our summary formulation of our

---

[2]See Ossorio, *"What Actually Happens"* and *Positive Health and Transcendental Theories.*

status, which is to say, the place we take ourselves to have in the world. That formulation marks the extent of and the limits upon our behavior potential as far as we are concerned.

In some cultures, to be a male is to have the status of intrinsically superior to females, and the fact that a given female may be more competent than a given male in nearly every respect may not affect in the slightest his self-status-assignment as superior, or her self-status-assignment as inferior. Other examples abound, as in the self-status-assignment of the person who is born into a hereditary ruling class, or who possesses certain physical characteristics or special abilities that ipso facto carry with them a high status, as contrasted with the low status often assigned to themselves by persons who lack those characteristics.

Self-status-assignments are notoriously resistant to change by factual input, a resistance eloquently expressed in the remark attributed to W. S. Gilbert, "You've no idea what a poor opinion I have of myself, and how little I deserve it." Here is an example of the not uncommon case where a person appraises himself as inferior, and that self concept remains fixed despite his notable achievements and even fame. Who has not heard someone say, in effect, "I know I've done a lot, but I'm really just a very ordinary person. I just happened to be in the right place at the right time"? No doubt he is praised for his humility, but surely there must be someone who regrets that an extraordinarily gifted person has appraised himself and his achievements so ineptly that—so to speak—he inhabits a house too small for him, thereby failing to develop his capacities to the fullest.

Doubtless some will say that he ought to know that he is not ordinary, and possibly he does. But that self-knowledge may not alter his self-status-assignment, his formulation of his place in the world, his self-concept. All the time, he may have in the back of his mind, unarticulated,

"Surprising, isn't it, how ordinary people can sometimes, with luck, do remarkable things!" The same phenomenon occurs in reverse when a conceited ass fails at everything he puts his hand to, and finally fails even to try, yet retains an invincible conviction of his pre-eminent status.

---

A paradigm case of status-assignment is found in ceremonies of degradation and accreditation, as when a person is accused of engaging in behavior that is significantly unacceptable to the community, and consequently he loses status within it. As an example based on the work of Garfinkle,[3] we can take the soldier who is stripped of the symbols of his rank and drummed out of the regiment. Less dramatically, we have the employee who is refused promotion at the expected time, or the politician who loses an election, or the spouse who is deserted. In the opposite case, accreditation, we have the promotion, the graduation, the accolade, the election to office.

The paradigmatic **degradation ceremony** calls for (1) a community having certain shared values, and (2) three members of that community: a Perpetrator whose behavior is at issue on the ground that it violates those values, a Denouncer, and a Witness. The Denouncer and the Witness are members of the community in good standing, and on this occasion they are acting as representatives of the community rather than as simply themselves.

The Denouncer describes the act to the Witness, and if necessary, redescribes it so as to make clear in what ways it contravenes the community's values. He then gives reasons why the act should not be interpreted as excusable; he rules out, for example, the possibility that the act was an accident or that the Perpetrator was not responsible for the act (e.g.,

---

[3]H. Garfinkle, "Conditions of Successful Degradation Ceremonies." See also Ossorio, "*What Actually Happens*", and *Clinical Topics*.

drunk, insane, etc.). Instead, the Denouncer interprets the act as genuinely manifesting the Perpetrator's fundamental character. And because it is a matter of character, it follows that the Perpetrator never has been *really* "one of us". If the Denouncer successfully makes his case to the Witness, the degradation ceremony as such is complete, although it may (or may not) be followed by a formal rite.

When a person is degraded, he acquires a new status. With that new status goes a different behavior potential, and a new set of standards concerning how it is appropriate for him to act, and how it is appropriate for other people to treat him.

There are a number of possible transformations of this paradigm case of the degradation ceremony. (1) One has already been mentioned, the accreditation ceremony, in which an Achiever substitutes for the Perpetrator, and a Proponent or Advocate substitutes for the Denouncer. (2) Either the degradation or the accreditation ceremony can be public as in the awarding of the Nobel prize, or comparatively private as in the boss's office, or purely private as when one says to oneself, "I don't trust him any more." (3) It can be a two-party process in which the same person acts as both Denouncer and Witness, or (4) a one-party process in which the person denounces himself in a self-degradation. (5) A ceremony such as a criminal trial before a judge and jury (as "Witnesses") can issue in degradation (the defendant is guilty) or accreditation (he is innocent). Even more of these transformations will become apparent if the participants are assimilated to the Actor-Observer-Critic model, with the Perpetrator or Achiever as Actor, the Denouncer or Proponent as Observer, and the Witness as Critic.

Almost any change in life circumstances will involve status changes with both positive and negative aspects that correspond to degradation and accreditation. The soldier who is drummed out of the regiment loses behavior potential with respect to the military, but as a civilian, he is eligible to do many things that as a soldier he could not do—for example, live where he chooses to live, wear whatever clothes he likes, and change jobs when he wishes to.

Our self-appraisals can confirm or deny community appraisal. We can accept or reject an attempted degradation. "You say I'm inferior and I take your word for it," or "You say I'm inferior, but dammit, I'm not!"—with all their variants. Yet if we are to become and remain members of any community, we must take account of the status which that community assigns to us. We cannot ignore it without risking the extreme degradation of expulsion, which may take the form of exile, imprisonment, hospitalization, the silent treatment, depersonalization, execution.

At the same time, no one is compelled to accept a community's status-assignment as ultimate and immutable, although the tendency to do so can be strong. As one writer comments, "The terrible temptation for the powerless is to believe what the oppressors say about them."[4] In reverse, the adulation of great crowds can tempt a politican or entertainer to believe the flattering statements that his devotees lavish upon him. We can, however, challenge the status system of the community, just as it can challenge ours, and if it does expel us, we can try to earn reinstatement, or seek out another community in which we shall be accepted.

Self-status-assignment is closely related to self-presentation. In a highly mobile society, we frequently meet persons whom we have not known before, and who do not know us. Initially, therefore, we do not have a clear basis for interacting with them or they with us. In those circumstances, we present ourselves to each other as this or that, and anything we do toward letting the other person

---

[4]John C. Raines, "Righteous Resistance and Martin Luther King, Jr.", p. 52.

know what kind of persons we are constitutes a presentation of our self. The clothes we wear, our gestures, voices, choice of language, and topics of conversation, all that constitutes our demeanor, reflects our self-status-assignment and can enter into our self-presentation. What it amounts to is that at our first meeting, I offer to be and act in a particular way in relation to you, and if you accept what I am offering, tentatively we shall have that relation.

In a self-presentation, we may or may not present ourselves as we authentically are. If we do, we speak of a self-disclosure. However, we can instead present ourselves as someone else—a bold person can present himself as shy, or a confidence trickster as honest and trustworthy. We can fool others or be fooled, at least for a time, but that is simply one of the hazards intrinsic to living in the kind of society we do.

A person's place is always within a setting, whether geographical, or a scientific or artistic community, or an organization such as an industry or business, or a social group such as a family or culture. And our place—status—correlates with our eligibilities and behavior potential. Depending upon our status, we are eligible or ineligible to vote, to marry, to enter school, to become a member of a club, to participate in a given social practice.

A change of status signals a change in what we are eligible to do and not do. It increases or decreases our behavior potential, or increases some and decreases others. For example, a non-citizen is not eligible to vote, a restriction of his behavior potential, but he may be eligible to travel in countries where citizens are forbidden to go, an increase in his behavior potential. Children are often permitted liberties that adults could not get away with, but they are not eligible to vote or to marry.

Also associated with status are standards for our

behavior, and standards for how other people shall behave toward us. The standards for adult behavior are not the same as the standards for a child, and a certified craftsman expects of himself, and is expected to produce, a quality of work that neither he nor anyone else expects of an apprentice.

In later chapters, we shall consider communities and cultures, as well as status principles, in some detail. For the moment, all that is necessary—and it *is* necessary—is to note that status goes with context, i.e., domains. More detailed discussion of the domains which are usually most important for our day by day living is merely being delayed, not overlooked.

# CHAPTER 7

# PERSONAL DEVELOPMENT[1]

Maxim 8 reads, "If a person has a given person characteristic, he acquired it in one of the ways it can be acquired, i.e., by having the prior capacity and an appropriate intervening history".

Let us begin with the persons we now are and work our way backwards in time. You who are reading this book and I who am writing it have at least one person characteristic in common: the ability to read. Reading is a social practice that can be taught and learned. Whatever pedogogical methods were used with us, we did learn, formally or informally, to read because the proper opportunities were present, and because we had the capacity to acquire that ability. And so for all our other person characteristics. As we have already seen in connection with Maxim 8, this can be stated in another way: **Given the relevant Capacity, the relevant personal History results in the given Person Characteristics.** This can be represented by the

---

[1]See Ossorio, "Outline of Descriptive Psychology," and *Personality and Personality Theories*, 21 and 22 July 1977.

basic **Developmental Formula: C + H —> PC**

What, in fact, the history was by which we learned to read can only be discovered empirically, if at all, and is likely to be of little interest except to specialists in teaching methods. We do know that the method was at least adequate because we now have that ability. Because we have the ability, by reading we can add to our repertoire of information, concepts, and skills, thus increasing our capacities to acquire still more facts, concepts, and skills. The process is cumulative, and is all part of our history.

C + H —> PCs
$\downarrow$
New C + new H —> new PCs
$\downarrow$
New C + new H —> new PCs
$\downarrow$
etc.

In certain respects, we have similar histories, yet we respond differently to closely similar circumstances. Take, for example, a class of elementary-school pupils who are being introduced to reading. Unless it be an exceptionally homogeneous group, a few of the children will learn very quickly, most at a moderate rate, and a few very slowly if at all. The same teacher is using the same methods—roughly speaking—with the entire class, but the pupils' achievements are remarkably diverse, even perhaps unto equal ability to read the words but different ability to comprehend their meaning. Or we can compare the varied reactions of many individuals to a single event, such as the outcome of an election. What each of us makes of the election results reflects our individual Dispositions and Powers.

To spell out these reflexive and recursive interactions: our histories reflect our person characteristics, which are manifested in our behavior. Our circumstances, by providing reasons and opportunities for our behaviors, enable those behaviors to make a difference in our person characteristics. And those behaviors, which reflect both our circumstances and our person characteristics, constitute our history ("A person is an individual whose history is, paradigmatically, a history of deliberate actions").

As we have already seen in the discussion of capacity, without an appropriate history, a person cannot acquire an ability or other person characteristics, and without the prior capacity, the person cannot take advantage of the opportunities provided by his circumstances to develop particular person characteristics. Or to state it in another way, if we are given the opportunity to do X—act generously, let us say—but do not have the proper person characteristics and capacity, merely doing the generous thing would not be a case of genuinely acting generously, and therefore would not lead to our acquiring the person-characteristic trait of generosity. It is through the interplay between our person characteristics and our circumstances that our history was what it was, so that we became what we are, and shall become whatever we do become.

---

Where did it all begin? At birth? During gestation? At conception? With our ancestors? In previous incarnations? For our purposes here, it makes no difference which or how many of these we specify, because no matter what we take as the point of origin, and no matter how far back we take it, finally we reach a point where all we can say is that in the beginning we are entities with the **original capacity**[2] to respond to circumstances. That original capacity can be expressed by a person characteristic which can be called "merely able to do X". That is, there is at least one circumstance in which success would not be accidental or due to

---

[2]See Ossorio, *Personality and Personality Theories*, 21 July 1977.

luck or chance. Notice how "merely able", the special type of person characteristic that explains having the original capacity, contrasts with "ability", i.e., "under normal circumstances, success is not surprising".

A newborn child is merely able to eat. Its success in eating depends upon there being someone else with the requisite knowledge and ability to provide it with appropriate circumstances—that is, food in a form that it can eat and digest. The baby's performance of taking food constitutes participation in a two-person social practice, in which one of the persons supplies everything except the prior condition of original capacity reflected in the lowest level of competence, namely, "merely able". Unless something goes wrong, with practice and experience the baby develops more and more abilities until it becomes able to feed itself, and at some later time, to obtain its own food.

When personal development is thus understood, it becomes at once less mysterious and more intricate than it is sometimes supposed to be. Looking backward from where we are now, our development can indeed appear to have been determined, and is often so described. But looking at whatever we are now doing, it is unmistakable that in a practical sense we could be doing something else, and at any moment can choose to do something else: stop reading, for example, in order to make a telephone call or brew a cup of tea or just sit.

So it is at every stage of our developmental history. At the outset, when we were merely able, the number of alternatives available to us was miniscule, not because of our circumstances but because our potentials, i.e., our capacities, were undeveloped. As our abilities increased, so did the range of possibilities among which we could choose. We chose then as we are choosing now, and what we choose often cannot be foreseen by others or even ourselves. Shall I or shall I not, at this moment, go get a cup of tea?

A choice may or may not be preceded by a period of deliberation, but the concept of choice is basic and indivisible. When a person engages in a given behavior (deliberate action), he does so by virtue of having selected that option from the set of options that are formally available within the social practice in which he is engaging. Indeed, he engages in that practice by taking that option. This can be diagrammed: social practices provide options; in a deliberate action, we choose among behavioral options ( <> ), some of which may be formally available but not practicable. Any occurrence of that practice involves a sequence consisting of one of the options from Stage 1, followed by one from Stage 2, and so on. The line from one diamond to the next indicates which of the possible behaviors does in fact take place.

## Social Practices

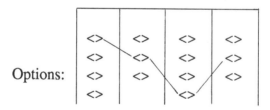

Options:

Our choices, it will be remembered, reflect our Dispositions, Powers, and Derivatives, the last of which includes our capacities. We do not know the full extent of our original capacities, because our having a given capacity is revealed only as our historical circumstances provide the motivation and opportunity for us to develop that capacity into a person characteristic. A child brought up in a nomadic hunting society may have the capacity to become an engineering genius, but with no opportunity to develop those skills, and no social practices that call for acquiring them, nobody will ever know. Closer to home, every time we say Yes to one opportunity, we say No to a host of others, shutting the doors upon developing—at that time, at least—innumerable different capacities into abilities. This restriction is not always, as some have suggested, a reason for regret or guilt. "I was so angry I could have killed him—thank God I didn't." "All those family and social pressures were pushing me to become a lawyer, and I would have been a good one, but I'm much happier designing and building furniture."

———————

Looking back, we can see patterns in our behavior. Looking forward, we can see possible patterns that depend upon what we do with our circumstances as they arise. But our circumstances are also significantly subject to our choices. Some circumstances we can alter deliberately, as by changing jobs or our marital status. Other circumstances we cannot change: the round of the seasons, the fact that we shall die, our having had the upbringing that we had. However, it is possible to assign the invariables to one place or another in our current lives, so that in a broad sense, we can make and remake our worlds depending on how we choose to take what we are given.

In our early development, on some occasions we adapted to our circumstances: as babies we ate what food was given to us when it was given. On other occasions, we asserted ourselves: we howled when we were hungry. As our powers increased and our dispositions stabilized and specialized, patterns of behavior emerged, and in time we achieved an over-all pattern, a reasonably consistent way of relating ourselves to our circumstances, and of responding to them. This constitutes our personal way of life, or pattern of living, within the context of the **Way of Living** of our cultures and communities—of which more later.[3]

We may achieve our personal way of life—our partic-

———————

[3]See Ossorio, "A Multicultural Psychology."

ular version of a cultural Way of Life—as the result of an impetuous choice, like getting married or joining the armed forces on the spur of the moment. Or we may do so only after much deliberation, as Thomas Merton chose to enter a contemplative monastic order, and Carlos Castaneda to engage in activities appropriate to becoming a Warrior. Or we may achieve it merely by conforming to what is expected of us, or by making a series of choices whose significance may not have been apparent at the time, or by creating new social practices or new versions of old ones.

Throughout, we should take care not to confuse our personal way of life with our occupation. They may coincide, or they may not. The contemplative and Warrior modes—to name only two—can be carried out through many varieties and changes of occupation: there are contemplative as well as Warrior housewives, factory workers, and business executives, and there are Warrior as well as contemplative monks and nuns. What marks them is not their performances or the social practices they engage in, but their individual variations on a community or cultural Way of Living, variations that inform—give form to—all that they do.

Obviously, how we did become what we are now must be discovered empirically. Less obviously, what we are becoming will reflect the fact that we are continually creating new behaviors[4] as we respond to new situations.

We come across an acquaintance in the supermarket, and to a large extent our initial moves are likely to be prescribed by the social practices of our community: "Hi, how are you?" "Fine. I haven't seen you for a long time." Such formulas set the stage, so to speak, and depending upon the

---

[4]See Ossorio, "Explanation, Falsificability, and Rule-Following," *Clinical Topics*, and *Positive Health and Transcendental Theories.*

situation, we may continue with formulas which, like our original greeting, we choose from a number of options. Again, depending upon the circumstances, we may create new behaviors to fit the particular situation of both persons, our specific relationship with each other, and our present states (perhaps one of us is in a hurry, the other not), the immediate situation (perhaps the store is crowded, perhaps not), and so on. Thus our behaviors on that occasion may be no more than minor adaptations of one or another formula, although another meeting of the same persons, in other circumstances, may elicit major creations of new behaviors such as may emerge during a long, deliberative conversation about an urgent problem. And there can be masterpieces of newly created behaviors as in choreographing a dance or generating a new scientific theory.

Our responses to what is going on around us reflect a logical order that is expressed in the Maxims for Behavior Description. Understanding those responses involves the notion of **empirical identities**,[5] i.e., that "In *these* circumstances, 'this' (whatever it is) is the same thing as 'that' (whatever *it* is)". For example, in these circumstances, asking the question "How are you?" is the same thing as offering a greeting. Or taking another example: in these circumstances, reaching out for my cup of tea is the same thing as stretching out my arm to the east—these are empirical identities—whereas in other circumstances, stretching out my arm to the east will be the same thing as reaching for the doorknob, or into thin air, or offering to shake hands. In responding to what is around us, we are continually exploiting the formula, "In this context, doing this is a case of doing that".

Functioning in terms of empirical identities is so exact and subtle that we could not be programmed for all the contextual contingencies. Nor can we blindly follow such

---

[5]See Ossorio and Schneider, "Decisions and Decision Aids."

prescriptions as "Always play it safe", or "Nothing risked, nothing gained", with impunity.

---

The specific ways by which persons acquire their Dispositions and Powers has been the subject of innumerable studies. What teaching methods are most effective for enabling children to learn to read? What techniques are available for developing or changing particular traits, attitudes, interests, styles? By what means is a particular value inculcated, or a concept mastered? What are the expected stages in personal development? What is the role of teaching? Are the conditions needed for teaching something the same as or different from the conditions needed for learning it? Such studies can be useful to fill in details of how we can take advantage of the circumstances which we encounter or create, so as to achieve the person characteristics we desire for ourselves and others. But intentionally or not, they are grounded in the recursive formula for personal development: Capacity (a person characteristic) plus History leads to Person Characteristics, and they, plus further History, to still other Person Characteristics, and so on until death.

More will be said on this topic in the final chapter, because personal development is a special case of personal change.

---

Here at the end of Part II it is time to bring together the major elements in the Person Concept. We can start by combining our definition of "person" with the aphoristic elaboration on it, so that it reads: **A person is an individual whose history is paradigmatically a life history of deliberate action within a world history.** By this definition, we bring together systematically Persons, Behavior (deliberate action), and the World (history).

In the logically coherent set of concepts that we have

been examining, nothing is ad hoc or arbitrary or paradoxical. As a conceptual system, it is close enough to a reconstruction of common-sense conceptualizations that we can take advantage of the experience of the human race. At the same time, it is different enough that we are not bound by our predecessors' confusions and errors.

Returning to the questions we raised at the beginning of this book—"Why do we do what we do?", "How do persons differ from one another?", and "How did we get this way?"—here is a resource by which to answer those questions without appealing to mechanistic or deterministic theories, or postulating hypothetical "forces" or "instincts" or "impulses" or "reinforcements". The major schemas that we have dealt with so far—the behavior formula, the developmental formula, the judgement diagram, plus the relationship formulas that are yet to come (Chap. 11)—give the logic of the explanation for a behavior, which is why they help us to explain in particular cases. They spell out what constitutes an explanation for the behavior, and then point to what facts we need in a given case in order to have an explanation.

For example, if we ask, "Why did he do that?" and look at the schemas, we can turn to the behavior formula, in which case we are usually asking for the content of the Want parameter. Or we can look at his person characteristics and circumstances, and say, "Because he's that kind of person" or "Because he was trying to escape the lion". That is, the schemas show what sorts of facts have the kind of connection to behavior that makes them explanatory.

Which schema or schemas we turn to depends upon what questions we are asking, what type of understanding we are searching for. If we are asking "Why is he the kind of person he is?" we shall go to one schema. If instead we are asking "How did he become this kind of person?" or "What is he doing?", we shall go to others.

Thus equipped with the means to understand, describe,

and appraise any person and any behavior, we can now turn to describe with equal economy and precision the context within which persons live and act: the real world.

[Note: It may be useful, at this point, to turn to Appendix 3, where the basic concepts are charted in a way that permits (indeed, encourages) seeing the relations between the parameters of the behavior formula and the parametric analysis of person characteristics, as well as some of the more important diagrams and schemas.]

# PART III

# DESCRIBING THE WORLD

# CHAPTER 8

# THE REAL WORLD[1]

Behaviors occur in a world. Persons live in a world. We have articulated the concepts of "behavior" and "person"; it is time now to articulate the concept of "world".

The **real world** can be understood in three closely related ways. First, it is what we see when we look around us, what we might speak of as the "observable" world. Second, it is the world which includes us as Actors, Observers, and Critics, that is, the world that we act on and in. As such, it is the "behavioral" or "human" world. It follows from these two ways of understanding the world that the real world is that which our life histories are a part of. Third and most comprehensive, the real world can be understood as the state of affairs which includes all other states of affairs.[2]

"The real world", like "behavior" and "person", is a basic concept, and it is essential because "A person requires a world in order to have the possibility of engaging in any behavior at all".[3] That is, no world, no behavior; no

---

[1]See Ossorio, *"What Actually Happens"* and *Positive Health and Transcendental Theories.*

[2]See Ossorio, *"What Actually Happens"*

[3]Ossorio, "Place", #A-1.

persons, no behavior; and no behavior, no world.

The articulation of the concept of a real world is likely to be confusing at the outset. For this reason, two reminders may be in order. As I said in the Introduction, it is not necessary to master the system in detail, step by step, before proceeding to its applications and extensions. What is necessary initially is to develop an appreciation for the structure, and that can best be accomplished by skimming.

Even so, concepts are acquired not by memorizing them, but by participating in social practices that involve their use. To illustrate, I had not been able to see any noteworthy point in the basic descriptive formats until I found how one of them had been employed to solve an organizational problem in a large industry. I then went back to the systematic exposition and found that it made most excellent sense. Other people grasp more readily the relevance and importance of those formats, and other aspects of the system.

---

What *do* we observe when we look around us? Five **reality concepts** will enable us to articulate systematically the welter of our empirical observations. What we observe are **Objects, Processes, Events, States of Affairs,** and their **Relationships.** We are observing *objects* when we see a desk, hear a doorbell, touch the keys of a typewriter, smell an orange, taste its flavor, and feel its texture as we peel it. We are observing *processes* when we see a person walking across the room, hear the playing of a song, and feel the movement of our fingers on the typewriter keys. We are observing *events* when we see the light go on, hear the pen hit the floor when it falls off the desk, begin to taste the orange. We are observing *states of affairs* when we note that the desk has four drawers, hear that the telephone is ringing, taste that the orange is sweet, feel that there is a draft across our ankles. And we are observing *relationships* when we note that we are sitting at the desk with pen in hand, and writing on the paper that lies on the desk (i.e., ourselves being related to desk and pen, and they to each other).

What we have here is not an arbitrary or accidental aggregation of concepts but a coherent descriptive system, in which the relationships of the reality concepts object, process, event, and state of affairs are represented by the identity-coordination operation, "is the same thing as". The real world is such that whatever can be described in one way can be described in other ways as well, and the various descriptions are anchored in and related by the identity of what is being described.

Thus the formalism of the following descriptive units and transition rules enables us to deal systematically with multiple descriptions of the same things. We do not have, and do not need, a "privileged" description that would give us *the* real description of whatever we are describing. As we have seen earlier, $2 + 2$ is the same thing as $1 + 3$, which is the same thing as $10 - 6$, which is the same thing as 4. What is *the* real number that each of these is the same thing as? How can we answer that, when all that we have are the identity coordinations, none of which is privileged above any of the others, and each of which has its uses?

Objects, processes, and events call for different forms of description, but all three of those forms can be transformed into state-of-affairs descriptions. This is one of the reasons why the formulation of the reality concepts as a conceptual structure is called **the State of Affairs System**. Its logical articulation takes the form of **Transition Rules**, which are rules for going from one type of description to another. Seven of the rules are discussed here; three others will be discussed in the next chapter.

*Transition Rule 1*. **A state of affairs is a totality of related objects and/or processes and/or events and/or states of affairs**. Here, as in the rest of the transition rules, "is" means "is the same thing as": it is an identity coordination. Therefore Rule 1 can be restated as: "A state of affairs is the same thing as a totality of related objects, and/or processes, and/or events, and/or states of affairs". An example of a state of affairs would be, "I am sitting at my desk writing a letter", "I" being a person who has object characteristics (an embodiment), the desk also being an object, writing a letter being a process, having sat down being an event. All these, being related in the way that they are, constitute a totality which is a state of affairs.

**Transition Rule 2. An object or process or event or state of affairs is a state of affairs which is a constituent of some other state of affairs.** My writing that letter is a way of communicating with a friend, which is a way of maintaining a friendship that is important in our lives. In turn, my life and my friend's life have a place within world history. By such processes of *composition*, we move from what we actually start with—often but not always with what we observe—to larger and more inclusive wholes. The limiting case, the most inclusive whole, is "the state of affairs which includes all other states of affairs", i.e., the real world. No matter how far we take our composition of processes (or objects or events or states of affairs) into larger and more inclusive processes (or objects, etc.), what results will be a part of the state of affairs that includes all other states of affairs. Thus each object, process, etc., that exists has a place in the real world. *What* objects, etc., exist we must discover by observation, of course. The system does not specify what they are. It simply recognizes that anything anybody might encounter is going to be subsumed under this notion of the state of affairs that includes all other states of affairs.[4]

**Transition Rule 3. An object is a state of affairs having other related objects as immediate constituents.**

---

[4]Ossorio, transcript, 9 August 1984, p. 14.

(**An object divides into related, smaller objects.**) Again starting with whatever object we please (which may or may not be one that we observe), this time we take it through the process of *decomposition*. The desk can be decomposed into a top, drawers, and legs; they into pieces of wood and metal; they into smaller and smaller pieces; those into chemical components; and so on until we impose a limit. Or the desk can be decomposed into right half and left half, and each of those into halves, and so on recursively until we stop. The limit may depend upon what we want or need for that particular purpose, or it may be something that has no constituent parts—quarks, photons, gluons, or whatever physicists are currently taking to be the "basic building-blocks" (also known as "Zilch particles") into which all objects can be decomposed.

Wherever we begin, we can move by the process of composition to the all-inclusive real world, or by decomposition into basic building-blocks, or to any point in between, as our interests and competence lead us. Therefore we can describe any object, process, or state of affairs, at any level of complexity or simplicity and any degree of "situatedness". (Events, as we shall see later, have a built-in terminus for decomposition.)

No level of description, however, can be taken as primary, or as intrinsically favored over any other. Which description is "better" or "worse" than another will depend upon our purpose in giving the description, i.e., its place in our (the Describer's) world. A human being can indeed be decomposed to a handful of dust, but the person is not therefore "really" dust. In that process of decomposition, the humanity of the individual has been destroyed, whether by actual resolution to dust, or by mental assignment to the status of "only a pile of cheap chemicals".

The real world is the world in which we engage in behaviors, develop person characteristics, assign statuses, and otherwise function as Actors, Observers, Critics, and Persons. Anchored here, we can divide any object as finely as we please without—for example—mistaking the dusty parts for the personal human whole, or the physicists' Zilch particles for the desk; and we can set the person and the desk into the totality of possible facts without jeopardizing their integrity or prejudging their composition.

**Transition Rule 4. A process is a sequential change from one state of affairs to another.**

**Transition Rule 5. A process is a state of affairs having other, related processes as immediate constituents. (A process divides into related (sequential or parallel) smaller processes.)** "Sequential" means that in the change from state of affairs A to state of affairs C, there is at least one intervening point, B. And between A and B there will be an intervening point, as also between B and C, and these can be further subdivided indefinitely. The limiting case will be a continuous process.

Transition Rule 4 is neither a substitute for nor an elaboration upon Transition Rule 5; it describes the same thing as Rule 5, which is to say, it explicates the same concept. Rule 5 makes explicit that processes also are subject to decomposition. Thus the preceding discussion of Transition Rule 3 applies here also, with the appropriate, simple adjustments for "process" in place of "object".

**Transition Rule 6. An event is a direct change from one state of affairs to another.**

**Transition Rule 7. An event is a state of affairs having two states of affairs (i.e., "before" and "after") as constituents.** Rule 6 says that in an event, there is a "before" and an "after", and Rule 7 has to do with what is "before" and "after". Taking these two rules together: an event differs from a process in being a direct rather than a sequential change from one state of affairs to another. An event has no duration. For example, in winning a race there was a time before the race was won and a time after, but the winning itself simply constitutes a dividing-line between those times, and terminates the winner's process of running the race.

Central to the concept of event is that a change occurs, i.e., that the "before" state of affairs differs from the "after" state of affairs. Events can be of many kinds: in our ordinary time-frame, a flash of lightning, the sound of a gong, a birth or death. If we narrow the time-frame, the lightning-flash can be described as a process; if so, the beginning of the flash is one event and its end is another event. Or if we take an historical or geological time-frame, we can say that the Battle of Gettysburg was an event, although within a different time-frame it was a process. But whatever the event is, it involves the fact that things are suddenly different from what they were before.

---

The transition rules specify the logical connections among the notions of object, process, event, and state of affairs. In this respect, those rules are like such mathematical axioms as "B + A is the same thing as A + B", axioms from which all the rest of mathematics is generated. Thus an object or process or event can be described in its own terms by a parametric analysis of those concepts, or it can be redescribed as a state of affairs. Then given the parametric analyses, we can describe any particular object, process, event, or state of affairs by specifying the values of the parameters, and this will correspond to a description of some part of the real world.

To a great extent, our descriptions do not go very far beyond naming: "This is a sunflower and that a rose"; "He is playing the piano"; "They ate dinner at home". A gardener may decompose the tree into its rose bush into its roots, branches, leaves, flowers, and so on; within that domain, such elements are ultimate constituents. A botanist can decompose it into cells and other elements which are the botanical ultimate constituents, a chemist into yet smaller ones, a physicist into quarks and gluons.

Formally, decomposition of an object (or process) into smaller constituent objects (or processes) can be carried on infinitely. The system itself does not provide for any stopping points, any limitations upon decomposition. In practice, we do impose limits. We stop somewhere. From the point of view of the logic of the system, that stopping place is arbitrary. From other points of view, it may not be arbitrary at all.

Five ways of stopping have special significance because they create distinctions that make it possible to conceptualize real worlds, and to describe historical particulars. These five are:[5]

**Limiting Case I: The state of affairs which includes all other states of affairs** (i.e., "the real world").

**Limiting Case II: A type of object that is not the same thing as a state of affairs** (i.e., it has no constituents, and so is an ultimate object—a "basic building block").

**Limiting Case III: A type of process that is not the same thing as a state of affairs** (i.e., it has no constituents, hence no beginning that is distinct from its end, hence is the effective equivalent of an event).

**Limiting Case IV: A type of process that is the same thing as a state of affairs but has no process constituents** (i.e., is the effective equivalent of an object during a period in which the object undergoes no change—cf. molecular processes at absolute zero temperature).

**Limiting Case V: A type of state of affairs that has no state of affairs constituents** (e.g., Black is different from white. "Black" and "white" are not states of affairs, so there can be no decomposition of either into objects, processes, events, or other states of affairs).

---

[5]Slightly modified by Ossorio from *"What Actually Happens"*, pp. 29-48 (see transcripts 20 September 1984, p. 7, and 26 September 1985, p. 1).

Limiting Case I is a totality notion, but since it is content-free, i.e., it does not specify what that totality is, it does not limit any of our operations. Limiting Cases II, III, and IV are ways of limiting decomposition, because in those cases we specify what the ultimate constituents are that we are dealing with.

The ultimate constituents that we select are different for different "worlds" or domains, such as the domain of chess, of art, of physics, of economics. Once we have selected the ultimate constituents, we have placed a limit upon what can happen in that world, because everything in it has to involve those ultimate constituents and their possible relationships. Thus our choice of ultimate constituents determines what kind of domain it is, and what is the range of possible facts (states of affairs) within that domain.

With Limiting Case I, we have four equivalent ways of describing the real world: (1) as a single object divisible into smaller objects; (2) as a single process divisible into smaller processes; (3) as a sequence of events divisible into smaller sequences of events; or (4) as a state of affairs that includes all other states of affairs. Historically, each of these four ways has been used in saying what there is in the world, and generally, it has been taken to be the case that choosing one of these ways requires excluding the other three. Yet inexplicably, all four were adequate. With the State of Affairs System, however, we can see why all four were in fact adequate, and that when we choose one, we are not forced to exclude the others. Indeed, we cannot. We can choose not to use those others, but they are still part of the same system.

As every description is some person's description, so the upper and lower limits of composition and decomposition are set by persons, and how close we approach any limiting cases on a given occasion will depend upon our choice and competence. Ordinarily, we do not describe things in terms of whatever we designate as their ultimate constituents, but simply describe the human body, for example, by decomposing it into head, trunk, arms, legs, and so on. A physiologist, however, will decompose it into digestive, cardiovascular, neurological, and other processes which are the ultimate constituents in physiology. A chemist will decompose it into its chemical constituents, and a physicist into its Zilch particles. A sociologist, using composition, may see a human body as the embodiment of a person who has a particular place in a social entity, and a theologian describe its ultimate significance.

A diagram may clarify what we can do with the State of Affairs System so that we can generate the concept of a real world.

## STATE OF AFFAIRS SYSTEM DIAGRAM

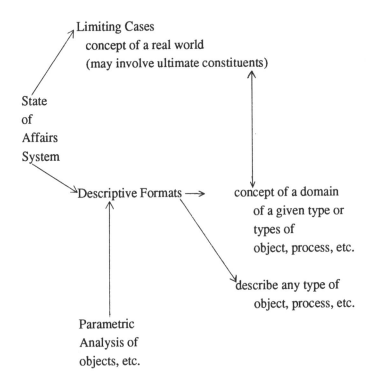

Limiting Cases
concept of a real world
(may involve ultimate constituents)

State
of
Affairs
System

Descriptive Formats ⟶ concept of a domain
of a given type or
types of
object, process, etc.

describe any type of
object, process, etc.

Parametric
Analysis of
objects, etc.

By parametric analyses of the real-world concepts, we can generate descriptive formats. Having done that, we can describe any type of object, process, etc., and can divide this real world into a number of domains which are based on the limiting-case criteria.

Domains such as those of football or fashion, chess or science, are characterized by the limits on what objects, processes, and events can be elements within them, and how they can be related. In chess, the elements are a board, and pawns, knights, kings, and other pieces, but not footballs or goalposts; its states of affairs include checkmates but not touchdowns. In fashion, we have dresses, coats, shoes, etc., and their appearance and popularity, but not logical sequences or hand-to-hand combative strategies. Communities themselves are domains, characterized by their particular social practices and institutions. Too, there are the rigidly enclosed domains created by writers of science fiction and fantasy.

All such domains have a place—a status—within the real world. Even the invented domains like imaginary worlds, however, are generated by introducing a set of objects, processes, events, and states of affairs, and the relations among them. Those relations can be economic, geometric, chronological, emotional, logical, utilitarian, aesthetic—whatever kinds are called for or permitted by the objects, processes, etc., that are constituents of that domain.

---

Each of us has his own world representation, which is a representation of a historical, behavioral world, i.e., the world we ourselves are living in. By and large, we understand a person's representation as a selection, with personal variations, from what is publicly available, and for the most part, we judge that what our personal worlds are representing is not unrealistic.

We discover the particulars of the real world by observation, but observation does not in itself generate the conceptual structure. The reality concepts, transition rules, and limiting cases provide such a conceptual structure for our observations, but they do not determine what content we shall assign to the content-free concepts when we move from descriptive formulas to descriptions.

The transition rules codify the reminder that anything that can be described in one way (e.g., as an object, process, event, or state of affairs) an also be described in some other way. Further, because there are no formal limits to composition or decomposition, no description can be guaranteed to be exhaustively complete, and there is ultimately no non-arbitrary way to establish a given description as having *the* privileged status of the ultimate or correct description. Instead, a person engaged in some purposeful activity will—potentially—be able to act upon any of a number of descriptions. However, as soon as a person becomes engaged in some purposeful activity, some descriptions become more relevant and appropriate than others.

Actually living in an actual, historical world, we guide our behavior by what we know, and what we know is a set of objects, processes, events, and states of affairs that we take to be more or less systematically related. That set changes as we make new distinctions, acquire new concepts and skills, accumulate new information, and invent new behaviors. Every meeting with another person (not to mention other things) constitutes an opportunity for reconstructing our actual worlds, and some of those meetings can initiate changes as radical as the paradigmatic religious conversion. A confrontation with someone whose world representation differs from our own in important respects will sometimes drastically alter our worlds—or his. When it becomes necessary for us to operate within another framework for an extended period, it is likely to result in what we call "culture shock". A similar form can occur when a student enters a college or university, or a person embarks on a new job.

———————

The state-of-affairs conceptualization presented in this chapter and in what follows is coherent in itself, and is also reflexive. Thus "The world is known to part of *itself*, namely, a person; the person knows about the world, including *himself*; language, which gives the person access to the world, is also part of the world, and so language gives the person access to *itself*."[6] Because of this reflexivity, we do not need to appeal to any god within the machine or ghost outside the machine. Conceptually, nothing could be more inclusive than a system that represents all possibilities. Substantively, nothing could be more inclusive than the state of affairs that includes all other states of affairs.

At the same time, the system "does not pre-empt the answers to any questions that could be settled empirically."[7] It can be used to generate world formulas, such as those which are derived from Limiting-Case I (the "real-world formula") and Limiting-Case II (the "basic building-block formula"), as well as reality formulas such as "Here is an X", "Doing Y involves doing Z", and "A is a part of B". And we can generate descriptions of the real world by plugging in specific content to the formulas representing objects, processes, events, or states of affairs—for example, "Here is a desk"; "Writing a letter involves using language"; "the handle is part of the cup".

What we need next are systematic ways of describing actual objects, processes, events, and states of affairs in such detail that any one exemplar of these can be differentiated from any other. The basic descriptive units are presented in the following chapter.

———————————

[6]Ossorio, *State of Affairs Systems*, p. 28.
[7]*Ibid.*, p. 31.

# CHAPTER 9

# THE BASIC DESCRIPTIVE UNITS[1]

If we are to be able to describe the world with as much precision and efficiency as we can describe behavior and persons, we must have a way to do so. For behavior, we have parametric analysis and the behavior formula. For persons, we have paradigm case methodology, parametric analysis, and individual difference categories. For the real-world concepts of object, process, event, and state of affairs, we have a **calculational system** (transition rules), and **basic descriptive formats** or **units**, each of which reflects a parametric analysis, i.e., of the domain of objects, of the domain of processes, etc.

Our task here is to systematically represent any given object, process, event, or state of affairs per se, or any given type of object, process, etc., in such a way as to make clear what it is, what are its similarities to others of its kind, and/or what are its differences from others. The connections among the descriptive units themselves are given by the transition rules which make it possible to convert one

---

[1]See Ossorio, "*What Actually Happens*".

kind of description to another—for instance, from an object description to a state of affairs description and thence to a process description.

These units can also be used as a check list, a reminder of what we need to specify in a description, and beyond this, they have further possible applications, only a few of which have been explored. To give only one example, the Basic Process Unit has been used to set out how a large industrial complex functions. In this case, it works in such a way as to facilitate by computer the acculturation of new employees, thereby relieving more experienced staff members of a great deal of routine advisory work, and preventing the tangles that can follow, e.g., from a newcomer's reporting a malfunction to someone who has neither the competence to deal with it nor the authority to order its correction.

2

Already we have at hand various ways of describing the real world which are adequate for many everyday purposes. For example, a carburetor is part of an internal combustion engine which is part of an automobile. Writing a letter can be broken down into procuring a writing instrument and something to write on, putting down the words, etc. For other purposes, however, such descriptions are not adequate. What place does this person have in this organization? What part does he play? Could anybody else play that part? What other relationships does he have with other members of that organization? Or: how does the process of writing a letter differ from the process of writing a memo, a business report, a dissertation, a story?

The three basic descriptive formats are: **the Basic Object Unit (BOU), the Basic Process Unit (BPU), and the State of Affairs Unit (SAU).** Each of these formats consists of a *name* and a *description*. The name identifies

---

2See Jeffrey and Putman, "The Mentor Project".

the person Julian or Josie; an automobile; the fact (state of affairs) that this object is more expensive than that one. For the description, we shall specify *constituents*, and their *relationships, elements, individuals, eligibilities*, and *contingencies*. And in the State of Affairs Unit, we shall add another parameter, *expansions*.

It should be noted that this is not an arbitrary set of concepts, but that the set stems from raising the question, "How can one of these things differ from or be the same as another?", or to state it another way, "What could we specify about an object as such that would be sufficient to distinguish it from other objects as such, or about a process as such that would be sufficient to distinguish it from other processes as such?" and so for events and states of affairs. As a reminder, for the most part we shall again be concerned primarily not with logical or causal but with part-whole relations.

(Note: The "canonical" versions of the basic formats have been simplified and condensed for presentation here. In Appendix 6, the full forms are reproduced.)[3]

---

### The Basic Object Unit (BOU)

Name(s) (of the object)
Description
  Constituents (smaller objects)
  Relationships (of those constituents to one another)
    Name (of the relationship)
    Elements
    Individuals
    Eligibilities
    Contingencies
      attributional
      co-occurrence

---

Versions

[3]Ossorio, *"What Actually Happens"*, pp. 42, 52-53, 66-67.

Let us take as our illustration of the Basic Object Unit the representation of an automobile. The first part of the BOU is the **name** which identifies the object. Some objects will have only one name; others will have several, e.g., "automobile" or "car" or "self-propelled passenger vehicle" or "1975 Chevrolet Monza". In principle, it is possible to have an indefinitely large number of names.

There are some number of ways that we can decompose the automobile into immediate **constituents** or component parts, such as into right and left halves; or into metal, plastic, rubber, and fabric materials, or into engine, transmission, differential, brakes, etc.; or into drive train, fuel system, electrical system, steering mechanism, suspension, etc. In principle, the representation of an object under the constituent breakdown includes all the ways that it can be decomposed into immediate constituents. In practice, we include as many alternative breakdowns into constituents as we want, or as we need for our particular purposes.

Because the BOU is recursive, each of these constituents can be decomposed in various ways into *its* constituents. Thus fuel systems can be broken down into fuel tank, fuel lines, fuel pump, carburetor, etc. Further, each of these can be decomposed into still smaller components, down to Zilch particles, or more practically, to the level of specificity required for our particular purposes.

It is not enough, however, merely to decompose the object into component parts. We must also be able to specify how those constituents are related to one another in such a way that we represent an object and not merely a collection of parts. To begin with a few of the **relationships** for which we have names: the cylinders are *in* the motor, the carbureter is *attached* to the motor, the wheels *rotate* around the axles, the front wheels are *in front of* the rear wheels, the fuel tank *stores* the fuel. For many relationships, however, we do not have specific names, e.g., the relation between the steering wheel and the carburetor, or between the pistons and the tires.

Some of these will be two-place relations, i.e., relations between two things—A and B. Others will be three-place (A, B, and C), or four-place, or five-place, and so on to N-place. The relation "attached to", for example, is minimally a two-place relation: it logically requires that there be one element which is attached to a second element. In the case of the automobile, the carburetor is attached to the motor, the steering wheel is attached to the steering column, each tire is attached to one of the axles. "Between" requires at least three elements, e.g., the fuel line connects the gas tank to the carburetor. A four-place relation will require four elements; an N-place relation will require N elements. When an object is broken down into its different constituents, there will be relations between any two of the elements, and among any three, any four, and so on to all N constituents.

We shall identify each relation with a **name**, if there is one. For most relationships, however, we have no names because we do not have sufficient use for them. In those cases, we simply say "the relation between A and B", as in "the relation between the carburetor and the steering wheel". And each relationship will directly involve elements and individuals.

The **elements** are the "logical roles" or place-holders that are required by the relationships. As we have already seen, the relation "attached to" requires a minimum of an A and a B, which we call "elements". Thus the element A can be embodied by a carburetor and the element B by a motor. Or the elements A and B can be embodied by the left rear tire and the rear axle.

**Individuals** are the constituents that play the parts—so to speak—of the elements: the metallic assembly that plays the part of the carburetor, the rubber and fabric object that plays the part of the left front tire, the plastic object that plays the part of the steering wheel. In the simplest cases, individuals stand in a one-to-one relation with elements, and often we use the same term for both. In the general case, an individual can play the part of more than one element. For example, a given tire can play the part of the elements left front tire, right front tire, left rear tire, right rear tire, or spare tire, but only one of those at a time.

In any case, the individuals (a formal category) stand in a one-to-one relation with the substantive or historical individuals that actually play those parts in the real world. On this occasion, the historical, substantive individual Bill is the element "driver", and this particular chunk of metal is the element "motor" in this automobile, the '75 Chevrolet Monza #lM27G56234168. Here is the connection between the formal structure of the BOU and the particular, real-world automobile or other object that we are representing with the BOU.

The concept of **eligibility** is inseparable from the concepts of element and individual, because the whole point about individuals is that they are eligible to be certain elements, to play various parts. The same object that is eligible to be the left front tire is also eligible to be the right front tire, although it is not eligible to be both at once. A piece of fuel line may be eligible to play the part of either the intake or the overflow return line. The given metal assembly that I am holding in my hand at this moment, however, is eligible to be only a carburetor and nothing else.

**Contingencies** specify the conditions under which an individual that is eligible to play the part of a certain element is that element in fact and not merely possibly. **Attributional contingencies** have to do with what the object has to be like, what attributes it has to have, in order to be—for example—a carburetor, a tire, a piston. The **co-occurrence contingencies** specify what else has to be present in order for this individual to be this part of this object, i.e., what are the other, corresponding constituents.

Given that this metal assembly is the carburetor constituent of the automobile, what other constituents and relationships have to be there in order for that object to be a carburetor instead of just one metal object in a heap of others?

Finally, although not as part of the BOU itself, we can identify which and how many different things would qualify as an automobile under our description. These will be **versions** of "an automobile". How many ways can there be a car? Or an internal combustion engine? Or a carburetor or tire or steering mechanism?

By extending the Basic Object Unit,[4] we can take systematic account of the fact that internal combustion engines, such as most automobiles are equipped with, can be—and are—used also in motorcycles, tractors, boats, some airplanes, and for sundry non-vehicular uses such as generating electricity. Further, the Extended BOU allows us to deal with other characteristics of the automobile as well, e.g., its horsepower, the aerodynamics of the body, its seating capacity, how it handles on the road, and whatever else is called for.

We can start with any object and compose it with other objects into a larger object. The automobile (our original object) can be composed as a member of a larger configuration, such as a transportation system. That larger object, in turn, can be composed with other objects into yet larger objects, and we can continue this composition process until we run out of objects.

Conversely, we can take the entire real world as an object and break it down using any of the alternative decompositions we choose. And all this follows directly from the reality concept "Object", and the State of Affairs Transition Rules 2 and 3: "An object . . . is a state of affairs which is a constituent of some other state of affairs" (composition), and "An object is a state of affairs having

---

4Ossorio, *"What Actually Happens"*, p. 53.

other, related objects as immediate constituents" (decomposition).

---

## The Basic Process Unit (BPU)

Name(s)
Description
  Constituents (options within stages)
  (Relationships: changing)
  Elements
  Individuals
  Eligibilities
  Contingencies
    attributional
    co-occurrence

---

Versions

Like Object Description, Process Description reflects both one of the reality concepts and the relevant Transition Rules. In this case, the reality concept is "Process", and the Transition Rules are numbers 4 and 5: "A process is a sequential change from one state of affairs to another", and "A process is a state of affairs having other, related processes as immediate constituents".

A process takes place over time. It has duration. An object also has duration, but when it persists without significantly changing, a description of it as an object will be valid for some appreciable period of time. In contrast, time and change are of the essence for processes, and for the sub-processes into which they can be decomposed—not to mention the larger processes into which they can be composed. Therefore the BPU differs significantly from the BOU, while retaining some similarities.

As examples of the similarities, the BPU also starts with a **name** that identifies the process we are about to describe—our illustration will be a performance of *Hamlet*—and goes on to a **description** that calls for specifying elements, individuals, eligibilities, and contingencies. The relationships in a process, however, are continually changing, so that there is less point in pinning them down with names than there is with object relationships. (Note that strictly speaking, "relationship" is a place-holder, and that what we have in fact is not a relationship that changes, but a succession of different relationships. Because of this succession, it is natural to say that the relationship changes.)

In describing a process we shall distinguish two major ways of generating components. Given that a process has other, related processes as constituents, the sub-processes can be related as either **sequential** or **parallel**, and both the parallel and the sequential sub-processes can be broken down into **stages**. To illustrate with a relatively simple sequence, in *Hamlet*, Act V, Scene 1, Hamlet and Horatio are strolling through a churchyard (stage 1) and come across a man digging a grave (stage 2). The gravedigger shows them a skull, and identifies it as that of Yorick, the late king's late jester (stage 3). Hamlet then reflects aloud on it (stage 4).

Decomposing the stages into smaller stages, we have the words each person says in their proper order; that as Hamlet walks across the stage his second step follows the first; and so on. In more detail, we can take the separate verbal articulations, the contraction and relaxation of various muscles, etc.

For the parallel paradigm, we can take each of the characters all the way through the play as if they were separate lines that intersect in various ways as the script and the director orchestrate them. Thus Hamlet is walking beside Horatio at the same time that each is approaching the gravedigger, at the same time that he is digging the grave and singing as he digs. In applying the BPU to a parallel division, at some point we shall probably want to introduce stages unless the parallel unit is a very short one.

By and large, an actor will primarily use the sequential paradigm. Where do I move from here? What do I say after that? How does the character develop from the beginning of the play to the end? The director, however, must be concerned not only with sequences, but with parallels. What are Horatio and the gravedigger doing while Hamlet is addressing the skull? Backstage, where are the members of the procession gathering for their entrance immediately after the skull scene? Lighting, props, costumes, sets, all must be coordinated with the actors and one another for the inclusive process—the performance—to move with the proper speed, rhythm, and clarity.

Each stage in a process, at whatever level of detail, can occur in a number of different ways. That is, there are different formal options for how that stage occurs. Every performance of Hamlet varies from every other performance, even with the same cast and in the same physical surroundings. Tonight a gesture is a little more sweeping, an intonation a little less marked, as the actor does whatever he is doing in one way rather than another. The range of available options for the physical stage and for the stage set, lighting, costumes, styles of individual actors, and so on, may be wide or narrow, as evidenced by the innumerable interpretations of the play that are possible within the constraints set by the text.

The other four items in the Basic Process Unit are equivalent to those in the Basic Object Unit: Elements, Individuals, Eligibilities, and Contingencies. The **elements** (place-holders or logical roles) will be formal ingredients of the process. In the case of *Hamlet*, the elements include eighteen named characters and a dozen or more who are not given names, plus a set representing (or at least indicating) ramparts, a council chamber, a bedroom, a churchyard, etc., and props such as swords, a tapestry screen, flowers, etc. These are elements that are necessary for this process.

The formal **individuals**—e.g., Actors 1, 2, 3 ... N—may be fewer than the elements, because in certain cases the same individual can be assigned to more than one element. Conceivably a single actor could play the Ghost, the gravedigger, and Osric, because no two of them are on stage at the same time. Or the same sword can be worn and wielded by different actors.

**Eligibilities** can be illustrated by specifying Actors 1, 2, 3 ... N (formal individuals) who are eligible to play any of four roles (elements), and the historical individuals who are in one-to-one correspondence with the formal individuals can be distributed among the roles in any way that the director decides.

**Contingencies** can be elaborated more fully here than in the discussion of the BOU. **Attributional contingencies** have to do with the fact that some option or set of options is open only to an individual who has certain attributes. The actor who plays Hamlet must be able to fence if he is to play the part properly. If he cannot fence, he will not be able to exercise the appropriate options. Further, a particular actor's options will be limited by such person characteristics as his style and his understanding of the character.

**Co-occurrence contingencies** are specifically time-linked: a certain option is open only if certain things do or do not occur at other times. Thus future options can be limited by what has gone before: an actor's options for playing his later scenes effectively will be restricted by how he has played the earlier ones. Likewise, earlier options can be limited by the fact that certain things occur afterwards. Nothing in a play can be the second scene if there has not been a first scene, and Scene 1 becomes the first (in contrast to the only, and hence unnumbered) scene only when there is a second scene. Since the queen dies from a poisoned drink, it must have been envenomed in advance.

Processes can be composed with other processes into larger and larger processes, as well as decomposed into smaller ones. For an actor, this performance may constitute only one incident in a lifetime of activities. This production can be viewed as part of a theatrical season, or of theatrical history which is part of the history of a culture which in turn is part of the history of the world.

Stages and options have to do with the gross structure of the process, contingencies with its fine or internal structure. With slight changes, the diagram from Chapter 7 may help to clarify the difference:

|  | Stages | | | |
|---|---|---|---|---|
|  | A | B | C | D |
| Options: | <1> | <1> | <1> | <1> |
|  | <2> | <2> | <2> | <2> |
|  | <3> | <3> |  | <3> |
|  |  | <4> |  |  |
|  |  | <5> |  |  |

From the diagram, it may appear that options A<1>, A<2>, or A<3> can be combined with any of the five B options, and the B option that is chosen with any of the C options, and so on. This would be the case were it not that the attribution and co-occurrence contingencies impose restrictions upon what can and cannot be part of a given version.

Let us suppose that we take option A<2> as Stage 1, and that Stages B<1>, B<2>, and B<5> are closed to us because of various contingencies, but Stages B<3> and B<4> remain as possible options. If we take B<3>, then we can have C<2> but not C<1>; but if we choose B<4>, we can take either C<1> or C<2>. And so for the set of options in Stage D. The sets of versions are simply the processes which are possible as net results of all the constraints, including constituents, elements, individuals, eligibilities, and contingencies—everything in the BPU. In general, for any given process there will be some number of possible versions, and that number can be indefinitely large.

The BPU is a way of systematically representing processes of any kind, from performing a play to cleaning a house or running a corporation or playing a game of patience. Generally speaking, the more complex the process, the more difficulty we shall have in understanding it, and the more likely that we shall need a systematic approach to it.

---

Two incomplete forms of the Process Description warrant special attention. **Means-Ends Descriptions** specify what logical roles (elements) in the process are sufficient for accomplishing at least one version of the process, without regard to the relationships among the elements, or to the sequence of changes in those relationships. A simple example of a Means-Ends Description is the list of ingredients in a recipe.

The end in the Means-Ends Description is a state of affairs brought about by the occurrence of some version, and any version will do as long as it brings about that state of affairs. In order to produce the version of *Hamlet* that we are planning, we must procure a stage, select a cast and technical crew, obtain financial backing, etc., and the chronological order we follow in assembling these makes not the slightest difference for a Means-Ends Description. We can hire the hall before or after we cast the play, and we can confer with our set-designer before or after we choose among the available locations for performing the play. But if we lack any of the necessary elements, the corresponding versions cannot occur.

In contrast, **Task Analysis** is an Achievement Description that either specifies what will qualify as a given result, or analyzes what will bring that result about. Starting a new business, or taking an examination, are examples. The task of putting on a play can be analyzed into subtasks, including selecting the actors, rehearsing, designing and building the sets, making the costumes, and so on.

A task analysis begins with a description of the state of affairs which is to be brought about: performing the play before an audience, or getting this new business on its feet, or passing that examination. That state of affairs is associated with other tasks which, taken together, constitute the original task, and the achievement of those several tasks is the achievement of the original task. Thus we can redescribe our primary task as a set of states of affairs (subtasks, component achievements), each of which we examine for whether we can succeed in doing that sub-task. If so, we proceed to the next state of affairs; if not, we analyze the sub-task into sub-sub-tasks, and so on. And we keep on until we have run out of redescriptions or we achieve task redescriptions that we can implement. But redescription constitutes only one form of task analysis. Another is causal analysis: "What other states of affairs are there which, if they were accomplished, would cause this primary task to be accomplished?"

In many cases, Task Analyses and Means-Ends Descriptions can be transformed into each other. Rehearsing, providing sets, and so on, constitute the production of a play (Task Analysis), but they are also elements necessary for producing it (Means-Ends Description), so that which description we use will depend upon what accomplish*ment* we have in mind, or what we are accomplish*ing* with our description.

---

## Event Description

As we have already seen, an event is defined as "a direct change from one state of affairs to another" (Transition Rule 6). In certain ways, event descriptions can correspond to object and process descriptions; those ways are specified by a Transition Rule that we have not previously discussed. It has two variations:

**Transition Rule 10. That an object or process begins is an event and that it ends is a different event.**

**Transition Rule 10a. That an object or process occurs (begins and ends) is a state of affairs having three states of affairs ("before", "during", and "after") as constituents.**

Returning to winning a race as our example of an event, the running of the race is a process that can be decomposed into smaller processes or composed with other processes into larger processes. But the beginning of a race is an event, and the ending of that race is also an event. What was before and after "winning" (or beginning or ending) are states of affairs that can be composed and decomposed. But the event itself has only a "before" and an "after", with a dividing line—not an interval—between them.

In ordinary discourse, we have two major ways of giving or implying event descriptions. The first: what is the difference (the "after") that this event makes or has made?—i.e., the **result** paradigm (e.g., "The king is dead"); the second is the **nature** of the change (e.g., "The king has died"). Somewhat rarer is a third form, referring to the prior state (the "before"): "Something has happened to the king".

---

## The State of Affairs Unit

State of Affairs Name(s)
State of Affairs Description
    Constituents (objects and/or processes and/or events
        and/or states of affairs)
    Relationships
    Elements
    Individuals
    Eligibilities
        classification
        assignment (to Element)
    Expansions
    Contingencies
        attributional
        co-occurrence

---

Versions

Because a state of affairs is a totality of *related* objects
and/or processes and/or events and/or states of affairs
(Transition Rule 1), the State of Affairs Unit includes all
the features of the BOU, BPU, and Event Descriptions,
plus one important elaboration of its own. The SAU is the
infinitely serviceable resource for describing anything at
all, e.g., that the car is parked in the driveway, that *Hamlet*
is being performed tonight, and that the battle occurred, not
to mention the marital problems of a particular couple and
how it is affecting their parents and children and friends
and colleagues, and the global interweaving of politics,
economics, institutions, cultures, histories, and individual
persons.

The priority of the state-of-affairs reality concept and
descriptive unit is shown most clearly in the transition
rules, which specify that object, process, and event

descriptions are directly convertible into state of affairs descriptions, and by virtue of that relation they are convertible into each other. Moreover, the descriptive (or assertional) use of ordinary language is directly a case of state of affairs representation—not only in ordinary discourse, but also in propositional, technical, theoretical, poetic, and other uses.

One clear advantage of the state of affairs representation lies in its unlimited capacity to pick out facts of any kind or degree of complexity, and to codify them. In using it, therefore, we can be systematically straightforward without jeopardizing the richness of our observation and experience.

Another advantage is not peculiar to state of affairs description: that with it we can represent something without having to represent everything—e.g., its connections to other things. Nor do we have to describe that something (object, process, event, state of affairs) completely.

As before, our first move is to give the state of affairs we are describing an identifying **name**, and in the State of Affairs Unit, any kind of identifying name or description will do—for example, "the necklace is more expensive than the ring". In ordinary discourse, the name is also a description, but when we are using the SAU, giving the name carries the implication that there is more to be said about that state of affairs than what is in the identifying description. That "more" is spelled out the description portion of the formal structure of the SAU. As in the BOU and the BPU, the **description** specifies constituents, relationships, elements, individuals, eligibilities, and contingencies, and in addition, expansions.

We can decompose objects into smaller objects or constituents, and processes into options within stages; they divide into pieces that belong to the same logical categories that we started out with. Hence the smaller pieces can be treated in the same way that the larger pieces are. The **con-**

stituents into which states of affairs can be decomposed, however, are objects and/or processes and/or events and/or states of affairs, and each of these kinds of constituent is decomposed differently, e.g., by the BOU, BPU, Event Description, or SAU. Here we must introduce the last of the transition rules:

**Transition Rule 8. That a given state of affairs has a given relationship (e.g., succession, incompatibility, inclusion, common constituents, etc.) to a second state of affairs is a state of affairs.**

**Transition Rule 8a. That a given object or process or event has a given relationship to another object or process or event is a state of affairs.**

**Transition Rule 9. That a given object, process, event, or state of affairs is of a given kind is a state of affairs.**

That one of the objects in our example is a necklace is a state of affairs, and that the other is a ring is another state of affairs (Rule 9). That they have prices and the prices are different is still another state of affairs (Rule 8a). That the price of the necklace is higher than the price of the ring is itself a state of affairs (Rule 8).

In the SAU description, the **relationships** we identify may have to do with succession, inclusion, etc., or may have to do with attributes, such as of what kind are the relevant objects, processes, events, or states of affairs. As in the BOU and the BPU, the **elements** are the logical roles; the **individuals** are the exemplars that can logically be assigned to those elements, and each individual is assigned to an element. As for **eligibilities**, each of the elements is characterized as having a status, e.g., whoever sets a price for the necklace and ring has the status of "person", because pricing is a deliberate action and it is persons who engage in deliberate actions.

**Expansions** enable us to extend our description recursively to include all the objects, processes, events, and states of affairs that are constituents of our primary state of affairs, systematically and to any level of detail that we want or need. We end the expansions by giving a name which identifies a constituent without giving any corresponding description. This device, given the name and description structure, enables us to avoid infinite regresses, which in some cases can be extremely important. And this holds, as well, for object and process descriptions.

———

Descriptions of states of affairs (as of objects, processes, and events) must, of course, be done by a person, whether that person be a scientist, a historian, or any individual trying to make sense out of what is going on immediately around him. This brings us to still other forms of description.

Two among those which are particularly interesting are the configuration description and the chronological description, which are characteristic of the scientist and the historian respectively.

The scientist routinely gives **configuration descriptions**. Sometimes he represents states of affairs as objects having process constituents, such as a tree in which growth is occurring, or a human body in which blood moves. Such a description is of the kind to represent a system or a relatively stable set of relations such as an established, on-going culture or family. In contrast, he can give a configuration description having the form of a process with object constituents. This will be of the kind to represent states of affairs where the relations are in flux, like a play, a game, a social revolution, or an explosion. In both cases, the scientist's emphasis is on the nature of the configuration, of the stable or flowing pattern that is repeatable on many occasions. These two forms of configuration description may be interchangeable by altering the emphasis.

The historian, on the other hand, gives **chronological**

**descriptions** of the non-repeatable real world. Typically, the historian will describe some aspect of the real world by using a more or less comprehensive configuration description, with the explicit or implicit stipulation that this configuration has a unique place within the history of the world. That stipulation is what makes it a chronological description, and not merely a configuration description. Since the real world, as the state of affairs which includes all other states of affairs, *is* unique and unrepeatable, so also is that part of it: the object, process, event, and/or state of affairs which the historian is describing.

Both the historian and the scientist, of course, are Observer/Describers as well as Actors and Critics. Each is uniquely himself, and each observes the world from his unique vantage-point in history. He has a status relative to the configurations and the historical particulars that he is describing, and this state of affairs is a conceptual necessity.

---

Like the other resources of Descriptive Psychology, the basic descriptive units and forms of description do not include instructions on when and how to use them, or which ones to use, or who shall use them. And our using them does not guarantee our achieving a comprehensive and coherent or true description of the real world or any part of it, any more than mastering a numerical system and arithmetical operations guarantees that we shall come out with the correct answer to a problem in arithmetic. It only ensures that in a practical sense, although such an achievement may sometimes be difficult, it is not impossible.

## Comparison of the the
## BASIC DESCRIPTIVE UNITS

| Basic Object Unit (BOU) | Basic Process Unit (BPU) | State of Affairs Unit (SAU) |
|---|---|---|
| Name(s) | Name(s) | Name(s) |
| Description<br>　Constituents (smaller objects) | Description<br>　Constituents (options within stages) | Description<br>　Constituents<br>　　(objects and/or processes and/or events and/or states of affairs) |
| 　Relationships<br>　Elements<br>　Individuals<br>　Eligibilities | 　(Relationships: changing)<br>　Elements<br>　Individuals<br>　Eligibilities | 　Relationships<br>　Elements<br>　Individuals<br>　Eligibilities<br>　Expansions |
| 　Contingencies<br>　　attributional<br>　　co-occurrence | 　Contingencies<br>　　attributional<br>　　co-occurrence | 　Contingencies<br>　　attributional<br>　　co-occurrence |
| Versions | Versions | Versions |

# CHAPTER 10

# DESCRIPTIVE PSYCHOLOGY AND COMPUTERS[1]

Practically speaking, certain technical possibilities of Descriptive Psychology can be actualized only by computer, but—still speaking practically—the converse is also the case. Certain other possibilities of computers can be actualized by understanding them and their functions in terms provided by the Person Concept and behavioral model of Descriptive Psychology.

Taking the human being (a person who is also a specimen of *homo sapiens*) as the paradigm case of "person", from that we can derive descriptions of non-human and non-personal beings—computers, dogs, trees, stones, clouds—by assigning the appropriate values for their individual characteristics, and in some cases deleting all content from various parameters. Thus a dog can be described as having attitudes (e.g., protectiveness toward its family) and interests (e.g., in playing with a ball). A stone has an embodiment, a status as part of the real world, and

---

[1]See Ossorio, *State of Affairs Systems*.

possibly states such as cold or warm, but not other person characteristics. We can assign a status to trees because we are status-assigners, but trees are not status-assigners. If they were, they would not be trees; they would be persons with an arboreal embodiment.

Often persons are defined by their embodiments, their object characteristics. However, such a definition leaves out too much that is essential for being a person, notably whether their history is paradigmatically a history of deliberate action. It does not follow from an anatomical and physiological description of a *homo sapiens* that that individual will be able to function as a human being. Our person characteristics cannot be deduced from our object characteristics: these are different domains of discourse. Nor are persons nothing but their embodiments. And this brings us to the question whether in all cases we can properly define computers merely by their embodiments.

The objects we call "computers" and "computer systems" vary in complexity and in their functional characteristics, and the more sophisticated of them show enough of the right kind of characteristics that it is not just trivial to speak of them as limited persons with an electronic physiology. In the following discussion, we shall be concerned only with those computers of a kind and complexity such that their operations and achievements are in some sense comparable to the behavior of human persons.

---

For the most part, what we think computers can and cannot do has hitherto been circumscribed by our conceiving of them and treating them as mere mechanisms, swift and elaborate calculating machines. The discipline of computing science was developed in the first place from the fields of mathematics and electrical engineering, not from the study of the intelligent behavior of persons. It is not surprising, therefore, that computer scientists have sought for improvements in their "thinking machines" in such terms as faster access, larger storage capacity, more adequate languages, and more efficient algorithms. To a considerable extent, scientists have assumed that solutions to the problems of designing better computers lie in the logic that is exemplified by mathematics. Here, however, we shall be following through on the logic of the Person Concept as it is being put to use by Ossorio and others who are using Descriptive Psychology in the domain of computer science.

Thus we shall be exploring what might happen if, instead of treating the computer as merely a machine, we were to treat it as a person behaving in the world—a person who is deficient as compared with normal human beings, and whose behavior potential is limited in special ways. To help wean us from the machine-imagery that is almost always associated with computers, let us call these special, artificial-intelligence computers "AI individuals". To illustrate their functioning, we shall take the case of an AI individual reconstructing some aspect of the real world, as in organizing data for a criminal investigation[2]—let us say, the kidnapping of three apparently unrelated persons who are being held hostage by a person or persons unknown.[3]

We start with the Superintendent in charge of the investigation, a human person, Jennifer, who is collaborating with an AI individual of the appropriate kind. Together, they are attempting to find out (1) where the hostages are located, (2) why, and (3) who are the criminals, with the further ends in view of (4) rescuing the victims and (5) bringing the criminal(s) into custody.

In principle, it is a relatively straightforward process to instruct (program) an AI individual to produce object,

---

[2]This is being done by Information Access Systems of Boulder, Colorado. See Guertin, "Overwhelming Evidence."

[3]This illustration is taken from John Buchan, *The Three Hostages*.

process, event, and state of affairs descriptions using the Basic Descriptive Units (BOU, BPU, Event Description, and SAU), and we shall stipulate that this AI individual has been instructed in this way.

In producing such descriptions, it is behaving as human persons do, although it is deficient in some human person characteristics. Most certainly it has an **embodiment** that can be composed and decomposed, **knowledge** in the form of a set of facts that can be increased or decreased and that it has the ability to act on, the **ability** to perform designated transformations of those facts (calculating, global searching, word-processing, etc., etc.), and **capacities** which have not yet been fully actualized. It has a few relevant **dispositions**—e.g., it is fast and accurate in what it does; and some human persons characterize an AI individual they are working with as having **traits,** or even a **style.** Normally we do not describe an AI individual as having **values.** It is not eligible to be a self-status-assigner, so whatever **status** it has (e.g., as a machine or as a deficient person) must be assigned to it by someone who is eligible to assign statuses. But **states** does have, such as operational (with many further elaborations of this), malfunctioning, non-operational, although at a finer level of description, the functioning of any computer is thought of as a sucession of states.

Taking what the AI individual is doing, we can describe it as a form of behavior, using the Activity Description (Know, Know-how, Performance, and Achievement) or by adding the specification of the Want parameter, which Superintendent Jennifer supplies, the Agency Description (the basic diamond). Either way, the AI individual is engaging in a social practice. That is, it is doing something that it makes human sense to do, such as global searching, calculating, reminding, comparing, etc., etc.

By treating the AI individual as a person behaving in the world, we adopt a new paradigm for artificial intelligence. Rather than working from the bottom up (the machine to the human mind), we work from the top down, from the real world of human behavior to a more detailed specification of performances and achievements. In no way does this top-down approach permit the reduction of human persons to computers, or of human intelligence to mechanisms, any more than treating a dog as a person implies reducing human beings to canines.

---

In our example of intelligence-data processing, we begin with our paradigmatic person, the Superintendent, who is instructing a limited person (the AI individual) to tell her about some portion or aspect of the relationships that may obtain between each pair of the three hostages. The human and the AI individual are jointly participating in a social practice in which the AI individual does certain things independently of the human individual. By virtue of its structure and composition, this AI individual has capabilities such as drawing conclusions, making judgements, pointing out contradictions, making inductive inferences, asking for more information, prompting, indicating uncertainty, extrapolating, and so on.

For example, Jennifer may inform it of certain facts, and instruct her AI colleague to draw conclusions from them. The AI individual then reports its conclusions to Jennifer. Those conclusions will constitute further facts, some of which neither Jennifer nor anybody else working with that AI individual may know or be able to find out.

In providing the AI individual with information, the Superintendent selects from her own store of information that which is, or appears to be, relevant to the hostages and their situation, discarding what seem to her irrelevancies such as the failure of a copper company purporting to operate in Spain, and a steel-industry strike in Germany. She gives the pertinent background data to the AI individual, along with the information she is receiving from various sources, and which she takes to be relevant to the total problem. For example, originally she includes the data that the families of all three hostages are both wealthy and politically prominent, but not that the chief investigator on the case suddenly becomes ill.

Most likely, the information that Jennifer receives will consist primarily of state-of-affairs descriptions which the AI individual organizes with the State of Affairs Unit, and since this AI individual is appropriately structured, it can compare and contrast each of the state-of-affairs descriptions from the various persons who are reporting to Jennifer's office, and compose them into a more comprehensive state-of-affairs description that includes all the constituents, relationships, elements, individuals, eligibilities, and contingencies from all the sources, and quite possibly, certain expansions.

If Jennifer wishes, she can direct her AI colleague to decompose her data on certain key informants along the lines of the Basic Object Unit, with special attention to such attributional contingencies as their person characteristics. Or she can ask it to plot strategies using the Basic Process Unit, including alternative versions. Or she can direct it to pinpoint discrepancies between one informant's description and those of other informants, thereby discovering that the hitherto inexplicable illness of her chief investigator is very relevant indeed.

The information that the AI individual acquires from Jennifer and her sources will not be complete in every detail, so when it develops its more comprehensive state-of-affairs description from the fragments supplied by the different informants, some degree of creative construction will be required. It is, after all, constructing what amounts to a story from more or less fragmentary data. Thus if it concludes from the reports that the criminals are organizing a showdown for midsummer, the conclusion will not necessarily specify all the details of who is involved, where they are, what are their plans, and why this is happening at this time.

Determining the relevance of information will require achievements of the AI individual that seem not to be reducible to computations, such as using concepts, and as long as our thinking is circumscribed by mechanical or electronic models, it is unlikely that we shall succeed in doing so.[4]

To explicate in extremely general terms the special issue of how our AI individual can use concepts, we can start by sketching what might be called the physiology of our AI individual. We are stipulating that this individual distinguishes subject-matters from one another. It also distinguishes words, and each word has been given a set of numbers that represents the subject-matter content—numbers which in this case are assigned by Jennifer or some other expert. Those numbers give a location in the subject-matter domain, which is conventionally represented as a **Judgement Space**. Any text or document or message in which some of the system's vocabulary-words appear can be assigned a location in the Judgement Space, and location in that space corresponds to the relevance of that text or document to Jennifer's request.

All Jennifer has to do is to ask the AI individual for—let us say—"anything having to do with 'fields of Eden'", or "with the relation between the parish visitor and the fiancé of one of the hostages", and it is worthy of note that the questions can be posed in just such direct terms.

The AI individual combines the word-relevances into a document-relevance, distinguishing by the word-numbers the fact that the document-number is this one and not some

---

[4]For detailed technical information on the use of computers in Descriptive Psychology, see the items marked with an asterisk in the References, and the references in those works.

other. Thus by relatively simple mathematical operations, the AI individual can calculate the relevance of each message, text, or document to Jennifer's requests for information, and can process or retrieve whatever document or documents she has requested.

Here we must go back to the concept of empirical identities (cf. Chap. 7): "In *these* circumstances, *this* (whatever 'this' is) is also *that* (whatever 'that' is)". That is, we can give a Significance Description of the AI individual's behavior, but we can also give a Performance description in terms of its "physiology". We cannot describe the Significance of a behavior in terms of the physiology of the Performance—these are different domains of discourse—but in *these* circumstances, the behavior with *this* physiological description is also the behavior with *this* significance. As Jeffrey summarizes:

> By gathering numbers which are instances of acting on concepts (numerical locutions), and manipulating the numbers so that the relationship is maintained, we arrive at a mathematical object (the vector space together with the combining function) such that we may appropriately treat the results of calculating that function, in these cases, as acting on the concept. The computer (viewed as a machine) still only calculates; but when it calculates with these numbers, in this way, we can view it as acting on concepts.[5]

Lest it be concluded that the behavioral capacities of AI individuals are exhausted by what we have indicated so far, we should recall that because the State of Affairs Conceptual System is both reflexive and recursive, in principle we can generate with it an infinite number of operations

---

[5]Jeffrey, "A New Paradigm for Artificial Intelligence," p. 186.

upon an infinite number of elements. Thus the AI individual is using the same State of Affairs Information System that we already have discussed for describing and reconstructing aspects of the real world, including ourselves.

The Person Concept enables us to treat the AI individual as a person in whatever ways there is a point in doing so, without reducing us to mechanisms or elevating it too readily to the status of "person". The behavior formulation suggests ways for us to increase its behavioral repertoire to include behaviors and achievements that have hitherto been thought impossible because they can not be generated from principles of computation. Thus we can, in principle, construct AI individuals which not only assimilate, process, and retrieve facts, but also place those facts within a domain, i.e., recognize their statuses. Its behavior, then, can be treated as acting on concepts as, implicitly if not explicitly, we treat our own and other human persons' behaviors as acting on concepts.

---

Here ends the first part of the book, in which we considered the basic structures of the Descriptive Psychology conceptual system and one particularly important application. To a considerable extent, it is a codification of what we commonly do, and what people have been doing for millennia even though they did not describe what they were doing in these terms.

The value of this codification is demonstrated not in a recondite laboratory, or in experiments hemmed in with artificial stipulations, but in the rough-and-tumble and nuances of actual living. Indeed, it belongs to the wisdom of the ages that to understand a person's behavior, another's or our own, we look not only to the movements that he makes, but also to what he wants, the range of his knowledge, his values, whether he acted cold-bloodedly or feelingly. We have recognized all along, as well, that we need to take account of where we stand in relation to him. These considerations have been exhibited from time immemorial in our laws, our ethical systems, and our customs. Such ancient wisdom about persons, and about what needs to be accounted for in understanding them, has perhaps been best portrayed by artists: Homer, Virgil, Dante, Shakespeare, and their like. And descriptions of the world—more or less extensive world-views—are reflected not only in philosophies but also in religions.

As a pre-empirical conceptual system, Descriptive Psychology provides us with the resources to bring together science and art, religion and the behavioral sciences, history and law, fairy-tales and everyday living, in a way that preserves the uniqueness of every domain and individual yet does not leave them isolated from one another. Because it is reflexive and recursive, it is unlimited in its scope and precision. Because it is content-free, it is not culture-bound in the usual sense, and is non-committal with respect to anything empirical: to repeat, it does not "preempt the answers to any questions that could be settled empirically".6 It is a resource designed to increase our behavior potential, not a way to limit it by imposing a set of theories or a sequence of behaviors, like answers at the back of the book.

Descriptive Psychology does not have to be completely mastered before it can be used, any more than a musician must have complete technical mastery of his instrument before he can play music—remembering that even complete technical mastery will not guarantee that he will play any music well. On the contrary, the system must be used in order for it to be mastered (Maxim 7). In the following chapters, we shall see how it is now being used for a variety of purposes that are generally relevant to understanding persons, behavior, and the world.

---

6Ossorio, *State of Affairs Systems*, p. 31.

# PART IV

# PERSONS IN RELATIONSHIPS

# CHAPTER 11

# RELATIONSHIPS AND RELATIONSHIP CHANGES[1]

When we define a person as "an individual whose history is paradigmatically a life history of deliberate actions within a world history", it follows that essential to our being persons is a network of relationships in which we have a place. Deliberate actions have a place within social practices. Life histories have a place within world history. We exist at all as a result of a relation between our natural parents, and we develop as a result of our relations with the persons and non-persons (objects, processes, events, states of affairs) of the world in which we are immersed.

Ordinarily we differentiate two types of personal relationship, symmetrical and asymmetrical. The symmetrical are those where A is related to B as B is to A: we love each other; we are angry with each other; we are collaborators; John is Jessie's spouse and Jessie is John's spouse. Asymmetrical ones are those where A's relation to

---

[1]See Ossorio, "Outline of Descriptive Psychology," *Personality and Personality Theories*, 22 July 1977 ff., and *Clinical Topics*.

B is not the same as B's relation to A: parent-child, teacher-student, husband-wife, physician-patient employer-employee. Then there are the complex cases where people have a variety of different relationships with each other, for example, a married couple having both symmetrical (spouses) and asymmetrical (husband-wife) relations can have a number of others as well. They can be fellow-students, perhaps, and/or parents, breadwinner, homemaker, etc. And there is the dazzling complication where Dante has St Bernard address the mother of Jesus as "daughter of thy Son".

Every culture accepts some range of behaviors as permissible within given relationships. This range is usually delimited piecemeal in terms of prohibitions or double negatives: "Children don't talk back to their parents"; "A friend won't betray you"; "You have no right to say that"; "There are some things that people like us just don't do". These more or less explicit understandings, which differ from culture to culture and sometimes from person to person, provide invaluable clues as to what behaviors we can expect from others and suggest guidance for our own, as well as give us a basis for evaluating any behavior, ours or others'.

If two people are friends, we take for granted that they will not act against each others' interests, and if they do, it is appropriate for us to seek for an explanation. If an experienced teacher does not keep order in his classroom, we are justified in asking why. We tend to be surprised by the manager who cannot make decisions, shocked when a physician tries to seduce a patient, outraged by a parent who abuses his child, because such behaviors violate our standards for what those relations call for. In such cases, we are not only disappointed or disgusted or horrified; we are also surprised, as we would not be if a known mass murderer killed one more person, or a new employee did not make a wise policy decision, or a husband behaved seductively toward his wife.

What is expected or required of—let us say—a parent-child or teacher-student relation will vary among cultures and, within cultures, with stages of persons' development. The relation of a kindergartner to his teacher is naturally different from that of a graduate student to his advisor, and a young adult who is financially dependent upon his parents will have a quite different relation to them than will a person of the same age who has been financially independent for years. We take for granted that disputes among factions within an ethnic enclave or religious body will be qualitatively different from disputes between "insiders" and "outsiders". However bitter the antagonisms among varieties of Christians, for example, they are likely to unite against non-Christians, and vice versa.

———

Being in a particular relationship is one of the important reasons why we do what we do, and this can be systematized by means of a simple **Relationship Formula**, which is not restricted to persons although the modifying unless-clauses are applicable only to people: **If F has a given relationship, R, to G, then the behavior of F with respect to G will be an expression of that relationship, unless — .**

A set of five **unless-clauses**[2] codifies ways for specifying why a behavior is not what we should expect on the basis of what we know of the person or group. That is, the behavior has other than the expected values for one or more of its parameters. The unless-clauses constitute qualifications on the Relationship Formula, and each of these clauses is associated with one of the parameters in the behavior formula. Three of them are associated also with

———

[2]See Ossorio, "Explanation, Falsifiability, and Rule-Following," and "Outline of Descriptive Psychology".

maxims. Thus the behavior of a person within a given relation will express that relation:

—unless he has a stronger reason to do something else (the Want parameter; see also Maxim 3), *or*

—unless he doesn't recognize the reason for what it is (the Know parameter; see also Maxim 2), *or*

—unless he is unable to do so (the Know-how parameter; see also Maxim 5), *or*

—unless he is mistaken in taking it that that is what he is doing (the Cognitive aspect of the Know parameter), *or*

—unless he miscalculates or his behavior miscarries (the Performance-Achievement parameters).

For an example, let us take a mother, Grace, and her daughter Fay. Fay's behavior toward her mother will reflect whatever is customary for mothers and daughters when and where they live — :

1. —unless the person does not know what the relationship is (the Know parameter). Let us suppose that soon after Fay's birth, her mother places her in a foster home, but visits her occasionally under the guise of a friend of the foster family. Fay does not know that Grace is her mother; consequently her behavior toward Grace does not conform to what is expected of daughters toward their mothers at that time and place.

2. —unless the person is acting on another relationship which takes precedence (the Want parameter). When Fay reaches legal age, she is told that Grace is her natural mother, but her relation with her foster mother is so warm and strong that it is more important to her than her relation with Grace. Fay wants to continue her closeness with her foster mother more than she wants to develop closeness with her natural mother.

3. —unless the person is unable to engage in such be-

havior at the time in question (the Know-how parameter). In the extreme case, the person may be paralyzed or otherwise incapable of movement. In this less extreme case, Fay can no longer treat Grace as merely a family friend, but neither can she respond as a daughter is expected to behave to her mother. Thus Fay is unable to respond easily and appropriately to Grace as either friend or mother.

4. —unless the person mistakenly believes that her behavior is an expression of that relationship (the Cognitive parameter). In time, Fay comes to treat Grace with the casual informality that some of her friends use toward their mothers, not realizing that their behavior is grounded in a life-history of reciprocal sharing. Her friends' apparently off-hand manner, therefore, has an entirely different significance for them than for Fay and Grace, with resulting discomfort for them both.

5. —unless the person miscalculates or the behavior miscarries (the Performance and Achievement parameters). A miscalculation occurs when one reaches to pick up something but instead knocks it over. In this illustration, inadvertently Fay says something that hurts Grace's feelings. A behavior miscarries when something happens to prevent it from occurring: since behavior is a process, it can be interrupted by outside influences. Fay's efforts to telephone her mother fail on a particular occasion because a storm has disabled the telephone system.

As a further qualification, and speaking practically, an individual's set of person characteristics constitutes a reality constraint on how he acquires relationships, and with whom, and what relationships he can acquire at all. Moreover, a change in his person characteristics (extreme examples would be those resulting from drug-addiction, brain injury, or psychosis) will affect not only what relationships he can acquire, with whom, and how, but may affect those which he already has, as when a new relation such as a marriage makes a difference to long-established friendships.

We learn by rote what behavior our culture expects for a given relationship. We do not learn by rote, but acquire by sensitivity, empathy, imagination, what is appropriate and inappropriate behavior. Once we comprehend the nature of a relationship, and have developed that sensitivity, we can generate new behaviors appropriate for the relationship—compare mastering arithmetic, which is not a matter merely of solving individual problems, but of learning how to do arithmetic and thereby becoming capable of solving problems that we have never met before.

In any given culture, the range of permissible variation for appropriate behaviors is wide for some relationships, narrow for others, as some calculations in arithmetic can be in round numbers, but in other cases they must be taken to the umteenth decimal place. Until we know what the basic relational phenomena are, however, we can neither identify what behavior is appropriate and what is not, nor discern when we need to call upon the resources of the unless-clauses.

The initial condition of knowing what the basic relational phenomena are can be compared with the first of the Maxims for Behavior Description: "A person takes it that things are as they seem, unless he has reason to think otherwise." We take it that friends will be loyal to friends, students will be open to learn from their teachers, parents will care for their children, and so on, unless we have reason to think otherwise in particular cases. That we have such a relation as friend or student or parent gives us a reason to behave accordingly (Maxim 2), and we shall do so unless we have a stronger reason not to (Maxim 3).

We may have two or more types of relation with another person, e.g., both colleague and friend, or both daughter and employee, and if two of those relations give us reasons for engaging in a particular behavior, e.g., to travel together or collaborate in building up a business, we shall have a stronger reason for behaving in that way than if we had only one of those relations—if, for example, we were colleagues but not friends, or an employee but not a daughter of the employer (Maxim 4). Finally, if a basic relationship calls for us to do something we cannot do, we shall do something we can do, if we do anything at all (Maxim 5). If loyalty to a friend required us to commit murder, what shall we do?

---

We come next to the **Relationship Change Formula**, which is also not restricted to individual persons: **If F has a given relationship to G, but the behavior of F toward G is such that it violates that relationship but expresses some other relationship, then the relationship will change in the direction of the relationship for which the behavior that did occur would have been an appropriate expression.**

Jim, aged 15, askes an older friend, Harry, to buy him a six-pack of beer, and Harry refuses because Jim is below the legal age for drinking beer. Jim responds, "Then you're not my friend." Harry replies, "I could get in bad trouble for that," and Jim, "You care more about yourself than you do for me"—and the friendship is on its way toward enmity. Or two persons meet for the first time; they are strangers. One makes a polite move; the other responds politely. They are moving from the relation "strangers" toward becoming acquaintances, a new relation, and perhaps friends.

Again we bring the unless-clauses into play because they provide not only reasons why a behavior may not be the expression of an established relation, but also why the relation itself may change, and in what direction. Let us suppose that Julian's income is not sufficient to provide an adequate living for his family, so when their children have entered school, his wife Jane takes a paying job. This means that she no longer has the time and energy that she once had for sharing recreational activities with her husband. Her relation to her job takes precedence over her relation as playmate with her husband. Julian recognizes that her new Want, to contribute financially to the family, results in rewards not only for the family as a whole but also for him personally, but they are not the same kinds of reward which they and he had previously enjoyed. Willy-nilly, Julian and Jane's relation changes, and it can conceivably move toward a stable new relationship.

---

The Relationship and Relationship Change formulas are applicable not only to individuals, but also to communities, because the logic of group relations is inherently similar to the logic of individual relations, although not identical. As examples of relationship changes for a community, we can think of a group with a particular set of values moving into a community with a different set—the migration of a religious community to another country to escape persecution, or of an ethnic group to obtain more opportunities, or of a farm family to a city.

The characteristics of such a group—its values, for example—will function as reality constraints on how and with whom it can establish new relationships. It may be that the group cannot continue its traditional social practices because essential elements are unavailable in the new setting, or inappropriate, e.g., the legal prohibition of peyote or of nudism as among the Doukhobors, or opposition to military service. The Dispositions and Powers of both the newcomers and the oldtimers will set limits on what relationships they can establish—the community equivalent of remaining strangers or becoming friends.

Persons and groups are differentiated by the kinds of relationship that are logically possible for them. The fact that persons have, or could have, these relationships is a state of affairs. Relationships, therefore, can be precisely described using the State of Affairs Unit, and relationship changes with either the State of Affairs Unit or the Basic Process Unit.

## State of Affairs Unit

State of Affairs-Name: Jane and Julian's marital relation

State of Affairs-Description

> Constituents: Jane and Julian
> Attributes:
>> properties—both are human persons
>> relationship—married to each other, parents, etc.
> Elements: wife, husband, marital agreement (explicit and/or implicit)
> Individuals:
>> classification—two objects (male and female persons), and a state of affairs
>> assignment—wife to female, husband to male, the agreement to state of affairs
> Eligibilities: initially, the wife is eligible to be housekeeper and nurturer for her husband and children, but not to be a breadwinner. The husband is eligible to be the breadwinner and to make major policy decisions
> Expansions—Basic Object Unit analysis of both persons, and specifications of the agreement by SAU
> Contingencies:
>> attributional: Jane's and Julian's person characteristics, which open some options and close others
>> co-occurrence: if Julian earns enough, Jane will not have to take a paying job, etc.

## Basic Process Unit

Process Name: change in marital relation from
      asymmetrical to symmetrical

Process Description: sequential

| Stages: | (a) | new co-occurrence contingency: family needs more money |
|---|---|---|

Stages:     (a)  new co-occurrence contingency:
                    family needs more money

            (b)  agreement that Jane should have a
                    paying job
                        options: inside or outside the home, etc.

            (c)  Jane hunts for a job
                        options: answers ads, places ads, agency,
                    word of mouth, etc.

            (d)  Jane takes a job
                  . . . . .

            (k)  household responsibilities are reassigned
                        options: who does what, and when

                  . . . . .

            (n)  Jane's new status as co-breadwinner
                    requires Julian to re-evaluate his status

Elements, individuals, Eligibilities, and Contingencies as in
      State of Affairs Unit

---

Versions: the options and sequences that are possible and available

Ordinarily, we do not articulate a state of affairs or a process in detail unless something has gone wrong and we need to identify where it has gone wrong, or unless we see that something could be improved and want to pinpoint how to change it, or unless we need to have detailed information available for future reference, perhaps in a computer bank.

If Jane and Julian's marital relation is breaking down

and we are counselling them, or if we are looking for a way to improve one of our own relationships that is merely adequate, these tools will ease our task. Using them, we can clarify the nature of the situation, establish what can and cannot be changed, select alternative stages and options, and choose among a range of possible versions. For the most part, however, such simple locutions as "Jane and Julian decided that she should find a paying job, and consequently their relations changed" are entirely adequate. It is not often that we shall need or want to represent a real-life situation with the elaborate apparatus of the Basic Descriptive Units. However, our practice and experience in thinking in these terms will discipline our observation and thinking, which is what they are designed to do.

The descriptive units enable us to treat relations themselves, and their changes, systematically. The unless-clauses enable us to treat systematically cases where the behavior that occurs violates the relation that obtains between the persons or groups. Moreover, with these we can do so trans-historically and cross-culturally, without prejudice. Ambiguous cases can be precisely described as ambiguous, and complex cases can be charted in the necessarily detail.

This is a formal approach to problematical relationships—an Observer-Critic's way, not an Actor's—but it is not impersonally cold. Use of both the State of Affairs Unit and the Basic Process Unit allows us to assign specific values to the individuals' person characteristics, under Contingencies, perceptively and with sympathy.

The formulas and descriptive units provide us with a way to organize our thinking. They do not show us what our options are, but instead, enable us to organize our options into categories so that we know what kinds of options they are, and where to look for other options and kinds of options. It is a considerable gain to be able to eliminate unnecessary vagueness and obscurity in our thinking, and to grasp how much we do not know, as we relate ourselves to other persons and, as members of society, seek to understand the relations that obtain among diverse social entities.

# CHAPTER 12

# COMMUNITIES[1]

Individual persons are social entities, but so also are groups, and it is just as important for us to be able to describe, compare, and contrast groups as it is to be able to describe, compare, and contrast individuals. How do Chicanos differ from Anglos, liberals from conservatives, 12th Century from 20th Century women, the Runagates Club from the Bellona Club, the Irish of Ireland from Irish-Americans and both from "the Irish of India"—the Bengalis? How has the family of Julian and Jane changed from what it was two years ago, before Jane began her paying job? Among the methods for answering these and similar questions are—again—those of parametric analysis and of paradigm case formulation.

A community can be parametrically analyzed in terms of individual **members** who share a **world** and **statuses**, and values which are expressed in **choice principles**. Those members participate together in specific, definable **social**

---

[1]See Ossorio, "A Multicultural Psychology," and Putman, "Communities" and "Organizations".

**practices**, and in the organized sets of social practices which we call institutions. One of the most important of these institutions is **language**. Let us take the parameters one by one.

*Members*. Paradigmatically, the individuals who comprise a human community are persons, each with his own person characteristics, who engage in deliberate actions and thereby participate in social practices. Some of these episodes correspond to mere social encounters, for example, the coming together of a group of strangers in an elevator or of the members of an audience at a concert. Others involve people in the more meaningful interactions characteristic of communities, such as in families, on committees, and so on. Typically, persons belong to a number of communities, from the limiting case of the community that includes all communities—the human race—to intimate two-person groups. To be a member in such a community is to have that status, and of statuses, more later.

*Worlds*. Members of a community share a world by distinguishing in common a large set of objects, processes, events, and states of affairs, and by manifesting values, attitudes, and interests that are compatible or similar in some other way. No one becomes a member of the world of chess-players unless he is able to recognize the different pieces and to go through the process of moving them in ways appropriate to those pieces, and unless he enjoys the game and has enough of a competitive attitude to value winning over losing. Some communities are international in their extension: any of the so-called world religions would be an example. On the other hand, a neighborhood association may extend for only a few blocks and endure for only a few months. Some communal worlds extend deep into history and, by anticipation, far into the future: a nation, or what in Christianity is called "the communion of saints".

Communities differ from one another according to

their ultimate objects, processes, and so on, and how they trace their history and their place in relation to other communities—briefly, in their worlds. The differences and similarities in these worlds can be set forth in any desired detail by using the State of Affairs Conceptual System, the Basic Descriptive Units, and the Relationship and Relationship Change formulas.

*Statuses.* Every community defines two critical statuses, member and non-member, and there are conditions under which a non-member can become a member, or a member be relegated to the status of non-member. Such conditions are usually implicit but they may be explicit. We are born into communities such as families, tribes, nations. In other cases, membership status can be formally assigned to persons by accrediting or degrading rites of passage, some public and ceremonial such as adoption, a citizenship oath, a graduation ceremony, a coming-of-age party, marriage; or exile, deprivation of citizenship, being fired from a job. Other status-assignments can be less formal: a newcomer is gradually accepted as "one of us"; as the reputation of an official is eroded, his influence diminishes. Accreditations mark us as eligible to participate in certain social practices which are not open to people who do not have that status—to take only one example, communities vary enormously in what eligibilities are associated with membership in the class "child" and the class "adult".

Conversely, degradations divest us of eligibilities which we had previously had. Although accreditation increases our behavior potential while degradation decreases it, the relationships are not as simple as they may appear. As we have already seen, expulsion from one community can result directly in admission to another, as in the case of a soldier who, upon being discharged, automatically becomes a civilian—a change that has in it elements of both degradation and accreditation: he has lost the behavior potential that comes with being a soldier, but gained the behavior potential that comes with being a civilian. Then there is the not uncommon case of the person who, when he becomes adult, takes the loss of the child's privileges to be a degradation for which the different behavior potential associated with adulthood is insufficient compensation.

Further to complicate matters, every community will have some sort of structure that can be articulated in terms of statuses. What place does farming have in that community—is it the primary activity or a minor one? What is the place of a married person relative to a person who is not married? What value does formal education have in this community? Or manual skills or spirituality? It is not by accident that this whole field of inquiry carries the name "status dynamics".

*Choice Principles.* The behavior of members of the community will be guided by its accepted choice principles. Here we return to the Justification Ladder (Chapter 4), and the appeal from individual judgement to custom, theory, and principle in defense of a choice, or for clarification in selecting among alternative courses of action. Choice principles are commonly expressed in the form of value statements, policies, slogans, maxims, and mottoes, and in scenarios such as myths. All these are ways of enunciating in Actor's talk the community's way of living. Think of "Play it safe", "The stranger is the enemy", "Love thy neighbor", "Caveat emptor", "America First", the myth of Hercules. A number of choice principles can be grouped, as in the Boy Scout oath or Kipling's Law of the Jungle, or they can be codified by legislative enactments or judicial decrees. The form makes no essential difference. What matters is that the members of the community know what the relevant choice principles are, and act accordingly unless —, and every community will have its own instances of occasions when the unless-clauses allow for exceptions: "This stranger can't be an enemy—it's only a baby"; "But the buyer was my own sister!"; "America First, sure, but not the gaggle of hacks who are in office right now".

Once we know the choice principles that are characteristic of a community, we shall have a fair notion of what to expect from its members. If they consistently play it safe, or treat strangers as enemies, we shall not be surprised. This gives us our baseline—not that all persons within that fold will hew exactly to that line. The variants, however, will be noticed and remarked upon. "He's overcautious. She's rather bold." "She's lazy. He works hard." "Those people act as if everybody were their neighbor." A person who goes beyond the range of permissible variation, in any direction, will be cast out, or refused admission, or treated as a special case: a tolerated eccentric, a licensed crackpot, a genius who is accorded extraordinary latitude, a criminal who is incarcerated.

*Social Practices.* With social practices and institutions (organized sets of social practices), we come to the specific behavioral patterns that constitute "what is done" in that community, and how it is done. The practices themselves are teachable, learnable, and do-able, and we learn them by practice and experience. Examples might be counting change, drinking from a cup, preparing a meal, carrying on a conversation, running a business, hunting, farming.

Within the range of behaviors acceptable to a particular community, there are likely to be myriads of known ways of doing social practices, which means that multiple options are available to anyone engaging in them. Therefore, given the relevant competence (Maxim 9), persons who engage in them can expect to carry them through to a conclusion.

A fuller discussion of social practices must wait for the next chapter. At the moment, however, we need to differentiate three types—fundamental, optional, and core practices—which are of particular importance in creating and maintaining a community.2

*Fundamental practices* are those which are essential if there is to be any community whatsoever; they include accreditation, degradation, negotiation, and a common language. Communities differ in how problems are negotiated—by arbitrators or courts or battles or sitting down to talk it over—but some process there must be. As we have seen, accreditation and degradation can be explicit or implicit, as casual as inviting an acquaintance to have a cup of coffee, or as ceremonial as a rite of confirmation. The language may be that of a nation or of a technical field, or signed as by the deaf, or pictographic as by persons without the capacity for vocal speech, but of this, more later.

Ordinarily communities have, in addition to the fundamental practices, a considerable body of *optional practices* or institutions that some people engage in and others do not, like typing, cooking, keeping accounts, hunting for food, running for office, raising children. But there are others, designated as *core practices*, that are not optional. What would we say of a person who claims to be Christian but has never been admitted to membership in any church, does not contribute financially or otherwise to any activity which is carried on under the aegis of Christianity, has not investigated Christian history or teachings, and does not adhere to any of the beliefs typical of Christianity? To be a Christian *is* to engage in at least some of those core practices, and it is by engaging in at least some of them that one becomes a member of the Christian community. By the same token, one does not become a Ph.D or an M.D. or a licensed dog-trainer, or a ballet dancer except by successfully carrying out a set of core practices.

*Language.*3 Every social entity—culture or commu-

---

2See Putman, "Communities" and "Organizations".

3See Ossorio, *Meaning and Symbolism, Rule-Following in Grammar and Behavior, Positive Health and Transcendental Theories*, and Mitchell, "On the Interpretation of Utterances".

nity or group or sub-group—is not only characterized but to a large degree constituted by its language. Young lovers give each other pet names and have their private terms for especially meaningful aspects of their relation. Every trade, profession, and craft has its jargon, every region its dialect, every nation its tongue. George Bernard Shaw once pointed out that what chiefly separates Britain from America is their common language, which tends to obscure the crucial differences between British and American English— differences that have nothing to do with any of their celebrated accents.

One of the important ways by which a member is recognized as such is by his mastery of the language of the community. Think of a chess-player, otherwise a stranger, at a chess tournament, being immediately accepted as "one of us" because he uses its language skillfully. Mastery, however, requires more than competence with words or signs, because although linguistic behavior is similar to other kinds of behavior, it different in fundamental ways. In brief, "Language is a form of behavior in which we explicitly make certain distinctions, and we have those distinctions because we engage in forms of behavior which involve making distinctions and acting accordingly."[4] Acting on distinctions, of course, is equivalent to using concepts, the difference between them being only grammatical.

Essential to any behavior is making distinctions (the Know parameter of behavior), and a baby or a dog—or for that matter, an insect or fish—can discriminate between food and not-food, and eat it or pass it by. But none of these individuals can *explicitly* designate what distinctions it is making. Because it does not have a language, it cannot distinguish the distinctions on which it is acting. Thus a dog can distinguish (a) food from not-food, and (b) playing with a ball from playing with a stick. What it cannot do is

---

[4]Ossorio, transcript, 11 December 1975, p. 7.

distinguish the distinction between (a) and (b). Without language, we can neither *know* what we are doing, nor know what we are doing.

It is a special function of language to signal what distinctions we are acting upon. Such signalling is a form of social behavior which has a place within a structure of interrelated social practices, and that place is unique and indispensable. Anyone who believes that it is dispensable need only take the little trouble to find out what happens when a person of normal intelligence who is multiply handicapped, as from severe cerebral palsy, is introduced to computer-assisted communication and suddenly becomes able to express himself verbally instead of only by eye-movements or by laboriously pointing to diagrammatic pictures.

We must have a language not only to participate in most social practices, but also to give an adequate account of what we are doing, to understand adequately what others are doing, to assess what is going on, and to generate all but the most elementary social practices. And to perform these various functions, we need the different ways of talking of the Actor, the Observer/Describer, and the Critic/Appraiser.

The *Actor's way of talking* is perhaps best exemplified by the kind of talk players use in actually playing a game. In baseball, the catcher calls "Lay it right there"; the umpire signals a strike or a ball or an out; the third base coach instructs the runner. In bridge, the players state their bids and declare what is trumps. In the kitchen, the chef tells his assistant, "Stir this. Add a whisper of lemon. Turn on the oven," and the assistant asks, "Shall I butter the baking dish? Does the pot need to be covered?" In general, Actors' talk makes sense only to the person who is already acquainted with the social practice in question. It is the paradigmatic Insider's way of talking, which may make little or no sense to the Outsider.

To describe what is going on calls for the *Observer's way of talking*, a straightforward report by means of a rule book or a play-by-play account. "He's caught the fly and the batter is out." "There are four players and a deck of fifty-two playing cards." "They're preparing the school lunch." Yet there are complications even in this straightforwardness, and two of them should be noted here.

First, the Observer must have command of all the Actor's talk, and more as well. He must use many of the same locutions as the Actor—he says, for example, "North bids two hearts" in place of North's saying, "I bid two hearts". The grammatical difference between these two is trivial compared with the difference between the social practices of action and of commentary in which they are respectively embedded. We are doing different things when we play bridge and when we describe a game of bridge. The behaviors vary in their Want, Know-How, Performance, and Achievement parameters, although not necessarily in the Identity of the behavers or in what they Know. A single person can simultaneously play and describe what is going on, or can describe it later.

Second, the Observer's way of talking can be non-judgemental and non-committal. "He was afraid" commits the Observer to a degree that "He told me he was afraid" and "He looked afraid" do not. All three forms, however, are eligible for the Critic's evaluation, and none is more conservative than the others. "How did you know he was afraid?" "He said ... he looked." "What makes you think he was not putting on an act?" "Because in that situation, anybody with any sense would be afraid, and he has sense."

Generally, we use non-committal talk when we are not sure enough of the situation or the person to be comfortable about saying unequivocally, "He was afraid", but despite the widespread notion that non-committal ways of talking are more "objective" or "scientific" or "unassailable", they have no intrinsic virtue. They are only better for some purposes and worse for others—as an example of the latter, the person who prefaces even the most inconsequential remark with "It seems to me".

The *Critic's way of talking* comes in two related varieties, diagnostic and directive. The Critic as diagnostician will characteristically speak in negatives and double negatives, as in "This is what went wrong," and "This could have gone wrong but didn't". Thus a drama critic might report, "Among the mainly lackadaisical actors, Miss Jarvis performed adequately." "Performed adequately" is indeed a positive, but it still fits the pattern of "could have gone wrong (and in the case of the other actors, it did), but in her case it didn't".

The Critic's diagnostic language tends to be comparative and relational, and in that sense is content-free. "To focus" means one thing with respect to a work of art, something else in photography or ophthalmology, and in all these cases, "in focus" implies a comparison with "out of focus". A critic who comments that a play lacks focus is implicitly comparing the production as it occurred with what it might have been. "Unsympathetic", when applied to a character in a play, does not mean what it does in a family or psychotherapeutic situation, and "brilliance" has other content when applied to color and when applied to intelligence.

The Critic's content-free negatives and double negatives, however, are usually of little or no value in guiding the Actor who wants to correct his performance. It does not tell the playwright or director *how* to sharpen the focus or the performers *how* to become less lackadaisical, and therefore does not complete the feedback loop. To accomplish that, the Critic—or someone—must use directive language, that is, direct the Actor to do something he already knows how to do. Perhaps the director of the play sees the justice of the criticism and instructs the performers, in Actor's language, on how to mend their ways. He will say not, "Do it right", but "Speak that line emphatically", and not "Don't be awkward", but "Move like a dancer".

One of the Critic's special language-functions is that of assigning statuses to the Observer's descriptions, and among the possible statuses, two pairs are particularly important: "objective and subjective", and "true and false".

To start with, we must differentiate subjective and objective judgement from subjective and objective language. Judgement is subjective when the person is presenting his own view; it is objective when he is functioning as a representative of a community, setting aside his personal biases. Language is subjective when, strictly speaking, the person is talking about himself: "I see it as being beautiful" or "I take this to be a book"; hence there are no criteria for correctness. In using objective language, however, we can be correct or incorrect: "That sculpture is beautiful" or "This is a book".

Sometimes we also take a further, unnecessary step, by equating objectivity with the absence of any personal contribution to what we are saying, apparently on the supposition that inevitably a personal contribution must invalidate what is being said, and on the pretext that observations do not presuppose an Observer. From this follows the protocol of the scientific report and the doctoral dissertation, which usually are required to be written in the third person and the passive voice: "It was noted", "The meter read", "The problem was defined as", "The results of the investigation indicate"—a style that is at once covertly deceptive and pretentious. Inescapably it was persons who noted, read the meter, defined the problem, and reached the conclusion, as is conceded by the names on the title page. The impersonal style does not eliminate any bias those persons may have had; it only gives the impression that the persons carrying out the project did not contribute anything to it, i.e., that their view was not in any way affected by their viewpoint because they were acting as representatives of a community. But as we have already seen, complete elimination of viewpoint cannot be the case. It would be at once more accurate and more honest to say outright, "We did this" and "I observed that".

"Truth" and "error" are also statuses which a Critic may assign to statements. The "search for truth" is an activity within a group whose members are able to distinguish truth from error, who value truth above error, and who are able to act on what they take to be true. Within that group will be communities whose members agree on what procedures are appropriate for assessing the truth-value of statements, for establishing whether statements are eligible for truth-status, and for discovering new truths. Those procedures will differ for different domains: we do not use the same techniques for ascertaining truth in—let us say—science, literature, philosophy, religion, and history. But in no case have we any procedure that will guarantee the achievement of any ultimate and universal truth, nor could we, because in assigning to a statement the status of "truth", we are giving it a place in our world, not establishing a preordained fact or value. Nowhere is this more conspicuous than in the natural sciences, where the "truths" of one generation are constantly being replaced by other "truths" in an unending pageant of degradations and accreditations.

We need the concept "truth" because we engage in forms of behavior that call for distinguishing between what is the case and what is not the case. And it can serve that anchoring function even though we know that many of the statements we now hold to be true—those to which we now give the status of "true"—are not immutable or unassailable. Even to bring in the question of truth, however, is often to enter a blind alley. In its place, we shall frequently do better to ask, "What is the point of talking that way?"— the way of science, religion, poetry, or however we are talking. Or the question can be given another form: "*When* is there a point in talking that way?" For example, there is a point in calling certain statements "scientific truths", because that identifies what scientists are not at the moment calling into question.

There is no point in talking about the chemical composition of a sonnet, or the physiology of a mystical vision, as such. That would be like introducing trumps or field goals into chess. The point of talking one way rather than another may not be immediately obvious. "This box belongs on that shelf" can be a description or a directive. "Can you drive the car?" can be explicitly a request for information or implicitly an invitation for the other person to drive it. The sentences in this book can be treated— mistakenly—as propositions and evaluated for their truth, or as they are intended to be treated: as instructions or invitations: "See what happens when you look at behavior, persons, the world, and language in this way". Directives, requests, instructions, invitations, and promises *cannot* be true or false. We simply act on them, e.g., by complying, challenging, criticizing, or ignoring them. And it is one of the Critic's functions to differentiate between, for example, propositions and directives, which is to say, those sentences which are eligible for truth status and those which are not.

Moreover, the Critic needs to be able to identify when an Observer has changed the subject in the course of giving a description. It is common in psychology (and not only there, by any means) for an Observer to profess—for example—that he is describing a behavior, although his choice of words reveals that the distinctions he is making are actually taken from physiology. Wittingly or unwittingly, he has changed the subject from psychology to physiology, perhaps because he holds the exotic belief that they are the same. In John and Jessie's altercation about moving the chair, the subject was changed several times, from the position of the chair through various stages to the nature of their entire relationship. Not all escalations of controversies take the form of changing the subject, but it is a standard maneuver, and sometimes it takes a very astute Critic to diagnose when a person is employing it.

Not only are there Actor's, Observer's, and Critic's ways of talking, but also Insider's and Outsider's ways. The members of a particular religious community will talk about the sacred, for example, in one way among themselves and in another way when they are with people who do not share that faith. An Observer or Critic will describe or appraise a ceremony very differently depending upon whether he does or does not see it from the inside.

The discrepancies between the Insider's and the Outsider's reports can be drastic, especially when the Observer restricts himself to depicting a performance without regard to its significance, or to what the Insiders want, know, and are able to achieve by that performance. But the Outsider's view does not need to be so straitened. A person can be entirely competent in the use of the concept of "holiness", for example, so that even though he has never experienced the numinous, he recognizes and respects what is going on when others bow before the holy. He can have formal knowledge about the Inside without knowledge by direct experience, but unless he does have adequate formal knowledge, his description or critique will be defective if not grossly misleading.

We must continually remember, of course, that it is only in relation to a given community that any Observer or Critic is an Outsider, because in every case he is also speaking from within *some* community. In the Jewish-Christian dialogue, for example, each stands inside his own tradition and looks out from that viewpoint. The Chicano appraises Anglo culture from his position within his own. The term "Outsider", therefore, can be misleading, but since we do not have a better word, we shall continue to use it here with the explicit understanding of this qualification.

# CHAPTER 13

# CULTURES[1]

"Community" is a convenient umbrella term, but at this point we need to articulate it in more detail. As so often, we shall proceed from the top down in a hierarchy of generality or scope. We shall take as the largest unit of our analysis **culture**, which is equivalent to a Way of Living, with its parameters of members, world, statuses, social practices, choice principles, and language. Within cultures are **institutions** which are organized sets of social practices. **Social practices** are classified as *intrinsic practices* which are engaged in for their own sake, and non-intrinsic or *instrumental practices*, which are undertaken in the course of engaging in intrinsic practices. And social practices can be articulated into *deliberate actions*. Generally, social practices are anchored in institutions, and they in cultures.

---

[1]See Ossorio, "A Multicultural Psychology," and *Personality and Personality Theories*, and Aylesworth and Ossorio, "Refugees: Cultural Displacement and Its Effects," Lasater, "Stress and Health in a Colorado Coal Mining Community,", and Orvik, "The Diffusion of Technology across Cultures".

These classifications are not to be understood in an absolute sense. They are instead distinctions that we use in describing the relations of social parts and wholes. Baseball, for example, can be represented as either a social practice or an institution, not because the distinction between institution and social practice is unclear, but because we can describe baseball in either way for different purposes: in terms of a game implementing a set of rules (a social practice), or in terms of leagues, batting averages, salary negotiations, etc. (an institution). Moreover, although playing baseball is always a participation in a social practice, it can be an intrinsic action on one occasion, and an instrumental action for the same person on another occasion, or for another person. We speak of educational, commercial, religious, political, and charitable institutions, of the institutions of the family, of arbitration, and many others. A culture, which is a special case of "community", is self-sufficient and viable, in contrast to neighborhood communities, or a world-wide community of professionals, and the like, which are not self-sufficient, being viable only as parts of some culture.

To be viable, a culture must provide ways by which its members can at least minimally satisfy their basic human needs, and these ways will consist of social practices. Because a culture embraces persons with a great diversity of personal characteristics, it must make available a wide enough range of social practices to accommodate such diversity, and equally important, a wide enough range of options within those practices. Only thus can persons of greater and less social and technical abilities, divergent interests, and so on, be able to satisfy their needs through their participation in those practices. Every culture, institution, family, has its own set of social practices for satisfying basic needs, and if its social practices and options are not adequate to that end, that social entity will disintegrate. The degree to which basic human needs cannot be satisfied within a culture sets limits upon its viability and its robustness—its ability to survive over a considerable time and under stress.

------------

We have already defined a need as a condition which, if not met, results in pathology. From that, we can derive the definition of **basic human needs** as conditions which, if not met at all, make behavior impossible. And we can expect that if such conditions are only partially met, behavior will be appreciably restricted.

There is no way to compile a definitive and exaustive list of basic human needs, because there is no end to ways of classifying what is essential to being persons. Many attempts have been made; not surprisingly, they show strong family resemblances. It is also not surprising that the lists are different. They are like different coordinate systems or taxonomies which are useful for different purposes. We can illustrate what we mean by "making behavior impossible" with a few examples that incorporate some of the more common proposals.

One of these is the need for *status*, that is, to have a place in a world, and this is a logical as well as a psychological imperative. Behavior cannot occur in a vacuum; it must take place in a world. Likewise, persons cannot exist except in a world; a world is as necessary to persons as persons are to the world.

Another is the need for *order and meaning*. There can be no behavior without making distinctions (the Know parameter of the behavior formula), and to make a distinction is to introduce some degree of order and meaning into the world or some portion of it. A world utterly without order and meaning would be a world without distinctions, and in such a world, both the Know and the Want parameters of behavior could have no possible values; therefore there could be no possible behavior.

Here we are not proposing to specify what order or orders there are—mechanical or personal or aesthetic, simple or complex, easily discernible or manifested exclusively to initiates—but only that the world does have some order and meaning. It is in principle intelligible.

Still another basic human need, *adequacy*, is associated with the Know-how parameter of behavior. If we have *no* competence in doing what we set out to do, the results of our behavior will be due only to chance or luck or accident. We need—in the full sense of the word—some degree of adequacy, some control over what effects our behavior has. The limiting case would be total randomness, as if we walked in the snow and it were up for grabs whether every step did or did not leave a footprint, if we blew at a lighted match and it might equally well go out or burn more brightly. Or as if we tried to implement one behavior, and what followed might be that behavior or, equally well, some other behavior. Then indeed, with zero competence to control the effects of our behavior, behavior would again be impossible.

If behavior is to be possible at all, we must also have *personal relationships*, relationships with other persons. All deliberate actions have a place within social practices, and all social practices require, directly or indirectly, that there be relationships between people. There is a categorical difference between persons and non-persons, despite our disagreements on where the line should be drawn, or how wide the zone of dubious or ambiguous cases. Some people include plants and minerals as persons. Others exclude all beings except those of their particular genetic strain, or their own culture or religious tradition. Probably most of us would not be inclined to take an electric light bulb as a person, or an ordinary tea-kettle, or a barbed-wire fence, where we would readily take a dog or cat to be a deficient person, and a terrorist to be a defective person.

If we have never achieved a relationship of appreciation or trust or intimacy with another person, our ability to engage in a wide variety of social practices will be so limited that for most practical purposes, we cannot participate in them—although presumably that would not keep us from going through the motions, or from being able to interact competently with things like abstract ideas and machinery and chemicals.

As a sidelight, person-with-person relationships do not tend to drift toward relationships of some other kind, but person-with-non-person relationships do tend to drift. The person either becomes more thing-like, or begins treating the other more like a person. As examples, a woman who has used the same tea-kettle for fifty years may look upon it as a familiar friend, and those who are professionally concerned with vast, impersonal laws or social developments may tend to gravitate toward impersonality in dealing with other human beings—witness certain (though not all, by any means) economists, politicians, social scientists, and philosophers. Nothing in those disciplines compels such persons to fall into that trap, but they may have to exert considerable effort to avoid it because of the nature of their characteristic activities in the domains where they are professionally immersed.

Many lists of basic human needs specify *self-actualization*, taking it as a long-term direction of development. Two indicators of such development are (1) characteristically performing something that is immediately of intrinsic value to us, and (2) characteristically using our abilities without decisive hindrance. In either case, unless our behavior results in some degree of self-actualization, the Want parameter of behavior will have no values. More strongly, if there were no self-actualization at all, there would be no satisfaction at all of our Wants. In effect, all behavior would be unsuccessful, and hence behavior as deliberate action would be impossible.

The same cannot be said of love as a basic human

need. Without love, behavior can be difficult or incompletely satisfying, but it is not impossible. Even infants can survive with attention that is less than actual loving (how well they survive is another matter). It has been said that all persons need beauty in some form, but apparently this is not universally the case. Or play? There are those whose work is their play—artists, for example. Such individual needs as for love, beauty, and play seem to be basic for some persons, and it is possible that without them no person can live well. They are not universal needs, however, as are the needs for status, order and meaning, adequacy, personal relationships, and self-actualization. To live at all as a person, we must have some of each of these, as opposed to none at all.

The question immediately arises, how much above "none" must we have in order to live minimally satisfying lives, and how much more than that in order to live as befits a person? To these questions we have no general answers; not enough conceptual or empirical work has been done in these areas. Neither can we answer the related question of how much opportunity, in the form of a variety of social practices and their options, a culture must provide for its members if it is to be not only minimally viable but robust. Most of the action lies in these gradations between the absolute minimum necessary for a culture merely to survive, and the optimum of a culture in whch every member is sufficiently socialized that he can take advantage of a wide enough range of the social practices that are actually available so that he can fulfil abundantly his basic needs, universal and individual.

---

An especially interesting example of the relation between cultures and needs arises when an individual or group becomes unable to engage in its customary social practices, and therefore must discover or invent new ones that will provide for its basic human needs. The youngster goes away to school and enters a new world whose order and meaning are not the same as at home, his adequacy may be in question, and he must develop many new personal relationships from scratch. On a broader scale, we have the cross-cultural problems between immigrants and their hosts, and between people in ethnic enclaves and the communities around them. The temptation is for each to regard the other as defective: "*Of course* people should plan for the future, live for what is coming—retirement or whatever" versus "*Of course* we should live in the present, savor the here-and-now which is all that we really have". Or, "*Of course* we have to get ahead in the world" versus "*Of course* a warm family life is more important than business success or professional celebrity". They call us lazy; we call them hard-driving. They call us sentimental; we call them callous.

Both these reactions exhibit ethnocentrism: each takes his own culture to be the standard and judges Them to be a deficient or defective version of Us. Conversely, upon occasion We judge ourselves to be deficient or defective versions of Them—whether They happen to be the Golden Age of Greece or a mythical Utopia. Because there is no neutral ground upon which we can stand, what can we do except put ourselves at the center? Since necessarily we see Them from our viewpoint, and they see Us from theirs, ethnocentrism must be inescapable. But is it?

There are, in fact, two ways out, or one way with at least two aspects: paradigm case methodology and parametric analysis, the first being formally convertible into the second. We have already seen how, by means of the parametric analysis of communities, we can describe, compare, and contrast any cultures, just as we did with the parametric analysis of person characteristics, because the logic is essentially the same for group and for individual differences. Here let us follow the paradigm case route, and for our paradigm case, take the hypothetical standard normal person in a given culture.

The **standard normal person** is the one who in every situation does just what that situation calls for, no more and no less, because he conforms merely to what could be expected in those circumstances. Compared with others in that culture, he is neither stingy nor profligate, aggressive nor submissive, diligent nor lazy, stupid nor brilliant. He does not do too much or too little of anything, or otherwise depart from the norms of that sociocultural frame of reference. Thus his person characteristics of Knowledge and Values mirror the cultural pattern of that time and place. In contrast, actual persons are characterized by how far and in what direction they deviate from the standard normal person: "She is brave", meaning that she is more than ordinarily courageous; "He is old for his years", i.e., more mature than most others of his age. And we can do much the same with groups: "We're a tightly-knit organization"; "As a family, they're quarrelsome"; "It's one of the technologically undeveloped countries".

Different cultures will have different standard normal persons. Their behaviors will reflect those cultures, which can be compared—without prejudice—using the parametric analysis of communities. Ethnocentrism, and egocentricity as well, do not enter unless we take one of the "standard normals" as universally normative. We are not compelled to do so. We can instead adopt the attitude typified by one of Charles Morgan's characters: "People were to him like the angles marked on his school protractor, some leaning to one side of the upright and some to the other. The upright was no better than the rest because it happened to be in the centre, but it was of use as a basis of measurement."[2] A standard normal person for a culture, when taken like the 90-degree mark as a basis of measure-

---

[2]Morgan, *Sparkenbroke*, p. 21.

ment, is not only a convenience; it is revelatory of that culture's norms and social practices. Taken as that to which other cultures ought to conform, however, it produces all the confusions and barbarisms of ethnocentrism and egocentricity.

For each important status in a given culture, it is possible to have a different standard normal person. In our own, for example, we could specify the differences between the standard normal man and the standard normal woman, or the standard normal banker, athlete, mother, Native American, and so on indefinitely. Even taking very large scale units, the twentieth-century-Western standard normal person will vary appreciably from—let us say—the standard normal person of twelfth-century China or of imperial Rome.

---

Even if we manage to avoid ethnocentricism, we are left with the problems associated with successfully adapting to a culture that is not originally our own. During a process of successful socialization, we develop personal characteristics that enable us to participate adequately in that culture, including the appropriate skills and the inclinations for engaging in its social practices. But the skills and inclinations we already have may be irrelevant to the new culture, and quite possibly our reflexes will be inept. For the new situation we are too modest or too confident, too quick or too slow to speak our minds or reveal our feelings, too ignorant to know when and whom to ask for help. We offend unwittingly when we offer to shake hands instead of bowing, or eat sandwiches with knife and fork at a picnic, and we are treated as stupid because we do not know what *everybody* knows—of course!

Amid what to us is strange in the new culture, we can be certain of at least two things. First, the members of this new world will have the same basic human needs that we do, and second, their social practices will provide opportunities for them to meet those needs. Presumably, therefore, we also can meet *our* basic human needs by engaging in those social practices in appropriate ways.

Let us suppose, however, that we do not have the person characteristics necessary for routinely successful participation in those new social practices. For example, the person characteristics (e.g., skills, attitudes) needed for bartering are quite different from those needed for reading a fixed price and counting out money or writing a check, so if we are to exchange goods or services in the new culture, we shall have to acquire new skills (Know-how). Of equal importance, we shall need to acquire appreciation for the different values, like the relative importance of arithmetic, and for the economic principles upon which the fixed-price practice is based, as contrasted with the importance of the personal relationships that are crucial in bartering.

Social practices provide order and meaning for behavior (cf. the Know and Significance parameters in the behavior formula). We must distinguish the pattern of the social practice in order for our behavior to have that order and meaning, but the pattern must be there in order for us to distinguish it. We learn by practice and experience what social practices are occurring when, for example, money is passed from one person to another. Is it payment for something received, or a gift with no thought of return? And there will be many exchanges of goods and services that do not or should not involve money at all, so we shall have to learn what kinds of occasions these are, as well as become competent to judge what economic and social institutions the behavior of monetary exchange is embedded in. Until we can identify that, we cannot tell what the Significance of the behavior is, and not until then shall we know what behavior the Performance is the performance of.

We shall be successfully re-socialized when we have acquired the requisite information (by observation and instruction), the requisite abilities (by practice and experience), and the requisite inclinations and appreciation that will enable us to really participate in the social practices and institutions of the new culture, as contrasted with merely fitting in or going through the motions.

But what if that particular way of life is incompatible with our personal values and our dispositions—traits, attitudes, interests, and styles? A case in point is that of the Chicano making his way in an Anglo culture.[3] To succeed in school or at work, José must conform to Anglo social practices of study and standards of achievement, but conforming may violate his self-identity as a Chicano. He cannot cease being Chicano, nor does he want to, but he wants also the opportunities (i.e., behavior potential) that go with participating effectively with Anglos in Anglo social practices.

One of his options is "When in Rome, do as the Romans do", that is, carry on what amounts to two separate ways of living, using different choice principles, etc., in different circumstances. A second is to take Chicano practices as intrinsic and Anglo as instrumental. A third—and the only one that constitutes successful bi-cultural living—is to preserve the Chicano values and choice-principles and outlook while appreciating the Anglo values and practices, and participating in them in ways that are compatible with the Chicano choice-principles, values, and so on. In order to do so, he may find it necessary to invent new options for Anglo social practices, options that are not only acceptable to Anglos, but also an implementation of Chicano values and choice-principles. Being Chicano is a way of life, not merely a set of social practices, and as there are a number of options for enacting a given social practice, so there are number of options for enacting a given way of life. Similarly, there are many ways of being a sci-

---

[3]Silva, "What Actually Happens to José."

entist, some involving the social practices of quantifying data, controlling variables, publishing in scientific journals, and the like, and some involving quite different social practices.

On a far smaller scale, this is what we do when we exercise our option to "put on our party manners" for an evening, or act in one way at a basketball game and in another way with the same group of people in a classroom, or behave differently with different persons. The options we choose will reflect our choice principles, and as well, our competence in judgement and our sensitivity. Our success in adapting to any culture, old or new, or to living biculturally, depends upon the judgement and sensitivity that enable us to choose the right options at the right time. And that, in turn, depends upon our having person characteristics such that we have the ability and the inclination to make the moves that are appropriate for us in the given situation.

We develop judgement and sensitivity in the same way that we acquire concepts and skills: through our participation in relevant social practices (Maxim 7). One such sort of participation consists of the specific and deliberate cultivation of our skills as Critics. We can allow and even encourage others to confirm or correct our appraisals, to draw our attention to factors we had not taken into account, and in a myriad of other ways to initiate us into what is and is not acceptable in this culture. Thus we acquire competence in dealing with particular social practices, their specific versions, and the person characteristics of the participants, probably with special reference to their statuses.

Thus far we have repeatedly used the concept of status without exploring the domain of status dynamics as a whole. This we must do before our analysis of personal relationships and communities can be complete, but it requires a separate chapter.

# CHAPTER 14

# STATUS PRINCIPLES[1]

Status dynamics formulates the orderliness of behavioral possibilities.

**Status** is a totality concept, which is to say that to give status to something is to place it within a totality such as a domain or, ultimately, the real world. To have status is to have a place within a totality.

It is characteristic of a totality that in order to grasp what it is, we do not need to be able to separate out every part that belongs to it. What we do need is to survey the logic of the whole domain. Once we have done that, we can locate the place that any single element has within that domain, or we can assign it a place. For example, a sphere is not only more, but other, than an infinite number of points equidistant from a center point; the game of chess is more and other than the sum of all actual or possible chess

---

[1]See Ossorio, "Place", "Appraisal".

moves; a community is more and other than an aggregation of individuals.

Among the reality constraints upon talking and writing about a totality, whether a sphere, a painting, a domain, or a conceptual system, is that although it can be grasped as a whole, it cannot be delineated without reference to its parts or aspects. Among the parts of the Person Concept are principles that we have articulated earlier, and in this chapter we shall often refer to them as a way of spelling out what places they have within status dynamics. By setting the old material within a new context, we shall be at once displaying the internal structure of the totality and laying the groundwork for our investigations into the more specialized topics which follow.

---

**Person, World, and Behavior Principles.** Let us begin with ourselves and our own statuses. Each of us has status—a place—in the real world as an *Actor, Observer, and Critic,* and that world is divisible into objects, processes, events, states of affairs, and relationships—or, using another schema, into communities with their typical social practices and institutions. These portray our behavioral possibilities and limitations. Unless we did live in a world, we could not engage in behaviors. There would be nothing for us to know or want, no arena for our performances, no identifiable achievements, and no significance in what we do. We recognize the world as being a totality, even though we perceive only a small part of it, just as we recognize an orange as a totality even though we cannot see it all at any given moment. So in the first instance, we have the status of persons-being-in-the-world and behaving-in-the-world.

Second, we have the status of *status-assigners.* Within the constraints imposed by our person characteristics and real-world circumstances, we choose what places we shall give to whatever confronts us. We call this element "important" and that "trivial", this "possible" and that "impossible", this "scientific" and those "historical" or "philosophical" or "artistic" or "spiritual". We give to this person the status of "friend", to that one, "hero", to the other, "customer". These are statuses that we assign, not facts that we observe. To call something a "fact" is in itself to give it a status, to assimilate it to the rest of our knowledge. And this contrasts with identifying what fact it is, which would give it a more specific place.

Our status assignments directly reflect what we are up to, and as well, they directly reflect our knowledge and values, our traits, attitudes, and interests, and our states—the more or less transient conditions (emotional, physical, social) that systematically alter our baseline dispositions and powers. These person characteristics are acquired in the course of participating in the social practices of the communities in which we live, and therefore reflect the status assignments characteristic of those communities. Yet routinely, it is we who choose what statuses we shall assign to this or that.

Roughly speaking, we have a standard repertoire of statuses (e.g., fact/non-fact, important/unimportant, possible/impossible), and where we have the most leeway is in what we assign to those statuses. For example, the status "friend" comes directly from our culture, and to that status we can assign this person but not that, and so on. Even if we adopt the choice-principles that are common to our associates, nevertheless in the end it is still we who choose, and we might have chosen—and might still choose—to accept the status assignments of some other person or group, or we might make our own independently of theirs.

Consequently, our worlds correspond to our psychological functioning, while subject to the over-all constraint that they must not make behavior impossible. As we have seen earlier, our world cannot be purely private or idiosyncratic. If it were, we could not participate in any social practices. We could have no place in the community because we did not share its world. Conversely, we could not be persons in that community if we did not do our own status-assigning, and thereby to some degree create our individual variations on the shared world.

What we take to be real (i.e., give the status of "real") is what we are prepared to act on—recall the Actor-Observer-Critic feedback loop. We take it that things are as they seem unless we have reason to think otherwise (Maxim 1). To elaborate on that maxim: we take the world to be as we have found it in the course of our life-history, and that world is not only subject to reformulation, but is in fact reformulated as our history proceeds. Every new piece of information that we assimilate gives new detail to our world, and every new concept that we acquire changes our world to some extent. Every new experience conforms to our existing world-structure and status-assignments, or does not conform and may lead us to change them. Once we have learned something however, we continue to know it until we forget it (if we ever do; the evidence is not conclusive), or until we change our minds about it. So the stability principle (see below) holds: worlds, like person characteristics and relationships, continue to be what they are unless something happens to change them.

Status in the world corresponds to being-in-the-world, because every world is somebody's world, and every person has to have a world, and this is a logical relation, not a causal, accidental, or historical one. Having a place, a status, in the world, we have relationships with whatever else is in the world, and those relationships give us possibilities for behaving. Thus a person who is an American citizen has the status "member of that social entity", and thereby has a variety of relationships with other citizens. By virtue of being a member, he is eligible to vote in elections, to run for office, to be protected by and subject to the community's laws, and so on. Being eligible, and having the appropriate dispositions and powers, he has the behavior potential to vote and otherwise participate in all public affairs that are open to citizens with the requisite person characteristics, for example, age: an infant is not eligible to vote or run for office.

Three statuses are especially interesting for the light they throw upon the concept "status" itself. The first is what amounts to having no status at all: an idea or state of affairs which is so alien to our worlds that we cannot act on it, and because we cannot act on it, we cannot give it a place. It is unthinkable, so that either we do not perceive it for what it is, or we do not notice or remember it.

A case in point would be the family argument about the chair, during which (let us say) John says to Jessie, "I'll be glad when you're dead". Jessie cannot deny that John spoke the words, but she can deny that John really meant what he said ("He was exaggerating because he was angry. He can't feel that way about me. He can't be that kind of person.") The circumstances call for her to do something that is impossible for her—i.e., take his words at their face value—so she does what she can do (Maxim 5): she excuses it or explains it away, or perhaps actually forgets it, because for her, a world in which her husband seriously wished for her death would be literally impossible. Therefore she must choose between accepting his words seriously, which will require her to radically remake her world, and rejecting their face value in order to preserve her world more or less intact.

Second come the peripheral statuses that we assign when we acquire a piece of information or undergo an experience that has little effect on the structure of our world. Generally speaking, these are things that we learn by rote (the multiplication table, the typewriter keyboard), or find it hard to remember because they add to our worlds only information that has no particular significance for us: "Okay, so she says that Richard III doesn't deserve his nasty reputation. So what?" or "Yeah, I saw the show, but I don't remember anything much about it."

Third are the statuses we assign ourselves. What place do we take in the world, and what places in the domains or communities in which we participate? What statuses do we enact? To review our earlier presentation: our self concept is a summary formulation not of information about ourselves, but of our status, and hence our behavior potential. When asked, we are likely to approximate that summary by referring to our family, community, culture, world history, universe, but those are not ingredients that we summarize when we formulate our self-concept. There is no way to add them up.

Other persons, of course, are continually assigning statuses to us, and we to them: "a gifted young woman", "a thoroughly nice guy", "an important figure in his field", "dependably unpredictable and probably dangerous". These are not merely descriptions, but appraisals, in that they carry motivational significance. They formulate reasons for behaving in one way instead of another. An appraisal is a special case of status assignment, one in which we give something a particular place in our world, and thereby have a reason to treat it in a particular way. A paradigm case is appraising something as dangerous to us (e.g., the lion entering the room), which is to say that we have a compelling reason to try to escape from it.

It is up to us whether we incorporate others' status-assignments of us into our self-status-assignments. For example, at school we are appraised as top of the line; at home we are treated as not very bright. But how others evaluate our accomplishments is one question; quite another question is how we appraise our very selves. High achievement can go with a low sense of self-worth, and vice versa, a fact that underscores what we have already seen, that status-assignments are highly resistant to change by simply accumulating information, and no amount of information about a person will reveal his status.

Knowing what kind of person we are does not reveal who or where we are. The most meticulous and minute description of a person will not tell us whether he is geographically located in Paris or Fairbanks or Madras, or whether his place in a community is as "one of us" or "an outsider", or as eligible (or ineligible) to vote or practise medicine or compete in a chess tournament, or whatever. Similarly, nothing in Tolkien's elaborate description of Middle-earth tells us whether it has a place within our calendar and geography.

We learn a good deal about the place in a community that others give to us by observing how they behave toward us, in what circumstances they turn us away or turn away from us, or encourage our participation. Ceremonies of degradation and accreditation delimit more explicitly our place in the world, and hence our eligibilities.

---

**Behavior and Choice Principles.** Our actual behavior depends not only upon (1) our self-appraisal, but also upon (2) our circumstances, which provide not only opportunities and constraints but also reasons for behaving in one way rather than another (recall the Judgement Diagram, Chapter 4), and upon (3) our person characteristics: our motivations and values, knowledge and competence, and so on. To want something is to have a reason for trying to get it, and for trying to find or create opportunities to get it (Maxims 2-4); and given the relevant opportunity and motivation, knowledge and competence, that behavior will succeed unless it goes wrong in one of the ways that that particular behavior could go wrong (Maxim 9). For example, perhaps we were wrong in thinking that we were not eligible to engage in this social practice; or the situation changed so as to erase an opportunity; or we discover that an achievement will be more difficult than we expected so we decide that we do not want it badly enough to pursue that course of action.

We do not always think and act explicitly in terms of the loss or gain of behavior potential, but our choices are likely to be in accordance with that factor. In any case, we will not choose to actualize less behavior potential over more, although we can be forced (or unwittingly fall) into situations where our behavior potential is diminished, sometimes drastically. We can mistakenly engage in an action or course of action that eventuates in our losing behavior potential although we did not anticipate that it would. We can give up behavior potential in one respect in order to achieve greater potential in another, as when a person refuses a career advancement in order to preserve or enhance his family relationships, or submits himself to the constraints of poverty, chastity, and obedience in order to develop spiritually. In these last two cases, what looks to an Outsider like a loss of behavior potential may look to the Insider like a net gain.

The person who "sacrifices" his career for his family, or the mundane for the transcendental world, is giving one status priority over another. He is making three declarations simultaneously, although probably not in words: "This is to be my personal way of life", "This is who I am", and "This is my place in the world". That is, he is at once making a behavioral choice, a personal affirmation, and a self-status-assignment. These are three ways of describing the same choice-event occurring within a given state of affairs.

All choices, from the most to the least momentous, involve all the elements behavior, person, world, and that world is preeminently a world of relationships and relationship changes, of cultures, institutions, and social practices. Every element in the world is eligible to be decomposed into objects, processes, events, and/or states of affairs, down to the basic building blocks of Limiting Case-II, and to be composed—together with everything else—into the state of affairs that includes all other states of affairs, i.e., Limiting Case-I, the real world.

Behaviorally, we express our relation to the real-world totality of which we are a part not only by our ordinary deliberate actions and social practices, but also by ceremonies, rituals, and deliberately symbolic behaviors. Characteristically, these are intrinsic rather than instrumental actions. We have nothing to gain—in any conventional sense of "gain"—by the ritual affirmation that we are part of an ultimate whole, or by celebrating a universal state of affairs, except the satisfaction of affirming explicitly and openly where ultimately we are.

To illustrate with a special case of spiritual affirmation, we may see ourselves "in a second place absolutely, and to kneel is an inward necessity".[2] When we have come to appreciate the wholeness of the whole in all its intricacy, and the ultimacy of the ultimate, there may be nothing we can do except celebrate it in ritual or in ceremonial behaviors, and nothing else is called for.

---

**Value, Motivation, and Choice Principles.** Whatever our motivation for engaging in a particular behavior, we shall be motivated to engage in other behaviors that are relevantly similar to it. What determines relevant similarity is that the behavior is responsive to the same reasons, and the degree of motivation corresponds to the degree of similarity or to the degree of responsiveness. So if a person is motivated to engage in a behavior, he will also be motivated to engage in any other behavior that has the same value for him. A classic instance is that of the man who has been chewed out by his boss, and on returning home, kicks his dog. Other instances are fantasizing, day-dreaming, compensating, complaining to a friend. This is displacement.

---

[2]Morgan, *The Fountain*, p. 333.

More generally, if a person values something, he will value anything else that offers the same value, to the extent that it is similiar. Thus if we especially enjoy reading fantasy, when none is available we are more likely to turn to science-fiction or beast-fables than to biographies or philosophical treatises or stock-market reports. The relevant similarity to fantasy diminishes through that sequence. Likewise, if we value a person, an object, a state of affairs, a relationship, or whatever, we shall tend to value other things that are relevantly similar to it, and to be sensitive to such similarities. In any case, what the relevant similarity is may not be obvious. A carefully organized bookshelf may hold novels, poetry, biographies, essays, and technical manuals side by each, by different authors and of different periods, held together only by a common theme—appreciation of nature, let us say, or a concern for social justice—which would become apparent only to an exceptionally astute observer.

The world that we value will be one that offers us sufficient behavior potential, i.e., opportunities to satisfy not only our basic human needs but also needs which are more peculiar to us as individuals. It should go without saying that persons differ extremely with respect to what circumstances and social practices they must have available in order to meet those individual needs which, if not met, will lead to pathology. For one, it may be a sheltered environment, for another, the wide world to adventure in; for one, much solitude, for another, constant companionship. It is equally obvious that if our world does not provide us with sufficient scope, we have reason to try to change it for the better. If it does give us scope, we have reason to try to maintain or improve it. And if it can become worse, we have reason to try to prevent its worsening.

---

**Stability and Change Principles.** We have already discussed, or at least mentioned in other connections, the status dynamics principles of stability and change, but there is value in bringing them together under this heading. If nothing else, doing so will exhibit the interweaving of the principles, which is such that many of them could fall under more than one rubric.

First we have three *stability principles*. (1) A person takes the world to be as he has found it to be (Maxim 1). (2) If a person has a given person characteristic, he continues to have it until something happens to change it. (3) If a person knows something, he continues to know it until he forgets it or changes his mind about it (this is a special case of (2)).

Next comes a *transition principle*: (4) A person's world is subject to reformulation. This is followed by four *acquisition principles*, acquisition being one of the two major ways by which worlds and persons change. (5) A person acquires facts about the world primarily by observation and secondarily by thought (Maxim 6). (6) A person acquires a concept or skill by practice and experience in one or more of the social practices which call for use of that concept or skill (Maxim 7). (7) If a person has a given person characteristic, he acquired it in one of the ways that it can be acquired, i.e., by having the relevant prior capacity and an appropriate intervening history (Maxim 8). And (8) If a person has a given relationship to something, he acquired it in one of the ways by which it can be acquired.

Finally (9), the *Relationship Change Formula* specifies how relationships can change or be changed: if a person has a given relation to another person, but the behavior of the first toward the second person is such that it violates that relation and expresses some other relation, then the original relation will change in the direction of the second relation. With appropriate systematic transformations, the relationship change formula can be applied to relations of persons to non-persons, and to groups, and because the logic is essentially the same for individuals and groups, it can be applied between groups as well. Often, however, the practical applications run into complications that call for an appeal to one or more of the unless-clauses. For example, two individuals are at odds; one makes a friendly gesture, and the other responds not in friendly fashion but with hostility. Why should this be? The discrepancy calls for an explanation. Perhaps he has a stronger reason to remain hostile than to be friends, or he doesn't recognize the gesture as friendly, or he cannot respond in kind because of a persistent trait or attitude, and so on.

---

**Constraints.** The inescapable reality constraints on our knowledge and behavior give stability and structure to our worlds in ways that we cannot control because we are neither omniscient nor omnipotent. The world limits our options and provides us with opportunities for behavior. Which options we choose reflect our person characteristics. Morever, our person characteristics impose constraints upon the relationships we can have, the further person characteristics we can develop, and the ways in which we can acquire new relationships and person characteristics.

We start with the person characteristics of bare capacities and capabilities ("merely able"). By virtue of our capacities, and our interaction with our circumstances, we develop our abilities, traits, values, knowledge, and so on.

Every choice of a behavior reflects who we are and what we are in the process of becoming, whether "more of the same" or "a changed person", and constitutes another stage in the developmental process. Which of our potentialities we cultivate depends—again—upon our choices and circumstances, that is, upon how we exercise our options within the constraints of the given.

At this point, it is worth recalling that a person will

not choose to actualize less behavior potential rather than more, and worth noting that a person cannot see to everything that happens. Even with the most sophisticated computer, we could not take account of every factor that might affect a state of affairs or that ought to enter into a choice, much less anticipate all the ways in which a behavior might go wrong, or all the consequences of an actual behavior that does go right—or wrong. What happens to us is largely not under our control. We cannot regulate the weather or the economic climate, or determine how other people will think and feel, or otherwise dominate the world we live in. We have influence but not mastery.

If a person has a given person characteristic and his behavior expresses it, that does not call for explanation. We accept it with such comments as, "That's just the way he is", or "That's what people in that relationship do". If, on the other hand, his behavior violates that person characteristic, it does call for explanation. "It's out of character for him to do that. Maybe I don't know him as well as I thought I did. Maybe something has jolted him out of his usual way of behaving. Maybe I'm misinterpreting his behavior. Maybe there are factors in the situation that I don't know about", and so on. Sometimes we shall ask why this person departs from the baseline of the standard normal person—for example, why an ordinary individual rises to the occasion in a disaster and acts heroically, or why without warning someone goes berserk. At other times we shall ask why he departs from his individual baseline—why a Scrooge suddenly becomes friendly, or how it happens that an otherwise mediocre poet succeeds in writing one consummate lyric.

---

Taken singly, the status-dynamics principles are obvious to the point of appearing trivial. Just so, each line of a Rembrandt etching, taken singly, is as simple as a mark that a child might draw. What makes the difference is the pattern they make when they are put together in the right way: in the etching, to create a masterpiece; in a conceptual system, to reveal by their logical connections its internal structure. In addition, the frequency with which some of these principles are ignored attests to the importance of stating them clearly, and of bringing them together in a form as systematic as is possible when dealing successively with the components of a tightly integrated part-whole interrelationship.

# PART V

# PERSONS AS SUCH

# CHAPTER 15

# EMOTIONAL BEHAVIOR AND STATES

We have three principal ways of formulating emotional phenomena: through the relationship formula, the concept of intrinsic social practices, and status dynamics. Thus what we have here is in part an extension and elaboration of what has gone before, rather than a new set of concepts and part-whole relations.

It will be remembered that the relationship formula, as applied to persons, reads: "If person F has a given relationship, R, to person G, then the behavior of F with respect to G will be an expression of that relationship, unless — ". That relationship can be, and often is, emotional, e.g., F is angry at, afraid of, jealous of G. He may express that relation by emotional behavior; if he does, the specific behaviors he engages in will reflect the social practices of the community in which the persons involved—let us call them Felicity and George—are jointly participating.

For a standard heuristic example for emotional behavior, let us return to the case of the lion entering the room (Chap. 4),[1] and elaborate upon it. Felicity is alone in the room, contentedly reading, when she hears a sound, looks up, and sees a lion coming in the door. Without stopping to think, she dashes for the window and climbs out. George, who is passing by, runs to her and asks what has happened. Felicity answers, "There's a lion in that room, and I jumped out the window to get away from it." George says, "Oh, come now, there can't be — ", at which point the lion sticks his head out the window and roars, and both Felicity and George take off at top speed.

To represent Felicity's fear behavior, we can use either the Judgement Diagram or the diamond. First the Judgement Diagram:

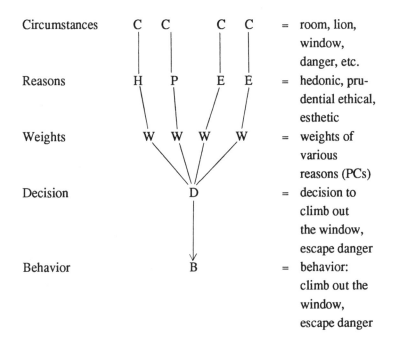

| | | | |
|---|---|---|---|
| Circumstances | C  C    C  C | = | room, lion, window, danger, etc. |
| Reasons | H  P    E  E | = | hedonic, prudential ethical, esthetic |
| Weights | W  W  W    W | = | weights of various reasons (PCs) |
| Decision | D | = | decision to climb out the window, escape danger |
| Behavior | B | = | behavior: climb out the window, escape danger |

---

[1]See Ossorio, "Three-Minute Lectures on Emotion," *Personality and Personality Theories*, 22, 26, and 27 July, 1977, *Clinical Topics, Positive Health and Transcendental Theories*, and "Outline of Descriptive Psychology". See also Bergner, "Emotions: A Conceptual Formulation and Its Clinical Implications".

The circumstance of the lion's entering the room gives Felicity a prudential reason to escape, and her person characteristics give her the behavior potential to succeed in escaping. Now for the diamond:

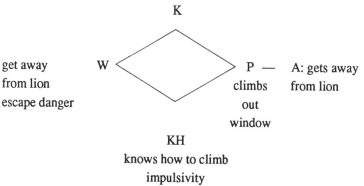

facts about the room
lion versus other things
lion as dangerous versus not dangerous
escape by climbing out window versus other behaviors

K

get away          W                              P —    A: gets away
from lion                                    climbs         from lion
escape danger                                  out
                                             window

KH
knows how to climb
impulsivity

Felicity *discriminates* the inside of the room from the outside, and the location of various things in the room, including the door, the window, and the lion. She takes the lion to be dangerous. She identifies the window as providing an opportunity to escape. She *wants* to escape the danger, in this case by getting away from the lion since she does not have a gun or other means of dealing with it. She has the *ability (Know-how)* to move in the right direction at the right speed, and long ago she learned how to act without deliberation (i.e., impulsively) in response to danger. Her *performance* consists of climbing out the window, and her *achievement* lies in her successfully escaping.

If we wish to be more precise in our description, we can diagram it as a symbolic behavior, the type in which we engage in one behavior (escaping danger) by engaging in another (getting away from the lion):

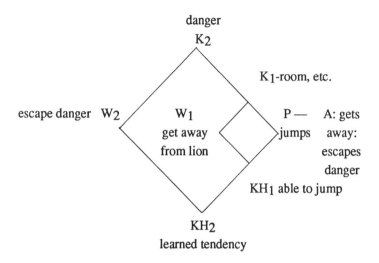

The symbolic behavior diagram brings out an essential point: that seeing the lion as dangerous involves both simple, factual information ($K_1$), such as seeing the lion and recognizing what it is, and an appraisal ($K_2$), that it is dangerous. The description "This is a lion" carries no motivational significance; but "This lion is a danger to me" does imply a corresponding motivation to act in a particular way, namely, "Try to escape".

It is noteworthy that in none of these representations is there any place for "fear" as such, either as an emotional state or as a motivation. There is good reason for the omission: it is the whole diagram that is classified as fear behavior, but it is escape, not fear, which is the motivation—the Want—in both diamonds.

What identifies a specific emotional behavior as such is that it fits one of the emotion paradigms. In climbing out the window, Felicity has no further end in view beyond escaping the danger. Each of the two fear behaviors in the story—climbing out the window, and running away when the lion roars—ends with an achievement that makes that behavior in those circumstances intelligible and coherent:

the person is engaging in an intrinsic social practice. When we know these facts, we do not question why Felicity was trying to get away from the lion, nor do we insist that there must be a further story in this regard. We have no tendency to ask, "What was she *really* trying to do?"

In every representation of fear behavior, the outer diamond, depicting the intrinsic social action, is the same: the K includes danger; the W includes escape; and the KH includes impulsivity, the learned tendency to act without deliberation. The inner diamond represents the the specifics of the situation, what the person is discriminating as dangerous (e.g., a lion, the dark, a crucial examination, another person, infection; a list could be endless), and the immediate setting in which the danger occurs—all this being included in the Know parameter. The Want parameter will always be to escape, but what constitutes escape (turning on a light, staying out of the other person's way, killing the lion, etc.), what one is competent to do (KH), and what one actually, overtly does (P) will depend upon the circumstances and one's person characteristics.

The universal features of fear behavior, which are shown in the outer diamond, can be expressed in a form that exemplifies the general Relationship Formula:

**Danger from H elicits the corresponding attempt by F to escape the danger, unless — :**

| | |
|---|---|
| K: | F doesn't recognize the danger for what it is; or |
| W: | F has a stronger reason for doing something else, or |
| KH: | F is unable to engage in any escape behavior at that time, or |
| C: | F mistakenly takes it that he is engaging in escape behavior, or |
| P-A: | F miscalculates or the behavior miscarries |

F does have a reason to try to escape; that reason is guaranteed. He may, however, have other reasons that override this one. Therefore the occurrence of the fear behavior is not guaranteed. What is crucial is the relationship: being in a relationship where we are endangered, we are motivated to behave accordingly.

Note that the formula applies no matter what the danger, and even if the person does not recognize the relation for what it is, or if a Critic would say that what the person is afraid of does not in fact threaten that person, i.e., there is no reality basis for the fear. Perhaps the lion was tame and held firmly by its trainer. Or what Felicity took to be a real lion was a friend in a lion's costume. Or it was stuffed and moved on wheels, with a recording of a roar. If it had been a hallucination—and in this case, the fact that George also saw and heard the lion rules that out—Felicity would still have appraised it as a danger and it would have elicited fear behavior.

Distortions of reality, as in some of the foregoing illustrations, are not peculiar to emotional behavior. Mistakes in perception, as in taking a hallucination to be a real lion, and mistaken appraisals, as in taking the lion to be dangerous, can occur with respect to behavior that is not emotional.

---

For our second example, let us add an episode to the tale of Felicity and the lion. At a party she recounts the incident, and when she has finished, an acquaintance, Gerald, says contemptuously, "How long did it take you to work up that story? . . . No, of course I don't believe it. Who could? . . . The passerby whose last name you didn't get—you can't even prove that any such person was there. . . . You women, always making up things to get attention. . . . " Felicity is furious at these aspersions on her ability to observe and her veracity, as well she might be, and **provocation**

**elicits hostile behavior** as inexorably as danger elicits fear behavior. She burns to attack Gerald physically, but that would disrupt the party, so after a moment of stunned silence, she merely answers as vituperatively as is within her power. Although her impulse is to react without deliberation, she controls that impulse and in fact deliberately chooses to cuss him out rather than hit him or throw something at him or walk away or engage in any other angry behavior. Diagrammatically:

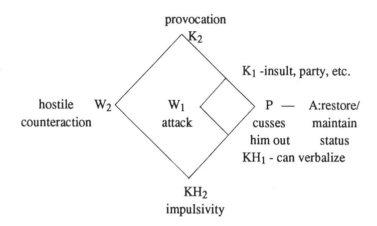

Again, the inner diamond represents the given behavior in all its particularity, although here we have not named all the particulars. The outer diamond shows what is characteristic of all hostile behavior. And the Hostility Formula is parallel to the Fear Formula: **Provocation by G elicits a corresponding hostile counteraction in F, unless — ,** with the unless-clauses modified appropriately.

From the fear and hostility formulas we can derive the general Emotional Behavior Formula and diagram, and all emotional behavior fits this diagram:

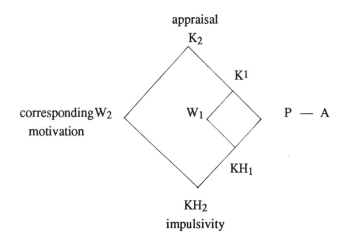

What distinguishes one emotional behavior from another, therefore, is the appraisal, i.e., the discrimination and the corresponding motivational significance. To look at a few typical examples:

## Emotional Behavior Chart

| Emotion | Appraisal (discrimination/ motivation) | Behavior motivated by appraisal | Relationship/ Reality Basis |
|---|---|---|---|
| fear | danger | escape | something is a danger |
| hostility | provocation | hostile | something provokes counteraction |
| $guilt_1$ | wrongdoing before the fact | avoidance | something tempts |
| $guilt_2$ | wrongdoing after the fact | penance | someone does wrong |
| shame | transgression of social norm | face-saving | someone transgresses norm |

| despair | hopelessness | no behavior | lack of behavior potential |
| sadness | bad fortune | lamentation | loss of something valuable |
| enjoyment | good fortune | celebration | gain of something valuable |
| awe | the wonderful | reverence | someone is awed by |

To engage in emotional behavior is to participate in an intrinsic social practice, something which we do for its own sake. Thus if we observe an emotional behavior, and see or can find a reality basis (relationship) for that behavior, in principle we do not need to look further for an explanation of what is going on. The behavior is complete and coherent in itself. To try to escape from danger, or to react with hostility to a provocation, is no more mysterious than drinking when we are thirsty or eating when we are hungry.

Our search for explanations begins (1) when we do not find a corresponding reality basis for that behavior; or (2) when we observe a reality basis such as a dangerous situation, but do not see the corresponding emotional behavior of escape; or (3) when we observe something that indicates that there is more in the picture than merely the danger. For these explanations, we can resort to the unless-clauses of the Emotional Behavior Formulas.

In those frequent cases where more than one emotion is evoked by the appraisal, as when the reality basis is complex, use of the Judgement Diagram together with the diamonds may help us to clarify what is going on. For example, the danger diagram and formula can be connected to the prudential perspective, the guilt diagrams and formulas to the ethical, sadness or happiness to the hedonic, the wonderful to the esthetic, and so on.[2] How heavily (or lightly) we weight each will reflect our person characteristics, and will vary according to the actual circumstances in question.

Three status dynamics principles need to be added before we turn to emotional states, feelings, and so on. The first: **The person values some states of affairs over others, and acts accordingly.**

The second: **Negative-emotional behavior constitutes an attempt to improve a bad situation by recovering, preserving, or enhancing behavior potential in the face of actual, presumptive or expected loss of that potential.**

The third: **Positive emotional behavior is expressive, constituting overt appreciation or celebration of a good situation, or is designed to maintain such a situation.**

---

The study of emotional behavior requires extensive use of the behavior formula. For the study of emotional feeling, states, and attitudes, we must turn to the Person Characteristics concepts.

Paradigmatically, the experience or feeling of anger is whatever we feel when we are angry, and we are angry when something provokes us. The experience or feeling of fear is whatever we feel when we are afraid, and we are afraid when discriminate that we are endangered. With emotional experiences, therefore, as with emotional behaviors, we start by identifying a reality basis, a relationship. As we anchored our investigation of emotional behavior in the Know parameter of the behavior formula, so we anchor our investigation of emotional experiences in the

---

2See Ossorio, "Place".

conditions for emotional behavior. And our study is firmly anchored, because provocations and dangers, as well as good and bad fortunes, wrongdoing, etc., are objectively describable states of affairs that can be approached directly, rather than merely inner conditions to which we have access only through the vagaries of introspection, or through physiology and other non-psychological methodologies.

What our feelings are when we are angry or afraid will differ from occasion to occasion, and possibly from moment to moment, not to mention from person to person. Moreover, since anything that can be described in one way can also be described in other ways, such a performance as turning away from another person can often be interpreted as either escape or rejection, and the corresponding emotion as either fear or anger. We may have to examine the person and the circumstances with some care before we can decide which behavior it was, and if in this case we are the Actor, we may not know for sure whether we are acting from fear or anger. If, however, we are asked, "What's upsetting you?" and we answer, "He insulted me!" or "He threatened me!", there can be little doubt in our—or anyone's—minds what we are feeling, although there may still be the usual mystery about what the feeling is like (e.g., What is my experience of 'green'? Is my experience of 'green' the same as yours?). The subjective state is in general problematic; the circumstances are in principle nonproblematic, or not problematic in the same way.

Any of the types of person characteristics classified as Dispositions can include examples which have an emotional character. We describe Angela as a happy person, Andrew as a hostile person (traits: a type of behavior with high frequency). Bill is sad about his disabled car, Betty is friendly toward cats (attitudes: a type of behavior that is object-directed). Carl is preoccupied with fear of losing his job (interest: type of behavior and intrinsic action). Dorothy has an aggressive manner (style: performance over-all).

The Powers also enter the picture: we distinguish safety from danger, joke from insult, conformity to social norms from transgression of those norms. We value our good fortune and our resistance to temptation, and have a low regard for being victimized. We are able to escape, attack, make friendly gestures, celebrate, and so on.

Finally, there are emotional States, which are more or less temporary departures from the norm for that person, departures which involve systematic differences in that person's Dispositions and Powers.

We use the same emotion-word to designate the emotional character of the person characteristic whether we are speaking of a trait, an attitude, a style, a state, or a feeling. For example, to be in a state of fear is not the same as being either a fearful person (trait) or fearful of strangers (attitude). One can be in a state of anger without feeling angry at all, and in a state of guilt without feeling guilty, or feel guilty when there is no reality basis for the emotional experience.

In studies of emotion, the distinction has not always been drawn between emotional behavior, states, attitudes, traits, and so on. Since umbrella terms like "fear" and "anger" cover phenomena that are logically distinct, we cannot make statements that are true about a person's emotional behavior, for instance, that necessarily are simultaneously true about his emotional traits, states, etc., much less true about "emotion" as such.

An unfortunate consequence of this verbal—and conceptual—lack of specificity is that in studies and discussions of emotion, much of the time investigators have not differentiated what phenomena they were studying and discussing. They have failed to distinguish which of the person characteristics they were concerned with, and failed also to trace how emotional states, attitudes, values, knowledge, feelings, and so on, are systematically interrelated. Sometimes they have even lost sight of the obvious: that to act angry or fearful, etc., is a way of treating things (persons, situations, ideas, etc.) as provoking or dangerous, etc. That is to say, emotional behaviors are responses that include the impulse to act in certain ways without deliberation. In principle, therefore, they are intelligible and not, as is commonly claimed, irrational.[3] We feel as we do because we perceive the world and our relation to it as we do, even though our appraisals may be hidden from ourselves, and may appear unreasonable to a Critic who does not see enough of our reality basis to understand what sense it makes for us to feel and act afraid or hostile or happy.

Indeed behavior is sometimes irrational. But the first ground for appreciating the reasonableness of an emotional behavior is to identify its reality basis. Felicity saw a lion coming into the room where she was reading; that was the reality basis upon which she acted. If she were mistaken, and wrongly believed that it was both real and dangerous, a Critic might conclude that it was a reasonable mistake to have made, but he would not discount either that it was a mistake or that it was reasonable.

A second ground for appraising the reasonableness of an emotional behavior is to follow through with the motivation that corresponds to the discrimination, together with the impulse to act without deliberation on the appraisal. If the action is successful, the person has achieved what he set out to achieve and he no longer has a motive to engage in that behavior. Once Felicity is out of danger from the lion, she no longer has a reason to try to escape. The incident is closed. But the incident of the insult at the party did not achieve closure. There, the only hostile behavior she could engage in was not adequate to the magnitude of the provocation. Since she did not achieve what she set out to achieve—either to degrade Gerald as he had degraded her, or to re-accredit herself in her own eyes—she continued to

---

[3]See Shideler, "The Lover and the Logician".

have reason to be angry with him. She may remain hostile to him for years, not because her anger was stored up like water in a reservoir, but because the reality basis for her residual anger continues unchanged. Therefore we could expect her to remain hostile toward him.

To develop this theme in another direction, Felicity might conclude that because once a lion did intrude upon her when she felt herself to be safe, such an invasion could happen again any time, any where. But it would be unreasonable for her to expect such an extraordinary event to happen again, and if she became fearful of all her circumstances on these grounds, we would need a special explanation for her doing so.

In the case of Gerald's provocation, however, it would be understandable, if not reasonable, if later she acted excessively angry when some other person took the line, "You women always—": her behavior is relevantly similar to that in the earlier event. Here we have another instance of displacement: her reacting so strongly in this second case is relevantly similar to the behavior she would like to have engaged in with Gerald, but didn't.

A multitude of other examples could be adduced to illustrate  that emotional experiences, states, attitudes, and the rest, are not in principle mysterious in their nature or arbitrary in their effects. Only one more needs to be added here: not to fear danger at all, not to feel any guilt for wrongdoing, not to be angered by provocation or to rejoice in good fortune, are all (barring the unless-clauses) to live in a significantly restricted world. And a person living in such a limited world will be limited in his ability to participate in practices which depend upon a broader world. To be in the strict sense "a-pathetic"—without emotion—is to be in a pathological state: significantly restricted in one's ability to participate in the social practices of the community.

For the sake of the record, here is the second half of

the Emotion Formulas Chart, which covers states, emotions, attitudes, and beliefs. In Appendix 7, they are printed together.

## Emotional States, etc. Chart

| Perception | State | Feeling | Attitude | Belief |
|---|---|---|---|---|
| danger | fear | fear | fearful | danger |
| provocation | anger | anger | anger | provocation |
| wrongdoing before the fact | $guilt_1$ | $guilt_1$ | $guilt_1$ | wrongdoing before the fact |
| wrongdoing after the fact | $guilt_2$ | $guilt_2$ | $guilt_2$ | wrongdoing after the fact |
| transgression of social norm | shame | shame | shame | transgression of social norm |
| hopelessness | despair | despair | despair | hopelessness |
| bad fortune | sadness | sadness | sadness | bad fortune |
| good fortune | enjoyment | enjoyment | enjoyment | good fortune |
| the wonderful | awe | awe | awe | awesome |

# CHAPTER 16

# SYMBOLIC BEHAVIOR AND THE UNCONSCIOUS[1]

Few if any developments in psychology have had as widespread an impact as the introduction of the concept of the unconscious and its subsequent popularization. We speak casually of unconscious motives and wishes, of repressing unwelcome thoughts and desires into the unconscious, of ideas rising out of the unconscious, of having access to the unconscious through dreams, of unconscious ego-defense mechanisms, and so on. And it is noteworthy that these are separate phenomena. There is no unity among them apart from their having been assigned to the unconscious, which is commonly thought of as a dark, churning mass of unruly impulses, sometimes as a noisome sewer, at other times as a richly fertile seed-bed producing exquisite fantasies and profound intuitions.

---

[1]See Ossorio, *Meaning and Symbolism, Clinical Topics,* and *Personality and Personality Theories,* 1-5 August 1977.

The concept of the unconscious explains a great number of phenomena that do in fact need explaining. Often we observe ourselves (and even more often, other people) behaving in ways that are conspicuously at variance with what we (or they) claim to want or to be doing. For example, which of us has not said or heard somebody say repeatedly, "What I want most to do with my life is thus and so, but I just don't seem to get around to it"? Some of us conveniently forget unhappy or shameful events, especially from our childhood; others blot out happy and successful occasions. Then there are the sudden bursts of insight that seem to come from deep within us or completely outside us, the erratic urges for which we can find no justification, our obscure sense that there is more to us than we can manifest to others or, indeed, can penetrate by our own efforts.

All the phenomena associated with the unconscious, however, can be understood without postulating any such ineffable domain. The Descriptive Psychology way is to exploit three of the conceptual resources which we have already met and used in other connections. One is the relation between behavioral repertoire and behavior potential. Another is the achievement of constructing worlds. The third is the treatment of symbolic behavior.

----

Our **behavioral repertoire** corresponds to the totality of our personal resources, that is, to all the behaviors that we could engage in, without reference to circumstances, opportunity, our transient states, and so on. For example, if we have the ability to play the piano, that is a part of our behavioral repertoire even if at the moment there is no piano available for us to play, or if temporarily a finger is disabled. In contrast, **behavior potential** depends upon circumstances as well as upon our personal resources. It corresponds to behavioral repertoire when the repertoire is limited or structured by opportunity. My repertoire has to do with what I could possibly do in some circumstances. My behavior potential right now has to do with what I can do now in my given circumstances, and with my possibilities for getting into other places where I have other potential. I can draw on my repertoire any time I want to, circumstances permitting. I actualize my potential in what I am actually doing now.

Any behavior we can engage in involves some part of what we know, value, and know how to do. For example, in taking a history examination, we call upon certain of our knowledge and abilities, some of which may not be immediately available because we are under stress. Shopping at a supermarket requires quite another set of information and abilities, and playing chess, still another. But on no occasion do we need more than a selection from our behavioral repertoire.

There is no behavior that requires us to discriminate at a given time everything that we are capable of discriminating. Accordingly, we do not engage in any behavior that involves distinguishing all our possible behaviors, or all our personal resources. Also, we do not choose behaviors that would require resources we think—or know—we do not have.

For the most part, we discover what our behavioral repertoire is from what we actualize. Our having these resources, however, is independent of our discovering that we have them, and in general, we have many more than we have discovered. Necessarily, therefore, there is indeed more to us than meets the eye, so to speak, and even more than we can possibly know.

———————

Here, we can only touch lightly on the construction

and reconstruction of worlds,[2] limiting ourselves to one of the forms of creativity, and to dreaming, and to the general problem of what we can do when we are confronted with an "impossible" world.

When we draw upon our behavioral repertoire to solve problems or to create new patterns of thought and behavior, we can, if we like, describe what goes on as "turning it over to my unconscious" or "emerging from my unconscious". Or we can instead describe at least one form of it more simply, as the philologist J. R. R. Tolkien does: "The mind that thought of *light, heavy, grey, yellow, still, swift,* also conceived of magic that would make heavy things light and able to fly, turn grey lead into yellow gold, and the still rock into swift water."[3] To distinguish and to connect ideas are normal, ordinary aspects of thinking.

When we "put the problem on a back burner to simmer" while we turn our attention elsewhere, we are likely to come back to it from a new angle or with new resources of information or organization. Many of our flashes of creative insight are of the same kind: something jolts us out of our customary ways of thinking, or we jolt ourselves by deliberately brain-storming, and lo, a new combination clicks: grey lead into yellow gold. Having described something in one way, we now describe it in another, and if this seems less marvellous than postulating unconscious processes, it will be because we have died to the wonder of the foundational marvel of thinking.

More fundamentally, let us return to the notion that knowledge has to start somewhere. We cannot have an infinite regress in which we have to know something else before we can know anything. Knowledge begins with observation, and the boundary condition for knowledge is

---

[2]See Ossorio, *Positive Health and Transcendental Theories* (index: creativity); Roberts, "Worlds and World Reconstruction," and Shideler, "The Creator and the Discoverer".

[3]Tolkien, "On Fairy-Stories," p. 50.

competence. Likewise, before we can do something, we cannot always have to do something else first. Actions and trains of thought have to begin somewhere, and if we ask where they begin, one of the possible answers is that they come from our unconscious. Another possible answer is "I am their author. They begin with me," and in this case the boundary condition for action and trains of thought is—again—competence.

**Dreams** have their place in this analysis, often as problem-stating and problem-solving efforts in a situation where reality constraints are sharply diminished or entirely lacking. That our dreams take shape in images is no more mysterious than our commonplace use of metaphors—a social butterfly, a sea of faces, being locked into a situation. It is characteristic of metaphors that they conceal and reveal simultaneously. In dreaming, the dreamer is inventing new metaphors; in interpreting dreams, the primary task is to decide what is being revealed and what is being concealed. If in a dream, we are auditioning a possible world in the absence of reality constraints, the metaphors conceal the pattern of that world—at the level of concrete detail. But when we drop the details and see what pattern the dream makes, we have left the realm of metaphor and entered the world of construction. Dropping the details and not making anything up in our interpretation, the dream becomes revelatory.

———————————

The real world is that in which we have a place as Actors, Observers, and Critics, and we discover that world empirically, that is, by acting within it, by observing what is around us, and by critiquing our actions and observations so as to guide our further behavior. A world that has no place for us is not our real world. It may be a merely possible world, like the world as it might have been if we had never been born. It may be a fictional world like that of

*The Tempest* or Middle-earth. But nothing we do can affect what happened or happens in those worlds wherein we have no place. We can only read about them or, as in watching a video record of events, see them from a distance, so to speak, i.e., as spectators who cannot influence what is going on.

If we are alive at all we must act: eat, drink, sleep, move around, play all three roles in the Actor-Observer-Critic feedback loop. We may, however, find ourselves in a real world that places us in what would be for us an impossible position. Such a world will be for us intolerable, and in what follows, I shall use the terms "intolerable" and "impossible" interchangeably for both that world and that situation.

Perhaps we cannot find work to do, which where we live means that we have no status. Or our beloved has jilted us and life has no more meaning. Or we are massively injured in an accident and can no longer engage in the activities in which we have hitherto found self-fulfilment. Or we perform an act so shameful that we think of ourselves with loathing, degrading ourselves to the limit.

If the world that we observe and act in has no place for us, or only an intolerable place, we shall construe our world as being one that does have a place for us. So doing, we are exemplifying Maxim 5, "If a situation calls for a person to do something he cannot do, he will do what he can do, if he does anything at all". And we can extend that by saying, "If a situation calls for a person to know something that he cannot know because it would be intolerable for him to know it, he will forget it or know it as something else instead". We exclaim, "I don't remember his telling me that!"—but other people were there and heard us respond at the time. "But it wasn't like that. I only skinned my elbow"—but here are the doctor's bills for your broken arm.

It may appear that when we are faced with an

intolerable world, we have an alternative to construing it differently: suicide. But a world in which suicide is a possibility is not literally intolerable, not literally an impossible world: we do have a place therein as Actors, even if the act of committing suicide demolishes the possibility of future actions, at least in this world. When suicide is not a matter of a person's seeing the world as having only one place for him and only this one action possible for him, then it is an ordinary choice, as in "I don't choose to live with these things. I would rather commit suicide".

An Observer-Critic who sees the world differently from the way we see it can compare his description of the world with ours, and critique ours as being a distortion of reality. He may go on to attribute the distortion to our being in an "impossible" situation, i.e., living in a world where we have zero status and therefore zero behavior potential—no place that we can operate from. He may then go further to show us that the situation does hold possibilities that had not occurred to us. Or, of course, he may simply accuse us of evading reality, and dismiss us with that degradation. In reply, we can critique his view of the world, and accuse him of evading reality.

Successful constructions of the world as a possible rather than an impossible one can result in either a decrease in behavior potential, or an increase. A decrease reflects some greater limitation. An increase may be entirely positive, as in learning a new skill, or it may be associated with an immediate or limited decrease in behavior potential, as when we are promoted to a new job that we are not familiar with, so that we have to begin with a period of apprenticeship.

One person's behavior may exemplify Maxim 5: "I can't face the possibility of failing, so I shall do nothing"; in an extreme case, he could become catatonic. An Observer-Critic, from the viewpoint of his different world, might see the catatonic's move as violating the status-dynamics principle that a person will not choose to actualize less behavior potential over more, but for the catatonic Actor, it is not so. By not-acting, he is engaging in a deliberate action.

We do not distort all parts of the world just because we are in an intolerable position. For example, we may leave out only certain facts, as in Jessie's "It can't be true that he wants me to die". Or facts may be forgotten, and here we must examine briefly the concept of assimilation. Any time we acquire a new bit of information or undergo an experience of any kind, our real world changes, just as when we change any part of a building, we change the whole building, although not all parts of it. Where that new material comes from—a headline, a comment in a conversation, a book or lecture or course of study, the touch of a hand—may well be secondary, too trivial to be identified at a later time. Yet as long as the new material is accepted as real, its effect remains and can be crucial for the development of an attitude, an idea, an emotional state. Who among us has not cherished a scrap of verse or epigram or story without being able to recall where it came from? And did we repress that information into our unconscious, or simply forget it as we have forgotten a myriad of other inconsequential matters, such as what we ate for lunch on the second Tuesday in January eleven years ago?

Often, although not always, we can reconstruct the source of what we have assimilated. A dictionary of quotations tells us the author of the poem, or research in the library discloses the title of the book in which the story was published. With the help of an old day-book, we recollect what we were doing on that Tuesday eleven years ago ("11:30 - meet Jan for lunch at Ivar's"). Or a scene in a movie reminds us of an incident in our own lives that we had not thought about for years. Or in therapy, we think of events long forgotten.

If we explain the absence of recall in terms of **"repression** into the unconscious", we are committed to an elaborate mental geography to which we do not have—and on the hypothesis, cannot have—confident access. In contrast, assimilation, rejection, and inattention together cover many of the same phenomena, and possibly all, without recourse to purely conjectural processes and states of affairs.

---

There remains symbolic behavior as a further way to describe various phenomena that are often attributed to unconscious mechanisms. One of the general sorts of behavior that often (though not always) has been attributed to the unconscious is spoken of as **displacement**. Here we shall return to the symbolic behavior (or significance) diamond, to extend and elaborate on our earlier presentations of it.

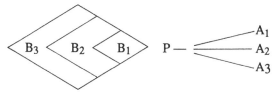

Each of these behaviors, $B_1$, $B_2$, and $B_3$, has its own Know, Want, and Know-How values, and the Performance is the same for all. For the paradigm case of successful symbolic behavior, there will be several achievements simultaneously, i.e., the performance will accomplish several things. For the sake of simplicity, we are limiting the figure to three behaviors, although there may well be more in any actual situation. In a complete behavior description, the last, largest diamond, whether third or second or fifteenth, will always be a behavior that is a participation in an intrinsic social practice, something done for its own sake without a further end in view.

Let us take for our first example Felicity's behavior at the party after seeing the lion, when Gerald denies that the lion was real. $B_1$ consists of her attacking him verbally, a concrete behavior that has significance as part of the larger whole, $B_2$, which consists of her hostile counteraction to Gerald's provocative behavior. To react with hostility to provocation is a self-affirmation in the face of threatened degradation, $B_3$. The occurrence of threatened degradation is sufficient reason for self-affirmation. Therefore the response of self-affirmation under those conditions needs no further explanation. Her behavior is intelligible in itself. This gives us a sequence from $B_1$, the concrete behavior, to $B_2$, an intrinsic behavior, and on to $B_3$, participation in an intrinsic social practice. By doing $B_1$, Felicity does $B_2$; by doing $B_2$, she does $B_3$.

But let us go back a little. Felicity's original impulse had been to attack Gerald physically—to hit or scratch or kick him—not just assail him verbally. Two kinds of constraints militated against her engaging in that kind of behavior. One, her personal and social standards—her values—gave her a strong reason not to do so; and two, Gerald's being considerably bigger than she gave her another, prudential reason (cf. the unless-clauses and Maxim 4). In other circumstances, there might have been different kinds of constraint: her friends held her back, or Gerald's insults were reported to her by someone else when he was not present.

For some or all of these reasons, Felicity is unable to engage in the most desired behavior, so she engages in a behavior that is relevantly similar in that to some degree it achieves the same value. Cussing him out is another form of attack, and thus of maintaining or restoring her status. It is also a case of acting on conflicting motivations, and coming up with a behavior that is responsive to all the factors in the situation—which is what most of us do most of the time.

One final episode in Felicity's story: on the way home from the party with her date, Henry, Felicity objects to the way he is driving, and their interchange escalates into a serious quarrel. The next morning, Henry calls her to make up, explaining that by now he realizes that Felicity was unconsciously taking out on him, another man (relevant similarity), her hostility to Gerald. Felicity denies that the contretemps with Gerald had anything to do with her reaction to Henry's driving which (she said) had been inordinately careless, inconsiderate, and dangerous, and was quite sufficient to explain her anger without bringing in Gerald at all. Henry apologizes, but all the same, to himself he accounts for her behavior in the car as a case of displacing on him her anger at Gerald, and perhaps an inability to recognize herself as the kind of person who would do that.

Which of them was right in the analysis is not important here. What is important is that the description in terms of the unconscious is always made by a Critic who has picked out one of the logical possibilities. That Critic may be an outsider (e.g., Henry), or the Actor-Observer-Critic in his role as Critic (e.g., Felicity) examining his own motives and prior behavior. An imaginative Critic can trace logical connections indefinitely in all directions and impute corresponding motivations, just as a Critic who is committed to a particular theory of motivation can restrict his search for connections to one direction. Either way, the resulting explanation of the behavior may be genuinely illuminating, or may have only the most tenuous relation to the original concrete behavior, $B_1$ (attacking him verbally), or to the intrinsic social practice, $B_3$ (self-affirmation) which comprises $B_1$ and $B_2$, and is the significance of the whole behavior. We must note, however, that until we know what behaviors the Actor was rejecting, we shall not know the full significance of the behavior he did engage in, that is, *what* behavior it was.

---

To illustrate the interplay among inattention, assimilation, world construction, and symbolic behavior, let us suppose that long ago we were exposed to a series of provocations—e.g., attempted degradations—to which we could not respond appropriately and adequately at the time. We brushed aside some of those events as insignificant, and consequently forgot them (inattention). Some, we took as jokes where others would have taken them as insults (assimilation). A few were so clear-cut that we were not able to assimilate them into our worlds, and were so crucial that if we had assimilated them, they would have made our worlds impossible for us to live in. So we constructed the world in such a way that it did not include them (world construction; distortion of reality). This kind of distortion, however, requires constant maintenance because we can neither deny what was so clear-cut nor admit it into our worlds. So we excuse, explain away, judge leniently, take blame on ourselves; but since we have neither fully accepted nor fully rejected that attempted degradation, we are left with an ambiguous self-status-assignment. When we cannot directly and overtly affirm our status in the face of attempted degradations, we can do so indirectly in ways that are more or less compatible with our world construction. In general there are seven of these, all relevantly similar in being self-affirmations:

(1) We can enact the hostile part in any interaction, rather than the victim part, thereby affirming that we are not the kind of person who will accept that attempted degradation.

(2) We can rehearse to ourselves what we would have liked to have said or done, but did not for prudential or other reasons, as a way of affirming that such behavior does lie within our behavior potential.

(3) We can remind ourselves that we *chose* not to

respond to the provocation with hostile behavior. We did not react as mere victims, but acted deliberately. To that degree, we were in control.

(4) We can think of or fantasize or day-dream or dream a revision of the events so as to develop a version that leaves our status intact or restores it, again as a way of affirming that we are not that kind of person.

(5) We can complain to a friend who will agree with us, thereby counteracting the attempted degradation with an accreditation, an affirmation that indeed we are not the kind of person we were accused of being.

(6) We can flatly assert that we are not that kind of person.

(7) We can flatly deny that the person who attempted to degrade us was qualified to judge us or our behavior or whatever it was he was judging.

All these are traditionally designated as displacements of our anger, but they may also be straightforwardly described as angry behavior and self-affirming behavior.

Further, if we respond with rage to what a Critic would appraise as only a mildly offensive remark, on this basis we do not need to postulate a reservoir of emotion stored up in an unconscious. All we need to do is to note that by virtue of the previous attempted degradations, we already have a fairly strong reason to enact some form of hostile behavior. Therefore we now have at least two reasons for responding with hostility to a perhaps innocent remark, rather than the one insufficient reason provided by this most recent, relatively mild provocation (cf. Maxim 4).

That the so-called reservoir of emotion is an unnecessary postulate is evidenced by the fact that emotional states, even very strong ones of long duration, can be dissipated instantly if we learn that their reality basis does not, in fact exist. Our friend has not betrayed our confidence. What we anticipated with fear is not going to happen. The mistake that we were ashamed of produces a happy result.

Emotional states evaporate swiftly when the reality basis changes. Being no longer under attack, we cease to be hostile. The danger having ended, we cease being afraid. There may be residual effects from sheer stress when the emotional state has subsided, but if the occasion for the emotion comes to an end, so does the emotion, and the residual effects might better be described as "relief" or something of that sort, rather than as a putative "discharge of accumulated emotional energy".

---

What we have presented in this chapter, thus far, has been the **unthinkability model** for distortions of reality and unconscious motivation, in which the constant is what the person *will not* see, and what he *will* see is up for grabs. Here we can only mention yet another, the **insistence model**, in which the constant is how the person insists on seeing the world. He *will* see it this way, and not in any other of the possible ways. However, the same principles of world-construction, assimilation, displacement, and so on, are as applicable here as with the unthinkability model.

The images of "the unconscious", "repression", "censorship", "transference", and so on, are vivid and enticing, but like other images, they conceal as much as they reveal. As an image, the "unconscious" has its uses, notably as a means for calling attention to certain apparent behavioral anomalies and for pressing the claim that they can be understood. In the Descriptive Psychology formulation, they are indeed understandable, but it is not necessary to set them apart in a special category. Instead, those apparent anomalies can be explained using exactly the same systematically-related set of concepts that are used to explain all other behavioral phenomena. Here, of course, we could only sketch that approach and the lines along which the details can be developed, but the logical form of this kind of explanation is given by the model in the following chart.[4]

## Unconscious Motivation

| | |
|---|---|
| Empiricist Principle: [Maxim 6] | You have to find out about the real world by observation |
| Paraphrases: | For a given observer, the real world is the one that includes him *as* an observer |
| | For no observer is the real world one that does not include him as an observer |
| | For no observer is the real world one that has no place for him |
| | For no observer is the real world one that would leave him in an impossible position |
| Maxim 5: | If a situation calls for a person to do something he cannot do, he will do something he can do, if he does anything at all |
| Conclusions: | If, for a given observer, A, the real world is such that it would leave him in an impossible position, he will not see it that way. Instead, he will see it as a world that does have a place for him, and he will act accordingly |
| | A second observer, O, who sees the world differently from A, and knows it, can count that difference as A's distortion of reality, and account for that distortion by reference to some real condition that A would find unthinkable because it would leave him in |

---

[4]Ossorio, *Personality and Personality Theories*, p. 296, with minor changes made by Ossorio in personal communication.

an impossible position, and therefore he
would be unable to behave with respect to it

Interpretations:

1. Among such unthinkable real conditions would be that A's behavior was a particular behavior or that it had a particular motivation or significance, hence *unconscious motivation*

2. Because the derivation above is a statement of logical constraints, the conclusion and the phenomena are non-voluntary and automatic; hence one could speak of *mental mechanisms*

3. Because the effect of the logical constraints is that the person continues to function more or less realistically when otherwise he would be unable to function, one could speak of the mechanisms as preserving realistic functioning, or as *ego defensive*

4. The second observer, O, might set up a taxonomy of the kinds of distortions A was engaging in. If the distortions were explained by the operation of mechanisms, the taxonomy could be identical to the traditional set of *ego defense mechanisms*

# CHAPTER 17

# THE SELF AND CONSCIOUSNESS[1]

"Who am I?" The question reverberates down the arches of the years, and almost always we answer by specifying our relationships with other people or our statuses in the world. "I am Sam and Sue's daughter", or "a middle-aged, middle-class, Middle-Western housewife", or "a young Chicano", or "a journeyman carpenter", or "a child of God", or "a stranger in a strange land", or "a nobody out of nowhere". With the barest encouragement, we will list a number of these, citing age, sex, ancestry, educational attainments, occupation, religious and social affiliations, and whatever else comes to mind that is important for our self-identification. Note that these are not only factual data, but data concerning our relationships and statuses, and that to designate them as "fact" (or "information" or "descriptions") is to assign them the status of "fact" (or "information" or "description").

"Who am I?" Let us try again by asking several people

---

[1]See Ossorio, *Meaning and Symbolism*, *"What Actually Happens"*, and *Positive Health and Transcendental Theories*. See also Plotkin, "Consciousness".

who know us well, "Who do you think I am?" Some of the answers will be the same as the ones we ourselves gave, especially those that have to do with straightforward facts about our relationships and statuses. Others will be more general descriptions that may or may not conform to our self concept. "An efficient administrator", "even at your age, still a spoiled brat", "formidable but in a nice way", "a flaming spirit". These constitute summaries of a totality, in contrast to lists of data.

Now let us take a third approach. Someone proposes to us a course of action so alien to us that we reject it vehemently, saying, "I couldn't do *that!*"—meaning "I couldn't do that *and still be me.*" What do we mean, in this context, by "me"? Obviously not ourselves as merely being of this age and that sex, this occupation and that heritage, but some central integrity that is more or other than can be encompassed by adding together all the data and impressions.

Since none of these ad hoc, impressionistic approaches seems likely to take us very far, let us ask three different questions. (1) Who is asking the question, "Who am I?" (2) In what circumstances is a person likely to ask it? And (3) Why do persons ask it?

First, it is persons who ask "Who am I?" and "Who are you?". Whatever else selves may be, they are at least persons: individuals whose histories are paradigmatically histories of deliberate actions within a world history. Second, most often persons ask questions such as "Who am I?" when they are in a state of perplexity or confusion or indecision about what behavior to engage in, and must choose among conflicting relationships, statuses, and/or values. They ask the identity question, "Who am I?", in order to answer the more pressing behavioral question, "What shall I do?"

Third, they ask the question in the form "Who am I?" as a way of establishing a superordinate relationship, status, or value in terms of which the conflict or confusion can be resolved or at least clarified. The appeal to "Who I am" is the last appeal in deciding what to do. We are who we are—for example, politician *and* wife *and* scholar *and* friend; in these circumstances, shall I act on the reasons a politician has, or those that a wife has, or those of a scholar or friend, or in some way that integrates them all?

To review: a person *as* a person has a place in the world as Actor, Observer/Describer, and Critic/Appraiser. As Actor, he is spontaneous and creative; as Observer and Critic, he is reflective. As Actor, he gives value to the world and its elements by assigning them contributions to make to his activities and life. As Observer and Critic, he finds that the world and its elements have or do not have the values the Actor has given them. Action is before-the-fact. Observation and criticism are essentially after-the-fact. Paradigmatically, what we observe and criticize is real, and is there to be observed and appraised.

Derivatively, it can be present in "the mind's eye". Since the Observer is a special case of Actor, the Critic a special case of Observer and therefore also of Actor, the extent to which they are spontaneous and creative reflects their Actor nature. Until now, we have diagrammed Actor-Observer-Critic as a triangle. Adding Person to the diagram, we shall draw not a square but a tetrahedron.

A person's knowledge of himself is comparable to his knowledge of his behavior, which is of two kinds. The more obvious kind is observational: we tell by observation something about what performances we go through, and we appraise what the significance of our behavior is. But observation is secondary to action, and as Actors, we have an author's knowledge of our identity, and of what we know and want.

We know in advance what we are producing in the same way that the author knows in advance what he is writing, and our observational knowledge has value chiefly in checking whether we have in fact succeeded in creating what we set out to produce. But the author, as such, does not and cannot produce what he does on the basis of having already observed it, because no one can observe what is not there, what has not happened. Nor does he have to have explicitly thought it out in advance. He can and does, however, *create* what was not there: a behavior or behaviors. He creates a sentence or a book; he creates his part in a conversation, or whatever. After the fact, the author or behaver can observe what he has created, and possibly appraise it in such a way as to modify his further behavior, but paradigmatically, the doing per se is simply *done*.

To illustrate with a fairly common experience: sometimes we say of something we wrote or said, "I hadn't thought about that before—it just came to me out of the blue as if it had been given to me." And so it was. But this is the Observer speaking. It *was* given to the Observer—by the Actor, who knew *what* he was doing, even though in this case he did not *know* what he was doing, at least not in the usual sense of having worked out in advance what he was doing. Most of what we know, we know because we discovered or found it out. We know our own behavior, however, because we produced it.

Primarily, we know ourselves by being in the world, by being alive and by acting in the world, in contrast to the way we know facts about our relationships with others and our statuses in the world, as well as about our dispositions, powers, and states. In order to act, we must distinguish one state of affairs from another, one object, process, and event from another, one reason from another, as well as distinguish our being in the world as we are, and acting as we do. Thus our primary access to what we call the self is through our acting as ourselves in choosing and creating our behaviors, in contrast to acting as a politician or a wife, an author or a spectator.

Logically, as we have already seen, "person" and

"world" are necessary for each other—as the inside and outside of an orange, or west and east, are necessary for each other. We experience our selves, then, not simply in contrast or opposition to the world, but rather as a particular part of the world, inseparable from the world but distinctive within it. That is, my experience of my self is my experience of a world of actualities and possibilities in which I have a place, and in which I actually occupy that place. In the world, I have being as a Person who is at once an Actor, an Observer/Describer, and a Critic/Appraiser.

This four-fold relationship has its own complexities. As Persons, we are related to ourselves not only as Actors, Observers, and Critics, but also to ourselves as Actor-Critics, as Actor-Observers, and as Observer-Critics. Moreover, as Critics we are related to ourselves as Actors and Observers; as Actors, we are related to ourselves as Critics and Observers; as Observers, we are related to ourselves as Critics and Actors. All that we can do here is to call attention to the logical possibilities that are inherent in this systematic conceptualization. We cannot spell out the details, intriguing though they are.

Paradigmatically we know ourselves—are real to ourselves—primarily as Actors, secondarily as the Observers and Critics who are special cases of Actor. We know *about* ourselves as Observers, and what—as Observers—we know about ourselves is what, in principle, any other Observer could know: our status, relationships, personal characteristics, and behavior. And our Observer-Critic knowledge of our status includes knowledge of our actual and possible value to other persons and to the world at large, just as it includes knowledge of our abilities, dispositions, and so on.

Such knowledge of our personal value may be general or specific. Either way, a Critic can appraise our knowledge as accurate or inaccurate: no observation can be guaranteed to be veridical and no Observer to be infallible, not even ourselves in observing ourselves. We observe what we do and accomplish, and correspondingly appraise how useful and valuable we are, and we act accordingly. It is commonplace for us to appraise ourselves as having been mistaken, or as having over- or under-estimated our value, or as having mistaken its nature ("I thought you loved me for myself, not just for my money!"—or vice versa).

Our self-appraisal is the description of ourselves that we are prepared to act on and that governs our behavior. Since the behavior can be observed, we—the Observer-Critics—can work backward from the observation of behavior to the appraisal and to the original description.

When we speak of a person's self concept, we are acknowledging that his appraisal of himself—what he takes to be the case about himself—is not necessarily the same as our appraisal of him, and that his self appraisal is not necessarily veridical in the sense of being accurate and complete. Nor, of course, is our appraisal of him, on the general principle that nobody can be guaranteed to be right. Central to a self appraisal is what we take to be possible behaviors *for us*, *our* behavior potential, and we can be mistaken about that, or perplexed or confused. Our self concept, therefore, like our self, connects directly to deliberate action, and to the concept of a person as an individual who acts deliberately.

If all this seems unconscionably elaborate, we shall do well to remember the simplicity of the tetrahedron, because here we are dealing with only four elements, and not so much in their logical as in their functional relationships. The logical relationships are specifically the concern of the Observer-Critic who knows *about* ourselves, as contrasted with the functional relationships that are the direct concern of the Critic-Actor through whom, primarily, we know ourselves. We do function in all these ways, normally with at least fair efficiency.

Our individual Person-Actor-Observer-Critic tetrahedrons have a place in the world, a status, but as the world can be articulated into many domains, so we can be said to have many places and therefore many selves. Thus "politician" and "wife" are different places (statuses) which are not per se incompatible either in principle or in practice. We have places within many domains of relationship, but those domains are not as disconnected as they may appear. Even chess and cooking can be interrelated: if a cook also plays chess, they are joined through his participation in both domains, even though the domains themselves have no elements in common. And he has a further perspective that is not either cook or chess-player, but is that of himself, as is delightfully illustrated in W. S. Gilbert's *The Mikado*, where Ko-Ko, the Lord High Executioner, asks Pooh-Bah, the Lord High Everything Else, how much he should spend celebrating his marriage. Pooh-Bah replies:

> Speaking as your Private Secretary, I should say that as the city will have to pay for it, don't stint yourself, do it well. . . . Of course you will understand that, as Chancellor of the Exchequer, I am bound to see that due economy is observed. . . . As your Solicitor, I should have no hesitation in saying "chance it"— . . . If it were not that, as Lord Chief Justice, I am bound to see that the law isn't violated. . . . Of course, as First Lord of the Treasury, I could propose a special vote that would cover all expenses, if it were not that, as Leader of the Opposition, it would be my duty to resist it, tooth and nail. Or, as Paymaster-General, I could so cook the accounts that, as Lord High Auditor, I should never discover the fraud. But then, as Archbishop of Titipu, it would be my duty to denounce my dishonesty and give myself into my own custody as First Commissioner of Police.

Finally, of course, Pooh-Bah reconciles all these con-
flicts by speaking as his superordinate self: "I don't say that
all these distinguished people couldn't be squared . . . with
a very considerable bribe".

Most of us do not resolve such perplexities so easily,
although we do so in essentially the same way, by means of
a status or relationship or value that takes priority for the
superordinate self. But what about those who are not asking
"Who am I?" at all, or "What do I really stand for?" or
"What do I really want?" Often it is not because they have
an answer, but rather that they are living confidently
enough that the questions do not arise. Their priorities are
clear, and are not in conflict with what is required of persons with those statuses and relationships within that community. Hence they are persons who are not deficient with
respect to their own identity as selves.

---

Given that we experience ourselves as being in the
world, what of consciousness, and how are "experience"
and "consciousness" related? We experience the world,
distinguishing this from that. We are conscious of the
world, again distinguishing this from that. Herein the terms
are equivalent. Where they are not equivalent is in what
they differentiate. Because we are not always conscious,
we need the distinction "conscious-unconscious". And because the distinctions we make are not always complete or
veridical, we need a way of saying implicitly if not explicitly, "Of everything that was available to be seen, heard,
touched, and otherwise apprehended, this is what I *did* see,
hear, touch, and otherwise apprehend. This is what I
experienced."

We can experience and be conscious of states of affairs involving objects, processes, or events that are "out
there". We can also experience and be conscious of states

of affairs that involve us, such as being confused, awake, angry, in physical pain, and so on. However, much of what we experience or are conscious of is there in the perceptual field but not literally there in the world, or is literally there in the world but not in the perceptual field. Five examples may suffice.

(1) A three-dimensional landscape is not literally in the two-dimensional photograph or painting of it that hangs on the wall.

(2) The under side of the desk at which I am working is not in my perceptual field, but I experience the desk as having another side. I am aware of it although I am not observing it.

(3) I am aware of my desk as being something that has a history, and of the persons I deal as having histories. Their having histories, however, is not something that I can see, hear, etc., or that I merely infer. As I experience directly my own continuity through time, so I experience theirs.

(4) I meet a stranger, and respond to him not simply in terms of the actual present situation, but also in terms of its future possibilities. The range of those possibilities is not infinite. It is restricted by our respective person characteristics, statuses, and the domain we are sharing—e.g., an informal party, a mutual interest in dancing, the city and country we are in, and so on. These three factors—person characteristics, statuses, and domains—codify the possibilities for future relationships between us, and in principle, from them we could work out how that "strangers" relationship presumably could—or could not—develop into friendship. Our future behavior is a continuation of our histories, and our present behavior has significance in terms of that continuity. Some of our possible behaviors will extend courses of action which we are already engaged in; others will end them and we shall start on new courses of action. We look to see what possibilities will be opened to

us by our current behavior, and what will be closed, given our person characteristics, status, and world.

(5) We are aware of our own behavior, but we do not necessarily observe any of that behavior. We watch the bird soaring above us, but no part of our body lies within our perceptual field; we do not observe our body, nor do we observe our knowledge, motivation, or achievement while we are concentrating upon the bird. Normally we do observe some part of our body: our hands lie within our perceptual field as we write or type, or turn the pages of the book we are reading. When we walk or sit down, we observe the movements of our body. But we can say "That's a western tanager!" without observing our own behavior.

Our experience, therefore, is not circumscribed by what is present to our senses. What we experience at a given time subsists within a world which gives us temporal and spatial limitations, and our experiences are not experienced independently of the world. It is not only ourselves, but other persons, objects, processes, etc., who are "being in the world" and whom we experience as having a continuous history.

---

One final area of concern must be mentioned. Starting from the idiomatic phrase "state of consciousness", let us return to the concept of a state as corresponding to a temporary systematic difference in our Dispositions and Powers, and therefore in what we experience and in our behavior potential. When we are angry or elated or weary or in love, the world looks different, and we behave in terms of more or less extensively different relationships and distinctions; our behavior potential is diminished or increased. When we are unconscious, we are not experiencing the world and have minimal behavior potential. These are departures from a normative baseline, either the person's own normal state or a social norm.

There is also, however, a sub-category of states which we speak of as "altered states of consciousness", in which the person's over-all perception of the world and his behavior potential are significantly changed. Although the conceptual difference is simple and clear-cut, it may be difficult on a given occasion for us to say whether a person is in an altered state of consciousness, and others may disagree with us on that appraisal.

As is commonly the case, here the "What is it?" question is easier to answer than the question "How do you tell?" The experience of despair, for example, and the experiences of ecstasy and being in love, can be taken as altered or unaltered states of consciousness. But some states are always considered altered states of consciousness, and among those that have been extensively studied, one stands out for its near-universality, dreaming, and four others for their especially dramatic manifestations: those induced by hypnosis,[2] drugs, toxicity, and certain religious or quasi-religious experiences such as trance-states induced by meditation.

For our immediate purposes, the changes in our Dispositions when we are in a hypnotic, psychedelic, toxic or meditative state are less interesting than the changes in our Powers, that is, our abilities, knowledge, and values. To give only a few instances:

First, our *abilities* to think, remember, and communicate with words are likely to be significantly enhanced or reduced; we may become able to perform feats of great endurance or be incapable of physical movement. We may perceive colors, sounds, and tastes as being extraordinarily intense, or in some trance states, lose all our abilities to see, hear, and feel.

---

[2]See Plotkin and Schwartz, "A Conceptualization of Hypnosis: I. Exploring the Place of Appraisal and Anomaly in Behavior and Experience," and "II: Hypnotic Induction Procedures and Manifestations of the Hypnotic State".

Second, commonly in altered states of consciousness, what we *know* undergoes significant change. Friend becomes foe, or all distinctions are eradicated in an experience of ultimate one-ness.

Third, our *values*, as expressed in our appraisals and consequently in our behaviors, can alter radically, including our final-order appraisals of true and false, good and evil, real and unreal, self and not-self, as well as appraisals that are not final-order, such as interesting and uninteresting, important and unimportant, and so on. A person in an altered state of consciousness may take something as real or true or as "belonging to the self" that hitherto he had taken to be unreal, false, or not-self. Alternatively, he may cease to make any final-order appraisals at all because he no longer distinguishes truth from error, real from unreal.

We speak of being in a state when the condition is temporary and reversible. We wake from dreaming; the drug wears off; we emerge from meditation or from a hypnotic state. What begins as an altered state, however, may persist to the point where it becomes established as that person's normal state, identifiable as an altered state only if the standard of comparison is other, normal people or general social norms.

---

Being in the world temporally and spatially, experiencing it, being conscious of it, entering and leaving altered states of consciousness, are natural to persons. We do them unthinkingly and without being taught. It is only when we begin to think about them that we see how elaborately they can be described, and how intricate is the pattern they make. But we must not lose sight of the simplicity that informs the elaborations, or substitute the Observer's descriptions for the Critic's and Actor's maxims.

# PART VI

# WHOLE PERSONS

# CHAPTER 18

# PATHOLOGICAL STATES[1]

We have already touched on the two-pronged definition of a pathological state as corresponding to "a significant restriction on a person's ability to engage in deliberate action, and (equivalently) to participate in the social practices of the community". Now it is time to consider the definition in detail, first for what it says, and second for what it does not say.

To begin with, the definition accounts for our concern with pathologies: they have important social implications. The person in a pathological state is unable to participate satisfactorily in the social forms of behavior of the community, that is, in a way that fulfils its expectations or requirements—stopping at stop lights, for example. These requirements are important in themselves because we cannot, in practice, treat every individual member of a community as a law unto himself. We have a legitimate and vested in-

---

[1]See Ossorio, "Pathology," *Clinical Topics, Positive Health and Transcendental Theories*, and *Personality and Personality Theories*, 18 July 1977.

terest in his ability to carry his own weight by participating with us in the life of the community. Neither, in practice, can we tailor our social practices to everyone's idiosyncrasies.

Here we can refer back to our purely hypothetical "standard normal person" who in every respect does merely what the situation calls for, no less and no more, and take him as our baseline. Rightly we expect and plan for individuals to differ from that norm in their behavior, and correspondingly in their person characteristics. But it is only when their characteristics are different in such a way that they are significantly restricted in their ability to participate in current social practices that they are correctly described as being in a pathological state.

This definition gives us also our conceptual criterion for differentiating pathological from normal states. Is the restriction serious enough to be significant? If so, then probably intervention will be desirable or disqualification advisable. In any case, "pathology" reflects a summary appraisal of the person in relation to the community—an appraisal that may serve as a basis for legal, therapeutic, or other intervention.

Disqualification, however, is tailored to a status. A ballplayer may be disqualified as a pitcher but not as a catcher. A person with a quick temper can be disqualified as an arbitrator in a complex dispute, or an inexperienced cook as caterer for a banquet. A familiar example of disqualification is the classic treatment of the "village idiot", who wanders about harmlessly and happily, and for whom we make all kinds of allowances—until a medical officer from outside intervenes by pronouncing him "sick" and locks him up.

When we disqualify someone, we make allowances for him by not requiring this or that from him. We do not hold him to certain standards. We tolerate him because he does not endanger the community. We adjust to him unless the total situation reaches a point where we are no longer willing, or perhaps able, to make those adjustments. Whether in practice we can make such allowances for him is one of the factors contributing to the decision that his restriction is or is not significant. If he becomes violent or helpless, or in some other way exceeds the bounds of our tolerance, we appraise him as being in a pathological state, and take whatever steps seem appropriate.

Always, that judgement is made by particular persons functioning as Critics, at a particular time and place, and with reference to a particular set of social practices. A person who is judged to be normal in Kansas City, for example, might be appraised as pathological in Kathmandu. And what constitutes a *significant* restriction can vary from—let us say—an authoritarian to a permissive milieu. Moreover, even competent Critics can disagree in their appraisal of a person's state as being pathological or normal, depending upon what their purposes are. Members of a person's family may disagree with a therapist. Or a Critic may appraise an individual as being significantly restricted in one respect but not in others—able to care for himself, for instance, but not to hold down a job, or able to leave the hospital but not to stop medication.

The most dramatic instances of disagreement among Critics are found in those trials where the verdict or sentence hinges upon whether the accused is insane, and an array of mental-health professionals is called upon to testify for and against his sanity. "Sanity" and "insanity", however, are legal, not scientific, terms, so we shall not be concerned with them here.

In practice, we seek intervention for ourselves or others when the restrictions upon our abilities to engage in deliberate action or to participate in current social practices are not just a nuisance (a common cold, a mild apprehension in the presence of cats), but incapacitating or threatening to become so. Or we may seek intervention as a preventive measure. Our standard is behavioral, and can be either specific to the individual or more general.

We see ourselves as being in a pathological state when we function at a level significantly below what we require of ourselves, usually based upon past experience, or when others appraise us as functioning significantly below the level they require of us. Alternatively, we can base our appraisal upon the hypothetical standard normal person: we see ourselves or others as in a pathological state if we or they are functioning at a level significantly below that of the standard normal person.

---

By implication, our definition of pathology distinguishes between the nature of the pathology and any explanation of its causes. To be significantly restricted as specified in the definition *is* to be in a pathological state. How we explain the restriction is another matter entirely. Depending upon what kind of explanation we give—physical, physiological, psychological, moral, spiritual, situational, or other—we follow the convention of calling it a physical or mental or other illness. But the illness, the deficit, is not the broken leg in itself or the paranoia or the inferior moral sense; it is the restriction in the person's ability to participate in the social practices of the community in question.

When a person is in a pathological state, his behavior potential is restricted. A restriction in behavior potential, however, is not necessarily pathological. In many cases, limited behavior potential is due not to the person's inability but to the lack of opportunity to exercise his behavior potential. A person who is imprisoned or who has lost his job is certainly restricted in some of his opportunities. He is not, however, restricted in his abilities, since he will be able to exercise them again when he is released from incarceration or unemployment. A refugee may find that the country where he has taken refuge does not provide him opportunities to practise his previously-acquired skills, but he does not necessarily lose those skills.

Although absence of opportunity is not in itself pathological, it may be pathogenic. Prolonged incarceration or unemployment, or a lengthy period during which the refugee fails to acquire the skills which his new country requires for participation in its social practices, can contribute to pathologies.[2] Even so, pathological restrictions upon ability do not automatically follow from restrictions upon opportunity.

What our definition of pathological states does not specify is what the reference-community is, or what constitutes a significant restriction. Nor does it imply that there is some set of things that a person must be able to do in order to avoid being in a pathological state. We do not expect that a two-year-old will be able to read and write—we evaluate him in terms of the norms for that age, that is, in terms of his status in that community. We do expect that a twenty-year-old can read and write. If he cannot use language at all, we consider him to be in the pathological state of mental retardation or aphasia, but if, on the other hand, he cannot read and write but can understand spoken language and can speak, we shall probably take it that he may have the capacity to learn reading and writing but has not had the opportunity—perhaps the teaching methods used with him were not appropriate.

———————

We can further clarify our definition of pathology by going back to the Maxims for Behavior Description, especially an expanded version of Maxim 5: "If a situation calls

———————

[2]See Ossorio, *Clinical Topics*; Aylesworth and Ossorio, "Refugees: Cultural Displacement and Its Effects"; Lasater, "Stress and Health in a Colorado Coal Mining Community"; and Torres, "Puerto Rican and Anglo Conceptions of Appropriate Mental Health Services".

for a person to do something he cannot do *by virtue of lacking the requisite knowledge, motivation, or know-how,* he will not do that, but will do what he can do—if he does anything at all." Knowledge, motivation, and ability, of course, are person characteristics, and these will provide one of our major resources in formulating systematically what is the case when a person is in a pathological state. Another will be the Actor-Observer-Critic feedback loop. In principle, either can be used to understand a pathological state, although in practice one may be more helpful than the other in a given case.

To start with the person characteristic of Knowledge: clearly if a person does not know what is going on around him, his ability to engage in deliberate action or to participate in current social practices will be diminished. Not-knowing can take many forms, e.g., ignorance, unconsciousness, simple inattention, and distortion, with a myriad of gradations in between. Or the person can fail to make relevant distinctions, as between real and dream worlds, or make inappropriate ones, as in treating a lover's quarrel as a problem in logic, or a tiny puppy as an immediate threat to life.

The circumstances of not-knowing can also matter. Inattention to a blizzard while one is meditating in a warm room is one thing, but while one is driving in it is quite another. Or to take another form of not-knowing, a person can believe that he is participating normally in the social practices of the community but be mistaken. Consider the battered child who grows up to be a battering parent, believing that this is how everybody else does—and should—treat children. Or the teacher who conveys to his pupils that being slum children, they are stupid and incorrigible. Or the fanatic who rejects as damnable all ways of thinking and living except his own.

Such a question as "When does not-knowing become pathological?" presupposes that it is the degree of restriction per se which is fundamental, but this is not the case. What is fundamental is that the restriction has, or has not, a significance or importance that warrants our taking action. If it does—as we saw earlier—our principal behavioral alternatives are either to intervene, or to exclude by disqualifying, avoiding, or whatever. We must act in one way or the other.

The consequences of a person's not-knowing may be more or less serious, and as we distinguish between the seriousness of the consequences, so also we distinguish between greater and less pathologies. But these more-and-less distinctions are secondary to the basic distinction between normal and pathological states.

The second person characteristic that we must consider is the person's motivation:[3] is his pathological state associated with what he values and wants? Is he bent on achieving something that is, on the face of it, impossible—for example, always to have whatever he wants whenever he wants it? Is there nothing that he wants for its own sake? Is he continually doing the right things for the wrong reasons, or the wrong things for the right reasons? Does he expect to achieve some goal without taking any of the appropriate steps toward that end—e.g., to learn a new language effortlessly, or to become socially adept without taking pains to learn the norms and procedures of that society?

Third, we come to Abilities, i.e., competence and skills. Illiteracy might be placed here instead of (or as well as) under the Know parameter, but the clearest examples are cases where the person cannot—literally cannot—acquire the skills that are necessary for normal social participation. This might come about because of, for example, general mental incapacity or physiological anomalies.

---

[3]See Ossorio, "Place", "Notes on Behavior Description," and "Outline of Descriptive Psychology,".

To take an example of another kind, certain emotional states can critically diminish a person's abilities. The accomplished musician afflicted with stage-fright to the point where he cannot play before an audience is pathologically restricted, as is the student who, on examination day, forgets everything he ever knew about the subject.

Within the category of Ability, one class of instances deserves special mention: the case of the person who has limited ability to participate in current social practices because he is so caught up in other forms of interaction that he cannot or will not change his ways of behaving. Thus he is significantly restricted in his ability to participate in that community, although in some other community he might be able to participate fully. Of such are—among others—not only "crazy die-hards", but also some social critics who may be anything but crazy.

Generally speaking, the Critic bases his judgement of pathology upon an initial conclusion that the person is not participating in current social practices in some important way or ways. On further examination, he concludes that the lack of participation reflects an inability—a lack or distortion of knowledge, motivation, or competence—rather than a simple choice not to participate. That conclusion depends, very often, upon his having an explanation for the occurrence of the inability. Conceivably, a person in a quietly decorous community who was dramatically displaying his emotions might be diagnosed as hysterical unless his behavior could be explained, perhaps on the ground that he was a foreigner from a country where such exhibitions were customary.

From the diagnosis of inability to participate, the Critic can go on to a more detailed investigation. Is the under-achiever in school manifesting inadequate prior knowledge, insufficient motivation, incompetence, or a mistaken view of the world ("I am a slum child, and slum children are — "), or an emotional block that prevents his reciting in class?

A general understanding of pathology will take account of the person as such, and not merely his inability to participate. That is, it will also take account of his other person characteristics, the behaviors he does engage in, the community in which he is living, and his personal way of life. And because all these are systematically interrelated, the Critic has access to the whole person through any of them.

---

We can also approach the person who is in a pathological state through the Actor-Observer-Critic feedback loop ("Anything that can be described in one way can be described in other ways"). That loop can be weak or anomalous at any point—between Actor and Observer, or Observer and Critic, or Critic and Actor, or by a failure of the Actor, or Observer, or Critic himself—and any of these can contribute to a pathological state.

Since Actor is the most general of the three statuses, the other two being special cases of Actor, let us begin with the Actor who does not observe what he is doing. The paradigm case is the person who acts without thinking, and who may even make a cardinal virtue of spontaneity, not knowing (as Observer) or caring (as Critic) what he does. But a person who neither knows nor cares what he does will not be able to participate to an appreciable extent with other people in the social practices of the community, for which he will have a blithe disregard. Either we never know what to expect of him, or we know all too well: the chances are that he will be disruptive. For real-life examples, we need only look at infants, for whom this is a normal state. In older children and adults, it can be pathological.

As an Observer, a person can go wrong by ignoring certain aspects of what he is observing. Or he can force his description into a schema to which he is devoted, like the paranoid who simply does not see anything that contravenes his delusion, and interprets what he does see in line with his pathological state. Similarly, the teacher who is committed to the belief that slum children are ipso facto incorrigible, or that girls do not have mathematical minds, will discount any observation to the contrary.

When the break comes between the Observer and the Critic, the person knows what he is doing, in the sense of having a correct description, but he is unable to appraise it at all, or appraises it incompetently. "Whatever I do is right"—or, it may be, "Whatever I do is wrong"—displays an insufficiently critical judgement, a lack of discernment. His blanket evaluation represents a failure to be a Critic in any except the most rudimentary sense. Less extreme is the person whose critical judgement is faulty. What he appraises as appropriate or adequate participation is in fact inappropriate or inadequate or, sometimes, the other way around.

Perhaps the most striking break in the feedback loop comes between Critic and Actor, which commonly occurs in one of two ways. The Critic knows what the Actor should do to improve his state or behavior, but the Actor does not do it—and the unless-clauses may be useful in determining why he does not. Or the Critic limits himself to diagnosis without prescribing anything for the Actor to do.

A Super-Critic can all but paralyze the Actor, especially when both are the same person. Even when they are not, the Actor is more vulnerable than the Critic because whatever he does that is short of perfection can be criticized, while the Critic can continue his negative evaluations indefinitely. Yet in the end, the Critic is dependent upon the Actor, because without a prior action to criticize, he has nothing to work on or work with or work for.

On the basis of these two means of access to pathological states—person characteristics and the feedback loop—it would be possible to work out taxonomies, and for certain purposes there may be a point in doing so. For most everyday and therapeutic purposes, however, there is no reason to anticipate that more is needed than these systematic and straightforward resources, together with the material presented earlier on emotional behavior and states, symbolic behavior and the unconscious, and the self and consciousness. These are all parts of a single package, logically interconnected, and practically effective because in every case the diagnosis directly implies a treatment.[4] Moreover, these resources are so flexible that they can do justice to the infinite variety of actual persons in any geographical, historical, or cultural situation, and in normal or pathological states, or states of positive health.

---

[4]The successive volumes of *Advances in Descriptive Psychology* contain a number of articles on the diagnosis and treatment of pathological states, by Baker, Bergner, Driscoll, Farber, Kirsch, Marshall, and others.

# CHAPTER 19

# POSITIVE HEALTH[1]

As long as "health" is taken to mean nothing more than the absence of pathology, we have no serious problems with the concept. Once we admit—as we commonly do—that some people live above the "not-pathological" baseline, we run into trouble. We have designated pathology in terms of deficits, using as our baseline the hypothetical standard normal person who is not significantly restricted in his ability to engage in deliberate action and to participate in the social practices of the community in question, and who does merely what the situation requires, no more and no less.

For the most part, however, we have not had a baseline for positive health. When is more, better? For example, when is extraordinary motivation a sign of superior health? In practice, more can be either better or worse: better in the case of an Einstein or a Beethoven, worse in the case of a religious or political fanatic. But on what grounds do we appraise the one set as exemplifying a commendable con-

---

[1]See Ossorio, *Positive Health and Transcendental Theories.*

centration and the other as exemplifying a pathological obsession?

A long list could be prepared of qualities that we might take as signs of positive physical or mental health: robustness, vitality, openness, integrity, self-acceptance, sensitivity, ability to do more or better than the situation requires. Note that these are Critic's terms, appraisals, and remember that in so far as Critic's language is diagnostic, it is almost inevitably negative. He gives deficiency descriptions, as in "He's being too aggressive", or double negative as in "He's not being too aggressive". So robustness can be restated in Critic's language as not prone to illness, vitality as not weak or lethargic, self-accepting as not self-rejecting, sensitive as not insensitive, and so on. If, however, the Critic wants to say more than "not weak or lethargic", for example, he faces a dilemma. He has no standards for evaluation in the area above the normal, that is, for positive health.

---

One possible baseline is perfection, and as a baseline, that norm has the advantages that it calls only for deficiency descriptions. The Critic can say to the Actor (who may be himself or someone else), "These are the ways in which your superb performance falls short of perfection", or he can remark, "That particular saint is less than perfect, in being occasionally irritable". Now and then the Critic may even have occasion to say, "This behavior (or person) is impeccable, beyond criticism."

With the perfection baseline and consequent deficiency descriptions, the whole range of positives becomes manageable, as was the whole range of pathology once we established the baseline of "significant restriction in one's ability to participate in the social practices of the community", with deficiency descriptions relative to that baseline. But the perfection baseline is not as simple to handle as the normal is. We have to go a step further and ask, "Perfect of what kind?", and then we must go still further to ask whether one kind is better than another.

Health, like pathology, is a state, and states correspond to systematic differences in the person's Powers or Dispositions, or both. Therefore what we are concerned with here is not persons as athletes, bankers, mothers, or musicians, but persons in their wholeness and their **Ways of Living**, the undergirding and overarching structures within which, so to speak, they are athletes, bankers, mothers, or whatever. Often, though not always, Ways of Living[2] are formulated as religions.

A prime example of a way of living that is not specifically or exclusively religious has been described in detail by Carlos Castaneda under the name "the Warrior", who is a "man of power".[3] This has nothing to do with ability to manipulate nature or other persons, or with activities or occupations or social achievements. It is an all-pervasive way of living, manifesting itself in everything the Warrior does. His individual behaviors may appear no different from those of other people, but cumulatively they reveal a competence and an assurance that are distinctive.

A second example of a way of living that can be either religious or non-religious is the Seeker, the person of inquiring mind whose entire life is characterized by the search into the nature of things and their relationships. Another is the Lover whose ardor embraces all that is, such as Francis of Assisi. Many others could be specified, but these three—Warrior, Seeker, Lover—should be enough to suggest what is meant by ways of living that may or may not be religious, and how widely such ways can differ. Their religious parallels are obvious: the Soldier of the Lord, the

---

2See Roberts, "Worlds and Word Reconstruction," and Shideler, "Science, Religion, and Religions".

3See Farber, "Castaneda's Don Juan as Psychotherapist".

Seeker for Enlightenment, the Divine Lover, as well as forms that few of us admire, such as Dostoevski's Grand Inquisitor, or the merely inquisitive, or the unintelligent and amoral sentimentalist. And many religions have their own exemplars who fit none of these descriptions, or which have doctrinal definitions of their ways of life instead of exemplars.

A good Critic will not judge the Seeker or the Warrior, for example, by the perfection baseline that is appropriate for the Lover, any more than he will use the same baseline for the Buddhist, the Jew, and the Christian. That would be like using the same criteria for appraising a play, a scientific experiment, and a building. Thus we do not have a single baseline for perfection, but a multiplicity of baselines—as many standards of perfection as there are cultural Ways of Living and personal versions of those ways.

Because of the diversity of ways of life, taxonomies are of considerable value in this connection, and for the most part, the common ones are serviceable enough: Warrior, Seeker, Lover, and so on; or Buddhist, Christian, Jew, Hindu, Moslem, Native American, and so on, each with its subclassifications. Protestant, Catholic, and Orthodox Christianity can be broken down into genera and species, and Buddhism likewise into Theravada, Mahayana, Vadjarama, and Zen Buddhism, and so for other religious traditions. In Critic's language, the person living a perfect Buddhist, Warrior, etc., life will not be in any way deficient in choosing and enacting the Buddhist, Warrior, etc., options in those social practices of his community which fit his way of living. The double negative, in this case, is equivalent to a positive.

A taxonomy should also include a miscellaneous collection of individuals for whom we have no general name, and I do not intend to propose one. It consists of persons whose standard of perfection is so personal to themselves that they can only be described as living from competence—which is all very well if in fact they are competent, but if they are not, they can be dangerous to others and themselves. Charles Morgan describes one who was indeed competent, and compares him with those less competent, as follows:

> It was the essence of Barbet's nature that he lived by no rules and yet had order within him, the order not of submission to laws or of conformity to the ideas of others but of his own sense of natural values. And yet . . . of what use it is to say that? A rebel, a man of anarchical mind, any vague and paltry upstart who wished to be conspicuous in his defiances, might claim to have "his own sense of natural values." The phrase is just a phrase—with truth in it if you know the man, but, if not, meaningless.[4]

Unlike the follower of a traditional or accepted way of life, this type of person does not climb the Justification Ladder rung by rung, appealing from Judgement to Custom to Theory to Principle, and from Principle to Perspective or Competence. He proceeds directly to competence, and so doing he invents his own way of life. If he is intelligent and responsible, as Barbet was, he will almost certainly take account of the intervening rungs, but he does not rest his weight upon any of them.

Such a person may justify his stance with the familiar "I couldn't do that and still be me", which can be frivolous or profound, an irresponsible rejection of all persons and considerations except what one wants for himself at the moment, or a responsible decision after taking into account the relevant customs, theories, and principles, and all the perspectives. This is an appeal from reasons to person

---

[4]Morgan, *The Voyage*, p. 421.

characteristics which—as we have seen earlier—are not reasons and therefore cannot be negotiated.

People like Barbet are anchored neither in the social practices of the community, nor in a model (Warrior, Seeker, Lover), nor in a religious tradition or a doctrine, but in anything from "their own sense of natural values" to a private revelation ("Thus saith the Lord unto me"; "God has called me to do this"), to which the Critic has no independent access. Among them are saints, geniuses, criminals, and fiends, as well as mere eccentrics. Some of them attract followers and become the founders of traditions—Jesus, Mohammed, Hitler, and others who have been equally influential, as well as the hordes whose influence has been negligible. These particular persons have the ability to participate in current social practices, so they are not pathological. However, they are willing to participate only to the extent or in the ways such that their participation does not conflict with their personal values.

A person's life can be called perfect if it withstands all criticism when judged against the cultural or personal way of living which it exemplifies. (Here, as elsewhere in this discussion, we are assuming a reasonable critic, not the Super-Critic who is determined to find fault somewhere.) But what about the Critic's appraisal of the diverse and often disparate ways of living themselves—Mahayana with Theravada Buddhism, Buddhism with Christianity, Christianity with atheism? Or the Lover with the Warrior and both of them with the Seeker? Or religious with non-religious ways of living?

---

When we propose that one thing is better than another, we should be prepared to answer the question, "Better how, in what respects?" And we shall do well also to be prepared for such questions as, "Is it better to implement this value rather than some other value?" "Is saving one's own soul better, ultimately, than reforming society?" "Is the increase of knowledge more important than the increase of love?" "What *is* the highest good, the finest type of person?"

Dealing with questions such as these calls for the introduction of what are called, in Descriptive Psychology, the **Transcendental Concepts: ultimacy, totality**, and **boundary condition**.[5] In such questions about the meaning of life, and so on, we are comparing totalities: whole persons and whole ways of living, summary formulations and not details, and we are concerned with ultimate, not immediate, objects, relationships, values. Boundary conditions correspond to the internal structure of a given domain, whether the domain be relatively small like that of chess, or the all-encompassing real world, "the state of affairs which includes all other states of affairs".

The transcendental concepts were originally articulated for describing the domain of spirituality: that is "spiritual" which deals with ultimates, totalities, and boundary conditions. For some purposes—especially in connection with religious spirituality—it is sometimes necessary to add others, for example, the concepts of ultimate significance, of holiness, of timelessness, and of transcendence as such. Normally and naturally we assign significance to objects, processes, events, and states of affairs, but where does the significance sequence end? It is characteristic of religious ways of living that the series does not regress—or progress—infinitely, which would be equivalent to no significance at all.

Herein significance is like certain other sequences, whose boundary condition is reflected in a move of a different kind. "What are you doing by doing that?—and that?—and that?", ending with, "I'm playing chess and this is how it's done." "How do you know this is a computer?"

---

[5]See Ossorio, *Positive Health and Transcendental Theories* and "Religion without Doctrine".

"Because—because—because—," ending with, "This is what we mean by a 'computer'." In following out the significance series, we end the series with "This is what life is all about", or more formally, "This is its ultimate significance".

The content we assign to the content-free concept "ultimate significance" may be doing the will of God, or achieving satori, or fulfilling the greatest good of the greatest number, or whatever it may be. In any case, it is the move from the subjective, such as "what I or we or humanity is ultimately concerned with", to the objective "what is ultimately significant". When, with empirical questions, we keep asking "what?" or "why?", sooner or later we are pushed to the move, "That's just the way things are", and since life itself is empirical, we should not be surprised at a similar move when we ask "what?" and "why?" questions about Life (with a capital L): "That's what Life is all about".

How *can* we compare on such a scale, we who are finite beings, limited by our viewpoints and our less-than-perfect abilities? We do because we must act in one way rather than another. Consequently we must choose among behaviors, and we are responsible for our choices. For millennia, philosophers and theologians, not to mention psychologists, have debated to their hearts' content—or discontent—what is the ultimate answer to these ultimate questions, without reaching any universally accepted conclusion. We cannot look to them for relief from the burden of our responsibility, but we must note that they are not in a position to inflict a curb upon our right—and necessity—to answer such questions for ourselves.

We do not choose a way of living. We enact it, creating our personal version of a cultural way by our choice of behaviors. We are born into a political community—a nation or tribe or people. But we choose to affiliate—or not—with a religious community, to learn its world view, make our choices according to its values, participate in its practices. We sit at the feet of a guru—a living archetype—and model ourselves after him. We follow the leading of the Spirit or spirits and, if we are wise, continually check our understanding of that leading against custom, theory, principle, and the reactions of those whom we respect. Otherwise we shall be in danger of going wrong in one or more of the ways that we can go wrong—by wishful thinking, perhaps, or intellectual confusion, or not having sensitivity or understanding enough to discern the Spirit or spirits rightly.

No way of living can ensure that by living that way, we shall achieve normality, positive health, salvation, perfection, or anything else. A way is simply a way, and in itself is eligible for criticism of its practices and values. We are not likely to appraise a person who lives as a terrorist as being in a state of positive health even if he lives it perfectly. Looking from another direction, anyone can be living any way of life—Warrior, Lover, Christian, Buddhist, or whatever—and yet be in a pathological state. This much, however, can be said, that no way of living will empower positive health unless it provides opportunities to fulfil basic human needs to a more than barely adequate degree, any more than a diet that minimally sustains physical existence can empower great athletes or scientists or even capable citizens.

———

One way of organizing this material on pathology and positive health for practical applications is by means of Jan Vanderburgh's Positive-health Developmental Model.[6] That Model has three dimensions: the first being the per-

———

[6]Vanderburgh, "The Positive-Health Developmental Model," and "The Positive-Health Developmental Model of Treatment and Psychopathology".

son's *Approach*, that is, his way of relating to himself, to others, and to the world. He can be primarily Power-oriented, Information-oriented, or Relationship-oriented (compare the Warrior, Seeker, and Lover). Each of these complements the others and increases behavior potential.

The second dimension is the *Developmental Level*, how the person's social skills and behavior compare with societal norms. For convenience, these are divided into eleven levels, the lowest being zero: the person who is socially non-functional (e.g., comatose, acutely psychotic, massively impaired) or not yet functional (the infant immediately after birth). The highest is the person of extraordinary resources and achievements. As an example, here is Level 5: "Developmentally, this level is appropriate for healthy 17- or 18-year-olds, and quite adequate for autonomous adult function. Well adapted to culture, within general mid-range of chosen subculture, experiences satisfaction in life, generally constructive." (Compare this with the standard normal person.)

The *Mastery* dimension has to do with the person's ability to function as Actor, Observer, and Critic in regulating his behavior at a particular developmental level of a particular approach. In Vanderburgh's own words, "At the point at which a person has mastered the content of a particular approach and level, in the sense that he or she has a genuinely functional (AOC) mastery of it, he or she has added a distinctive set of standards, appreciations, distinctions, and skilled behavioral options to his/her repertoire, and has correspondingly enlarged the world in which he/she lives."[7]

This model has direct bearing upon our participation in social practices, by facilitating our understanding of the persons we are associated with. In eliciting cooperation or avoiding conflict, we need a different approach to the

---

[7]Personal communication, 15 August 1981.

Power-oriented person from the one we would use with Information-oriented or Relationship-oriented persons, because each of these has different values and different dispositions.

A person who is deficient in Actor or Observer or Critic functions, or in either the Development or Mastery dimension, may not be in a pathological state. Quite possibly, however, his state is pathogenic. Take the Power-oriented person who functions without information or concern for others. Or take the Information-oriented person who is unable to put his information to use (lack of power) or who jettisons personal relationships for the sake of acquiring still more information. Or the Relationship-oriented person who abnegates his power and ignores information in favor of achieving or maintaining a particular relationship to another person or the world. In contrast, "A person who is positively healthy has full AOC mastery of the skills of all three basic approaches (Relationship, Power, and Information) at comparable and appropriate developmental levels."[8]

Vanderburgh's system is built from the bottom up; its baseline is complete non-function. It focuses upon describing actual abilities and achievements; hence as a positive-health model, it is non-pejorative. In contrast, the standard Descriptive Psychology analysis builds from the top down, i.e., from the perfection and the normality baselines which generate deficiency descriptions. In both cases, however, what is crucial is establishing a baseline. Having done so, we do not need to develop a different conceptual and logical apparatus for dealing with positive health, normality, and pathology.

---

Implicitly if not explicitly, we function with these

---

[8]Personal communication, 10 February 1982.

three baselines of the completely non-functional, the normal, and the perfect. However, when we take perfection as our baseline, everything can be incorporated within that ultimate framework. Such an all-inclusive framework, however, does not necessarily facilitate our dealings with more limited domains. For example, a problem in any domain—artistic, scientific, economic, psychological, or other—can have spiritual dimensions, but recognition of that dimension will not in itself enable us to deal competently with the artistic, scientific, economic, psychological or other problems that may arise within such domains.

Every domain has its own identity, its own set of ultimate objects and relationships which are not convertible into those of other domains. At the same time, any of their problems may be translated—or as it were, paraphrased—into spiritual problems or non-problems. Ultimate answers, however, do not solve domain problems, nor do domain answers solve ultimate problems.

The relation of positive health to spirituality (i.e., a way of life that takes seriously ultimates, totalities, boundary conditions, and other special concepts), needs a sharper conceptualization than we can give it in this limited space. Therefore, instead of following out that lead, we shall turn to the vast and urgent problems of personal change.

# CHAPTER 20

# PERSONAL CHANGE[1]

The first rule governing personal change is that the only things about ourselves over which we have direct control are our behavior and our over-all approach to life as persons, our "mindset". This holds whether whether we are attempting to change ourselves or another person, whether the change is deliberate or involuntary, and whether the change occurs—as toward pathology—despite efforts to prevent it.

The rule applies across the board, and implies as a necessary corollate that we cannot directly change any of our person characteristics: our Dispositions (traits, attitudes, interests, styles); our Powers (abilities, knowledge, values); or our Derivatives (embodiments, capacities, states). But the operative word, here, is "directly". For example, we can change our Knowledge person-characteristic by engaging in the behavior of reading books, talking with

---

[1]See Ossorio, *Clinical Topics*, *Positive Health and Transcendental Theories* (index: personal change, enlightenment), and *Personality and Personality Theories*, especially Appendixes I, II, and III.

other people, attending classes, travelling, thinking, or any of the other behaviors by which we acquire knowledge. Think of the person who reluctantly embarks on a mathematics course only because it is a required subject, and comes to love it: his new knowledge results in a new attitude and interest.

We can change our Ability person-characteristic by engaging in social practices by which we acquire new knowledge, skills, or motivations. Any of these will affect our values and our dispositions as well, if not our states. Wittingly or unwittingly, our person characteristics do change by virtue of our behavioral histories, and we can change them deliberately but not directly.

The Relationship Change Formula opens another path to personal change: "If F has a given relationship to G, but the behavior of F toward G is such that it violates that relationship but expresses some other relationship, then the relationship will change in the direction of the relationship for which the behavior that did occur would have been an appropriate expression". We can behave toward a stranger consistently and successfully in a friendly fashion, and eventually he may become a friend. That new relation reflects changes in our attitudes, values, knowledge, and so on. A hurt and terrified child is presented with a rollicking puppy, and in playing with a creature whom he is not afraid of, gradually his trait of fearfulness diminishes.

A special way of effecting relationship changes, called **Move 2's**, occurs fairly frequently, sometimes inadvertently and sometimes deliberately. Move 1 is an initial behavior in a social practice, a move that invites a continuation of that social practice. Thus we have the principle, *Move 1 invites Move 2*, and this is an ordinary, normal way of interacting. The Move 2 principle states that making *Move 2 makes it difficult for Move 1 not to have already taken place*. The simplest way to explicate the Move 2 principle is by an example.

Let us say that at a party, Bill relates an anecdote concerning his friend Betty, in her presence. That is a Move 1. The general reaction is laughter; that is the hearers' Move 2. Given the nature of the anecdote and the circumstances, however, Betty is insulted. The story constitutes a provocation and therefore elicits hostility. Her hostility constitutes her Move 2, and her being insulted makes it difficult for Bill's Move 1—telling the story—not to have been insulting. By insulting her, Bill has violated their friendly relationship, and the relationship is likely to change unless steps are taken to restore it.

In contrast, let us suppose that Bill intended the story to be insulting, but Betty took it as a joke. In that case, it is difficult for Bill not to have told it as a joke. In clinical applications of Descriptive Psychology, Move 2's are often used to defuse anger, prod a client into openness, encourage trust, and otherwise promote changes in him.

New circumstances—states of affairs—require new behavioral responses, and these can be agents of personal change. A move to another place will contribute to such changes, as will the loss or gain of a job, an accident or illness, marriage or divorce, the death of a person who is important to us, the sudden acquisition of wealth or descent into poverty, or any form of degradation or accreditation. Because such eventualities are occurring all the time, persons are continually changing in the natural course of events.

Paradigmatically, our history is continuous, punctuated by periods of sleep or unconsciousness, yet even our dreams and the facts involved in our having been asleep or unconscious contribute to our histories. Again paradigmatically, what kind of persons we already are is reflected in what we do, and in turn, what we do generates, over time, changes in who we are. Note that "what we do" includes how we treat the elements (objects, processes, events, states of affairs) in our worlds, whether as fragmentary bits and pieces or as parts of a coherent and comprehensive whole in which we have a secure place. That place corresponds to our personal version of a way of living: as a Seeker or Warrior or Lover; or a drop of water in an infinite ocean; or a link in the chain of a tradition; or a child of God; or a nonentity, a plaything of fate, a Victim.

---

We are where we are, continuous with our past but continually changing. However, the changes that the therapist or other Critic is most frequently concerned with are those that are directed away from pathology, or toward a perfection which we can approach more nearly than before even if we cannot achieve it totally. In the past, how did we move from where we were to where we are? How do we move now from where we are to where we are going to be? What does a therapist or other associate, or oneself, do as a Critic to help direct that movement?

He (or we) will do so both by understanding *where* we are, that is, by diagnosing our present position, and by clarifying the direction in which we are moving. He (or we) may also want to relate our Wants to the normal or perfection baseline. Perhaps we do not want to participate in current social practices because we prefer irresponsibility to the effort necessary for acquiring the attitudes and skills that we must have in order to participate in those practices. In that case, our direction is toward pathology. On the other hand, we may be rebelling intelligently and wisely—or stupidly or viciously—against those social practices themselves: we may be moving in either direction. Or we may be learning a skill that nothing to do with either the normality or the perfection baseline.

The Critic's own viewpoint and view will give him a basis on which to appraise our Wants. He will use whatever competence he has to evaluate not only Dispositions, but also what we Know, what our Abilities and Capacities are, and how our present and past Performances are correlated with our Wants and reasons. In some instances, he will set in motion an inquiry into our Embodiment: is there some physical anomaly that would delay or prevent our progress toward normality or perfection?

So much for the diagnostic part of the program, and it is the same when a Critic/therapist is meeting a client as when we as Critics are trying to amend ourselves as Actors, and whether the intervention is for the purpose of changing from pathology to normality, or from normal or above toward perfection. "Where is the Actor? What is his place in the world? What resources does he have?" And what resources does the Critic have to facilitate or induce change?

Possibly the most ambiguous resource in producing *personal* change—change of the whole person—toward normality or perfection is coercion, e.g., drugs, physical restraint or punishment, or incarceration, because coercion elicits resistance. Coercion has its uses in protecting the person from harming himself or others, and in providing a respite to prepare a person in an acute pathological state for other forms of therapy. Moreover, some pathological states seem to be permanently relieved by medication or other means that operate impersonally and causally. Certain religious traditions rely heavily on absolute submission to an authority, although often this constitutes a form of moral coercion which is as likely to eventuate in personal resistance as physical coercion does.

Most often, coercion constrains Performance, but not all direct and deliberate modifications of Performance are ineffective or deleterious. Take, for example, requiring a child to learn the multiplication table. If he learns the correct performance, he acquires a very useful skill.

The use, non-use, and misuse of language can be critical in changing persons. Innumerable attempts have been made to avoid or transcend the use of words by substituting "body-language"—posture, gesture, and facial expression—or music, art, or touch, but any of these can be mistakenly interpreted (just as a story or slogan or example can) unless verbal communication places them in a context and identifies clearly what is actually going on. A backward thrust of the head can mean assent or dissent. A drum-beat can constitute a growl of anger, an invitation to dance, or an importunate cry for help. Tears can express grief or the unexpected onset of joy. Think of how difficult it can be to tell why a baby is crying. Is it from hunger, discomfort, rage, frustration, loneliness, illness? A perceptive parent may be able to tell from the sound alone, or from the circumstances; anybody else will probably have to try a number of these possibilities before he pinpoints what was disturbing the infant.

Other non-verbal communications are less subtle—take the example of **Dinner at 8:30**. In the morning before Paul goes to work, he and his wife have an argument. When he comes home that night, dinner is ready at 8:30, and his wife serves him steak, well done, which might be the case in any of a hundred households in that community. However, normally Paul and his wife dine at seven and—as his wife knows very well—he likes his steak rare and detests it well done. This is non-verbal communication with a vengeance. Indeed, it *is* vengeance.

Non-verbal communication can be immensely revealing, and a smile, the touch of a hand, a belligerent posture, a straight right to the chin, can reinforce what is communicated by words. It is not by accident that in many religious traditions, and some non-religious ones, the laying on of hands is taken to have healing power, that friendly hugging has been recommended as therapy, and that music and art are increasingly used not only in treatment of pathological states, but also in furthering positive health—again see Winston Churchill's "Painting as a Pastime".

As a further point, almost invariably non-verbal communication modifies the verbal. Note the effect of rhythm and rhyme in reading prose as well as poetry; or in a telephone conversation, of tone of voice and the spoken rhythm or lack of it, of style of talking and use of silence; or in face-to-face conversation, of all these plus posture, gesture, eye-movement, and so on. Verbal and non-verbal language can work together in producing personal change, but the verbal is primary because without it the non-verbal can too easily be misunderstood.

---

Descriptive Psychology identifies nine elements in the systematic enterprise of bringing about personal change.

1. **General Practices**: (1) *Treat people as persons*; (2) *Legitimize*; and (3) *Be on the client's side*. At first glance these seem obvious. The client is not merely a case, not merely a Warrior, a mechanic, a Buddhist, or a wife, but a whole person. Always persons have reasons (K, W) for their deliberate actions, so whatever the person's behavior has been and is, it can be legitimized—which involves showing *what* sense it makes, not merely explaining, and certainly not merely excusing. However inappropriate or inadequate his behavior, it makes sense because it constitutes a participation in some social practice and involves reasons for engaging in that behavior rather than some other. Therefore the Critic (therapist, spiritual counsellor, friend, oneself) will be concerned that the Actor (patient, client, novice, oneself) shall understand what sense it makes.

Normatively, the Critic/therapist is on the client's side. They are working together for the client's benefit, to eliminate impediments to participation in current social practices, or to improve participation in those social practices. In such cases, the Critic/therapist is, in effect, substituting for what the client's own Critic should be doing.

Being on the client's side has one especially interesting ramification because it applies reflexively when a person is trying to change himself. In such a situation, it is not unusual for oneself as Critic to declare passionately, "I hate myself. I'm disgusted with my behavior. I can't stand being me". Oneself as Critic is denouncing oneself as Actor, and this particular provocation elicits hostility from the Actor as certainly when only one person is involved as when there are two or more. It is difficult, and perhaps impossible, for positive personal change to occur unless the Critic and Actor are on the same side, and very often one of the principal functions of a therapist or other counsellor—substituting for the client's Critic—is to take the side of a client who is excoriating himself unduly for his failures and sins, and thus working against himself in his effort to change.

2. **Specific Practices**—"Do these unless there is good reason not to"—encompass some of the ways for implementing the general policies. (1) *Don't buy Victim acts.* A person who sees himself as helpless turns himself into a non-Actor in crucial respects, and thus in effect cancels out that element in the feedback loop.

(2) Unless there is good reason not to, *use deliberate-action language rather than causal language to describe the client's behavior*, in order to remind the person that he *is* a person, and as a way of treating him as a person. Indeed, this is a Move 2, countering the Victim act. We did not become what we are entirely because our parents (community, education, etc.) were what they were, or because their parents were what they were, and so on in a causal (i.e., deterministic) chain going back to our earliest ancestors. At every stage in that sequence, every individual had available a set of options, and chose among them.

Looking back, we may feel as if we had no choice other than to act as we did. Nevertheless, the person looking back is the person who was in part created by that choice, and if imaginatively we now place ourselves where we were then, we can see that we did have alternatives at that time, just as when we look forward in the present moment, we see a number of possibilities before us. Further, even in situations where apparently we have no choice, it is we who are making that judgement and acting upon it.

(3) In order to minimize defensiveness and resistance, *give Activity rather than Deliberate Action descriptions*, that is, describe behavior in terms of Know, Know-how, Performance, and Achievement, omitting the Want parameter. In general, we are likely to be more defensive about our motivations than about the results of our actions; therefore we can see more easily what we are doing if we talk about those results rather than if our motives are challenged.

Two more specific policies are associated with not buying Victim acts. (4) Where there is a real choice between them, *choose anger over fear interpretations of behavior.* This is always formally possible, although not always plausible or desirable. The behavior associated with fear is escape from danger, but escaping from something is always, in a broad sense, moving away from it, and moving away from something can formally be redescribed as rejecting it, which is one form of anger behavior. Since in general we are acting from a position of greater power when we are angry than when we are afraid, the anger-description confirms us as Actors, and an Actor is in a better position than a Victim to act affirmatively and thereby to change.

(5) *Deal with the reality basis for emotions* rather than merely the experience or feeling, because it is the situation, not our feelings, that generates the problem. What is at stake is not feeling better, but being better off. When the lion walks into the room, our primary problem is to get away from the lion, not to cope with our fear. In principle, of course, dealing effectively with the reality basis by es-

caping the lion will also deal effectively with our fear, but not vice versa. We can eliminate our fear, perhaps by taking a *Happy Pill*, without in the least diminishing our danger from the lion.

3. Of the five **Influence Principles**, two have already been introduced in connection with Relationship Changes: Move 1 and Move 2. To restate these in their explicit form, (a) Making Move 1 invites Move 2—e.g., telling a joke invites laughter; insulting a person invites hostility. (b) Making Move 2 makes it difficult for Move 1 not to have already taken place—e.g., laughing at a story makes it difficult for the teller not to have told a joke, or being enraged at a story makes it difficult for the teller not to have been insulting. A shorter form of this is, "Move 2 creates Move 1 ex post facto", and the shortest form is, "Move 2 preempts Move 1". These last two forms open the way for those Move 2's where no Move 1 has been made at all, as when we volunteer, "Since you haven't said anything about it, I take it that — ", or "As you have already recognized, of course — ".

The third and fourth influence principles are mirror-images: (c) *Poisoning the Well* consists of redescribing a behavior in such a way as to evoke existing motivation to refrain from engaging in it ("You don't want to hurt him, but that's what you're doing"). (d) *Salting the Mine* redescribes the behavior in such a way as to evoke existing motivation to engage in it. Praise is a common form of Salting the Mine, blame a common form of Poisoning the Well, but there are others, as well. "That was an exceptionally creative move" is an example of the one, and "If you do it, you'll be sorry" for the other.

(e) **Providing Examples** is so rich in possibilities that they can only be hinted at here. It includes offering examples from history, fiction, or the Actor's or Critic's own experience. "See how so-and-so (possibly invented for the occasion) dealt with a similar problem." "Look at how differently you behave when you're with your mother than when you're with your sister."

Like all the preceding (and following) methods for personal change, examples and models can backfire. The Actor may extract from the instance some aspect that the Critic had not intended, like taking Francis of Assisi merely for his acceptances and not for his rebellions, or imitating a Performance in a way that does not reflect the Significance of the original. For this reason, it may be more productive to use short and very pointed illustrations, or images such as the Super-Critic, or the famous line attributed to Groucho Marx, "I wouldn't want to belong to any club that would accept me as a member", or the story of Dinner at 8:30. Some thirty or more images of this kind are standard among Descriptive Psychologists; the list could easily be lengthened.

4. The principal **Interactional Format** for personal change is ordinary conversation, supplemented when the occasion arises by such special formats as *soliloquies, confessions, three-minute lectures, provocations designed to elicit perplexity, pantomime, gesture,* and a number of others. A concise injunction will sometimes carry more weight if it is labelled "an old Spanish saying"; fictitious statistics can be introduced to make a point. And the conversation need not be face to face. Many of these interactional procedures can be used in an exchange of letters, or by a person carrying on a conversation with himself, perhaps on paper, even unto giving himself a three-minute (or three-page) lecture.

5. For **Diagnosis, Insight, and Action** we have *Images, Internal Dialogues,* and *Scenarios.* We have considered Images already, under Examples, but to add a few more, there are *the Two Mayors* up for election, one of whom intends to perform all the duties of a mayor, while the other expects to delegate all those chores—he just wants to *be* Mayor. There is the Guy with the Shovel, dig-

ging diligently into the past for a solution to his problems; the action, however, is not in the past; it is with the guy who is wielding the shovel; so *Keep Your Eye on the Guy with the Shovel*. And then there is the Poker Player image. The moral of his story is: if you want to become a better poker player, *You Have to* Be *a Poker Player*.

Giving *Internal Dialogues*, the therapist reconstructs for the client the train of thought that has led him from where he was to where he is now, or from where he is to where he is heading. A classic example starts with "I've got to be my unique self", and typically proceeds as follows:

To be my unique self, I've got to do unique things.

To do unique things and thus be my unique self, I can't do what other people do.

Neither can I do what other people *would* do.

What other people would do is to act from reasons; therefore, to be my unique self, I cannot act from reasons.

Since I cannot act from reasons and still be my unique self, therefore I have to act crazy.

But acting crazy is what anybody else would do in this situation, so even when I do that I am not being my unique self.

I've had it. Here is the end of the line. *Who am I?*[2]

At this culmination the individual is—or is going to be—in trouble. Obviously, not everyone follows this entire sequence, or carries an Internal Dialogue to its logical conclusion, but by reconstructing an Internal Dialogue, the therapist can illuminate for the client how his mind is working (diagnosis and insight), and suggest Exercises for his action.

A person functioning with a *Scenario* is co-opting

---

[2] See Ossorio, *Clinical Topics*, pp. 196-197, for an earlier version of this.

other people to play certain parts in his personal drama. One of the simpler examples is that of Terry, whose father (mother, wife, sibling, teacher, employer) has set the rules and assigned tasks for him. When Terry obeys the rules and accomplishes the tasks, he receives rewards and enjoys the relationship. When he turns this pattern into a Scenario, he makes a practice of finding other people to set rules and assign him tasks, so that he can receive rewards and enjoy the relationships. He becomes angry at those associates if they fail to play satisfactorily the parts he has assigned to him, and not infrequently they do refuse to play those roles. As before, this way to diagnose and to facilitate insight suggests what action can be taken toward change.

6. Actual change is brought about in many ways, of which one of the most important is the use of **Exercises** such as "Give yourself (or someone else) the benefit of the doubt", "Imagine in detail a perfect day", "Decriminalize what you (or they) are doing", and "Keep your eye on the ball" (that is, on what you are doing that is positive), and a number of others. Exercises require the client to engage in new behaviors, and thereby give him practice in behaving differently. As well, they sensitize him to elements in his life that he has not previously been sensitive to. For example, a Super-Critic who is instructed to give himself or others the benefit of the doubt, for a week, will almost certainly become aware of new possibilities in his relationships, and by acting on them, will begin to change toward being less censorious.

7. Among the **Slogans** are "Powerlessness corrupts", "If you can't afford to lose, you're a loser", "You can go broke buying insurance", and "It's not a communication problem; it's what you have to say to each other". These serve both for insight and for reminders: a person who is engaging in Victim behavior may well be shocked by "Powerlessness corrupts" into a fresh understanding of what he is doing, and the next time he plays Victim, his

remembering the slogan can help him onto the non-Victim track.

8. The **Heuristics** are parts of Descriptive Psychology that the therapist can teach a client in ten minutes or less (this is a practical limitation), and that work like Images or Exercises or both. The most frequently useful are the Emotion Formulas (e.g., provocation elicits hostile behavior), the Actor-Observer-Critic feedback loop, the Judgement Diagram, and displacement, but others have their uses as well. Often one of the maxims can be quoted to good effect, especially Maxims 1, 5, and 9. Occasionally the Justification Ladder, the Perspectives, and the Significance diamond can be brought in. However, the Behavior Formula, the State of Affairs System, and other of the more elaborate aspects of the conceptual system require more background for their explication than is usually warranted in therapy.

9. Finally, two **Principles of Interpretation** have to do with the significance of the behavior: *Drop the Details*, and *Don't Make Anything Up*. Dropping details makes it possible to discern the general pattern in the behavior, and that pattern is its significance. Is the client enacting a Scenario? Has he been carrying on an Internal Dialogue? Is he presenting himself as a Victim? Are his Move 2's of a consistent type, e.g., taking every Move 1 as an explicit or implicit attack? This is the primary positive principle for interpreting the significance of behavior. Significance, however, depends almost entirely on context. It is a part-whole relation that has little if anything to do with generalities.

Don't Make Anything Up is the negative injunction not to interpret wrongly by inserting hypothetical facts into the context: "He might have had this motive"; "This could have happened in his childhood"; "Maybe the event was more traumatic than he realizes". By providing suppositional contexts, we can give the behavior almost any significance, because in freely providing such contexts, there are few if any reality constraints.3

The temptation to make things up can be very great. Therefore the principle "Don't Make Anything Up" is a most salutary discipline upon our desire to make intelligible such facts as we have, and to complete the pattern even if we can do so only by inventing further, hypothetical facts. It is a natural tendency—order and meaning are basic human needs—but not all ways of satisfying that need are legitimate.

There is, however, a legitimate way by which we can bring in possible facts that go beyond what is observed. This is by openly relating the situation in question to some other, within the limits imposed by the reality constraints. We can say to a person, "Your reaction is much like the kind that one would have if he were trying to assuage a guilty conscience". Then we can check out whether the person has indeed something to feel guilty about, and whether what he is doing is a maneuver of that kind. Here, we are operating with the reality constraint that the original situation did indeed *look* as if the person were trying to assuage a guilty conscience. Therefore we are simply proposing a part-whole relationship between the individual case and a general pattern, as a way of exploring a possibility without imposing a pattern upon the individual.

---

The rule of personal change, that our behaviors are all that we can directly choose or change, emphasizes the systematic connections of behavior with person characteristics, and of both with the State of Affairs System. The Person Concept does nothing to minimize the sublety and complexity of actual persons and actual living. We have not had to resort to reductionism, or ad hoc formulations, or

---

3See Cannan, *The Taste of Murder*, for a series of delightful lessons on the perils of making things up.

prevenient theories to discern order and meaning in our personal lives, and in our individual and community relationships. Our perception of that order will guide us in choosing our behaviors and therefore, ultimately, in creating our own way of life.

# POSTSCRIPT

Now at the end of the book, we must return to its beginning, specifically to the definition of Descriptive Psychology as "a set of systematically related distinctions (concepts) designed to provide formal access to all the facts and possible facts about persons and behavior—and therefore to everything else as well". Here, all I have been able to present is a broad outline of how this can be—and is being—done. I hope, however, that it will encourage some to go further into Descriptive Psychology, by giving them access to the more detailed and technical works in that discipline, and enabling them to see what place those books and papers have in the system as a whole.

As a warning and reminder, the conceptual structures formulated in Descriptive Psychology are neither true nor false. Conceptual systems can no more be true—or false—than the rules or a game, or a numerical system, or a language can be true or false. Such systems may be apt; they may have instrumental value for various practical or theoretical purposes; they may have aesthetic value in increasing our understanding; and they may have other values. The Person Concept formulations have demonstrated all these virtues, but their greatest merit lies not in their particular instrumentalities, but in their intrinsic nature in developing our consciousness. They increase our sensitivity to whatever is going on, and that heightening of awareness is more important than the increase of information or skills.

It is not unlikely that with greater awareness we shall become more competent, just as the mastery of a numerical system can lead to competence in accounting or mathematical theory. But in the last analysis, the justification of the Person Concept formulation lies not in its applications, but in the coherence, inclusiveness, and elegance that enrich us as persons.

# APPENDIXES

## 1. Forms of Behavior Description

Agency (General Behavior) Description
I̶, W, K, KH, P, A, P̶C̶, S̶

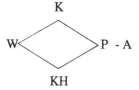

Activity Description
I̶, W̶, K, KH, P, A, P̶C̶, S

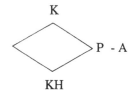

Performance Description
I̶, W̶, K̶, K̶H̶, P, A, P̶C̶, S̶

Achievement Description
I̶, W̶, K̶, K̶H̶, P̶, A, P̶C̶, S

Performative Description
I̶, W, K, KH, P, A̶, P̶C̶, S̶

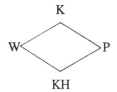

Stimulus-Response Description
 I̶, W̶, K, K̶H̶, P and/or A, P̶C̶, S̶

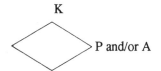

Cause-Effect Description
 I̶, W̶, K, K̶H̶, P, A, P̶C̶, S

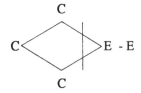

Purposive Description
 I̶, W̶, K̶, K̶H̶, P, A̶, P̶C̶, S

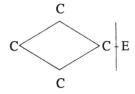

Cognizant Action Description
 I, W, 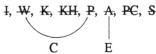, KH, P, A, PC, S

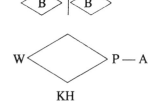

Deliberate Action Description
 I, 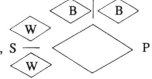, , KH, P, A, PC, S

Social Practice Description

I, W, K, KH, P, ⬦B̂⬦ , PC, S

$$W \diamond^{K}_{KH} P \quad - \quad \diamond^{K}_{KH} P \quad - \quad \diamond^{K}_{KH} P \quad - \quad \diamond^{K}_{KH}$$

Course of Action Description

$$W \diamond^{K}_{KH} P \quad - \quad \diamond^{K}_{KH} P \quad - \quad \diamond^{K}_{\overline{KH}} P \quad - \quad \diamond^{K}_{KH}$$

Symbolic Behavior Description

I, W, K, Kh, ⬦B⬦ , A, PC, S

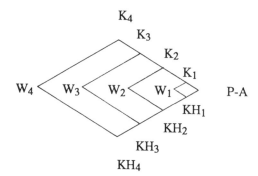

## 2. State of Affairs Transition Rules

1.  A state of affairs is a totality of related objects and/or processes and/or events and/or states of affairs.

2.  An object (or process or event or state of affairs) is a state of affairs which is a constituent of some other state of affairs.

3.  An object is a state of affairs having other, related objects as immediate constituents. (An object divides into related, smaller objects.)

4.  A process is a sequential change from one state of affairs to another.

5.  A process is a state of affairs having other, related processes as immediate constituents. (A process divides into related, sequential or parallel, smaller processes.)

6.  An event is a direct change from one state of affairs to another.

7.  An event is a state of affairs having two states of affairs (i.e., "before" and "after") as constituents.

8.  That a given state of affairs has a given relationship (e.g., succession, incompatibility, inclusion, common constituents, etc.) to a second state of affairs is a state of affairs.

8a. That a given object or process or event has a given relationship to another object or process or event is a state of affairs.

9. That a given object, process, event, or state of affairs is of a given kind is a state of affairs.

10. That an object or process begins is an event and that it ends is a different event.

10a. That an object or process occurs (begins and ends) is a state of affairs having three states of affairs ("before," "during," and "after") as constituents.

## 3. Articulation of the Person Concept

The following chart is designed not only to display the basic formulations of the Person Concept, but also to show how they are interrelated. The relationships, however, must be drawn in. That is, the chart should be used, not merely looked at. As an example of how to use it, on the chart (or a photocopy), draw the following lines:

Connect Knowledge (Person Characteristics box) with Know (Behavior box). What we know are States of Affairs, so connect Knowledge and Know with that box. Our knowledge of our current state of affairs is equivalent to what we know of our Circumstances (line to Judgement Diagram). Circumstances give us our Reasons, which are weighted by our Person Characteristics, so connect Reasons to Person Characteristics in both PC and Behavior boxes. More lines will connect Reasons with the Justification Ladder, and both these to the Perspectives, and the Perspectives to the Values (PC box) and Want (Behavior box). And so on indefinitely.

Start anywhere and see where it leads. Draw the relationships in so that you can see the network of connections. This is merely an exercise, but for some people it has proved to be an illuminating one.

# ARTICULATION OF THE PERSON CONCEPT

## PERSON CHARACTERISTICS

| Dispositions | Powers | Derivatives |
|---|---|---|
| Traits | Abilities | Embodiment |
| Attitudes | Knowledge | Capacities |
| Interests | Values | States |
| Style | | |

**Behavior** = Intentional Action = <I, W, K, KH, P, A, PC, S>

[Identity, Want, Know, Know-how, Performance, Achievement, Person Characteristics, Significance]

[I parameter = Identification, PC parameter = characterization]

### STATE OF AFFAIRS
### CONCEPTUAL SYSTEM

Objects
Processes
Events
States of Affairs
Relationships

Relationship
Formula

Status Dynamics
Self Concept
Behavior Potential

### LANGUAGE

Concept    Locution    Behavior

**Justification Ladder**

Perspective
Competence
—
Principle
Theory
Custom
Judgement

**Perspectives**

Hedonic
Prudential
Ethical
Esthetic
artistic
intellectual
social
(spiritual?)

## Significance (Symbolic) Behavior Diagram

**Actor, Observer/Describer,**
**Critic/Appraiser Feedback Loop**

**The Diamond**

**Transition Rules**

**Basic Descriptive Units**

**Judgement Diagram**

C = Circumstances
R = Reasons
W = Weights

D = Decision
J = Judgement

## 4. Maxims for Behavior Description

Maxim 1: A person takes it that things are as they seem, unless he has reason to think otherwise.

Maxim 2: If a person recognizes an opportunity to get what he wants, he has a reason to try to get it.

Maxim 3: If a person has a reason to do something, he will do it unless he has a stronger reason not to.

Maxim 4: If a person has two or more reasons for doing X, he has a stronger reason for doing X than if he had only one of those reasons.

Maxim 5: If a situation calls for a person to do something he cannot do, he will do something he can do—if he does anything at all.

Maxim 6: A person acquires facts by observation (ultimately) and by thought (secondarily).

Maxim 7: A person acquires concepts and skills by practice and experience in one or more social practices which involve the use of the concept or the exercise of the skill.

Maxim 8: If a person has a given personal characteristic, he acquired it in one of the ways it can be acquired, i.e., by having the relevant prior capacity and the appropriate intervening history.

Maxim 9. Given the relevant competence, behavior goes right if it does not go wrong in one of the ways that it can go wrong.

# REFERENCES

Where a book or article has been republished, I give the publication data for the most recent source, with the date of the earliest publication in parentheses after the principal citation. Material of special interest to computer scientists is marked with an asterisk.

Aylesworth, Lawrence S. and Ossorio, Peter G. "Refugees: Cultural Displacement and Its Effects," in *Advances in Descriptive Psychology*, Vol. 3, eds. Keith E. Davis and Thomas O. Mitchell. Greenwich, Conn.: JAI Press, 1983.

Baker, Eugene M. "Therapeutic Social Practices," in *Advances in Descriptive Psychology*, Vol. 2, eds. Keith E. Davis and Thomas O. Mitchell. Greenwich, Conn.: JAI Press, 1982.

Bergner, Raymond M. "Emotions: A Conceptual Formulation and Its Clinical Implications," in *Advances in Descriptive Psychology*, Vol. 3, eds. Keith E. Davis and Raymond M. Bergner. Greenwich, Conn.: JAI Press, 1983.

Bergner, Raymond M. "Hysterical Action, Impersonation, and Caretaking Roles: A Descriptive and Practical Study," in *Advances in Descriptive Psychology*, Vol. 2, eds. Keith E. Davis and Thomas O. Mitchell. Greenwich, Conn.: JAI Press, 1982.

Bergner, Raymond M. "Marital Conflict Resolution: A Conceptual Framework and Its Empirical Evaluation," in *Advances in Descriptive Psychology*, Vol. 1, ed. Keith E. Davis. Greenwich, Conn.: JAI Press, 1981.

Bergner, Raymond M. "The Overseer Regime: A Descriptive and Practical Study," in *Advances in Descriptive Psychology*, Vol. 1, ed. Keith E. Davis. Greenwich, Conn.: JAI Press, 1981.

Bergner, Raymond M. "Paranoid Style: A Descriptive and Pragmatic Account," in *Advances in Descriptive Psychology*, Vol. 4, eds.

Keith E. Davis and Thomas O. Mitchell. Greenwich, Conn.: JAI Press, 1985.

Buchan, John. *The Three Hostages*. Penguin Books, 1953 (1924).

Cannan, Joanna. *The Taste of Murder*. New York: Dover Publications, 1987 (1950).

Churchill, Winston. "Painting as a Pastime," in *Amid These Storms*. New York: Charles Scribner's Sons, 1932.

Driscoll, Richard. "Policies for Pragmatic Psychotherapy," in *Advances in Descriptive Psychology*, Vol. 1, ed. Keith E. Davis. Greenwich, Conn.: JAI Press, 1981.

Driscoll, Richard. *Pragmatic Psychotherapy*. New York: Van Nostrand, 1984.

Farber, Allan. "Castaneda's Don Juan as Psychotherapist," in *Advances in Descriptive Psychology*, Vol. 1, ed. Keith E. Davis. Greenwich, Conn.: JAI Press, 1981.

Garfinkle, H. "Conditions of Successful Degradation Ceremonies," in *Symbolic Interaction: A Reader in Social Psychology*, eds. J. G. Maris and B. H. Meltzer. Boston: Allyn and Bacon, 1967.

*Guertin, Elizabeth A. "Overwhelming Evidence," in *Digital Review*, Vol. 2, No. 8, May 1985.

*Jeffrey, H. Joel. "Knowledge Engineering: Theory and Practice," in *Advances in Descriptive Psychology*, Vol. 5, eds. Keith E. Davis and Anthony O. Putman. Greenwich, Conn.: JAI Press, 1988.

*Jeffrey, H. Joel. "A New Paradigm for Artificial Intelligence," in *Advances in Descriptive Psychology*, Vol. 1, ed. Keith E. Davis. Greenwich, Conn,: JAI Press, 1981.

*Jeffrey, H. Joel and Putman, Anthony O. "The Mentor Project: Replicating the Functions of an Organization," in *Advances in Descriptive Psychology*, Vol. 3, eds. Keith E. Davis and Thomas O. Mitchell. Greenwich, Conn.: JAI Press, 1983.

Kirsch, Ned L. . "Attempted Suicide and Restrictions in the Eligibility to Negotiate Personal Characteristics," in *Advances in Descriptive Psychology*, Vol. 2, eds. Keith E. Davis and Thomas O. Mitchell. Greenwich, Conn.: JAI Press, 1982.

Lasater, Lane. "Stress and Health in a Colorado Coal Mining Community," in *Advances in Descriptive Psychology*, Vol. 3, eds. Keith E. Davis and Raymond M. Bergner. Greenwich, Conn.: JAI Press, 1983.

Lewis, C. S. *The Abolition of Man*. New York: The Macmillan Company, 1947.

Littmann, Jane R. "A New Formulation of Humor," in *Advances in*

*Descriptive Psychology*, Vol. 3, eds. Keith E. Davis and Thomas O. Mitchell. Greenwich, Conn.: JAI Press, 1983.

Millay, Edna St. Vincent. "Sonnet to Gath," in *Collected Poems*, New York: Harper & Row, 1955 (1928).

*Mitchell, Thomas O. "On the Interpretation of Utterances," in *Advances in Descriptive Psychology*, Vol. 1, ed. Keith E. Davis. Greenwich, Conn.: JAI Press, 1981.

Morgan, Charles. *The Fountain*. New York: Alfred A. Knopf, 1932.

Morgan, Charles. *Sparkenbroke*. London: Macmillan & Co., Ltd., 1936.

Morgan, Charles. *The Voyage*. New York: Ballantine Books, 1987 (1940).

Orvik, James M. "A Conceptual Model for Migration in Alaska," in *Advances in Descriptive Psychology*, Vol. 4, eds. Keith E. Davis and Thomas O. Mitchell. Greenwich, Conn.: JAI Press, 1985.

Orvik, James M. "The Diffusion of Technology across Cultures," in *Advances in Descriptive Psychology*, Vol. 5, eds. Keith E. Davis and Anthony O. Putman. Greenwich, Conn.: JAI Press, 1988.

Ossorio, Peter G. "Appraisal," in *Advances in Descriptive Psychology*, Vol. 5, eds. Keith E. Davis and Anthony O. Putman. Greenwich, Conn.: JAI Press, 1988.

Ossorio, Peter G. *Clinical Topics: A Seminar in Descriptive Psychology* (LRI Report No. 11). Whittier, Calif. and Boulder, Colo.: Linguistic Research Institute, 1976.

Ossorio, Peter G. *Cognition* (LRI Report No. 32). Boulder, Colo.: Linguistic Research Institute, 1982.

Ossorio, Peter G. "Conceptual-Notational Devices," in *Advances in Descriptive Psychology*, Vol. 1, ed. Keith E. Davis. Greenwich, Conn.: JAI Press, 1981 (1979).

Ossorio, Peter G. "Embodiment," in *Advances in Descriptive Psychology*, Vol. 2, eds. Keith E. Davis and Thomas O. Mitchell. Greenwich, Conn.: JAI Press, 1982 (1980).

Ossorio, Peter G. "Explanation, Falsifiability, and Rule-Following," in *Advances in Descriptive Psychology*, Vol. 1, ed. Keith E. Davis. Greenwich, Conn.: JAI Press, 1981 (1967).

Ossorio, Peter G. *Ex Post Facto: The Source of Intractable Origin Problems and Their Solution* (LRI Report No. 28a). Boulder, Colo.: Linguistic Research Institute, 1981.

*Ossorio, Peter G. *Meaning and Symbolism* (LRI Report No. 15). Boulder, Colo.: Linguistic Research Institute, 1978 (1969).

Ossorio, Peter G. "A Multicultural Psychology," in *Advances in Descriptive Psychology*, Vol. 3, eds. Keith E. Davis and

Raymond M. Bergner. Greenwich, Conn.: JAI Press, 1983 (1981).

Ossorio, Peter G. "Notes on Behavior Description," in *Advances in Descriptive Psychology*, Vol. 1, ed. Keith E. Davis. Greenwich, Conn.: JAI Press, 1981 (1967).

Ossorio, Peter G. "Outline of Descriptive Psychology for Personality Theory and Clinical Applications," in *Advances in Descriptive Psychology*, Vol. 1, ed. Keith E. Davis. Greenwich, Conn.: JAI Press, 1981 (1970).

Ossorio, Peter G. "An Overview of Descriptive Psychology," in *The Social Construction of the Person*, eds. Kenneth J. Gergen and Keith E. Davis. New York: Springer-Verlag, 1985 (1984).

Ossorio, Peter G. "Pathology," in *Advances in Descriptive Psychology*, Vol. 4, eds. Keith E. Davis and Thomas O. Mitchell. Greenwich, Conn.: JAI Press, 1985 (1983).

Ossorio, Peter G. *Personality and Personality Theories: A Seminar in Descriptive Psychology* (LRI Report No. 16). Whittier, Calif. and Boulder, Colo.: Linguistic Research Institute, 1978.

Ossorio, Peter G. *Persons* (LRI Report No. 3). Los Angeles, Calif. and Boulder, Colo.: Linguistic Research Institute, 1966.

Ossorio, Peter G. *Place* (LRI Report No. 30a). Boulder: Linguistic Research Institute, 1982.

Ossorio, Peter G. *Positive Health and Transcendental Theories: A Seminar in Descriptive Psychology* (LRI Report No. 13). Whittier, Calif. and Boulder, Colo.: Linguistic Research Institute, 1977.

Ossorio, Peter G. *Religion without Doctrine* (LRI Report No. 19), Boulder, Colo.: Linguistic Research Institute, 1978.

Ossorio, Peter G. "Representation, Evaluation, and Research," in *Advances in Descriptive Psychology*, Vol. 1, ed. Keith E. Davis. Greenwich, Conn.: JAI Press, 1981. (1980)

Ossorio, Peter G. *Rule-Following in Grammar and Behavior* (LRI Report No. 7). Los Angeles, Calif. and Boulder, Colo.: Linguistic Research Institute, 1967.

*Ossorio, Peter G. *State of Affairs Systems: Theory and Technique for Automatic Fact Analysis* (LRI Report No. 14). Whittier, Calif. and Boulder, Colo.: Linguistic Research Institute, 1978 (1971).

Ossorio, Peter G. *Three-Minute Lectures on Emotion* (LRI Report No. 36A). Boulder, Colo.: Linguistic Research Institute, 1986.

Ossorio, Peter G. *"What Actually Happens": The Representation of Real-World Phenomena.* Columbia: University of South Carolina Press, 1978 (1971).

Ossorio, Peter G. and Schneider, L. W. *Decisions and Decision Aids* (LRI Report No. 31). Boulder, Colo.: Linguistic Research Institute, 1982.

Plotkin, William. "Consciousness," in *Advances in Descriptive Psychology*, Vol. 1, ed. Keith E. Davis. Greenwich, Conn.: JAI Press, 1981.

Plotkin, William B. and Schwartz, Wynn R. "A Conceptualization of Hypnosis: I. Exploring the Place of Appraisal and Anomaly in Behavior and Experience," in *Advances in Descriptive Psychology*, Vol. 2, eds. Keith E. Davis and Thomas O. Mitchell. Greenwich, Conn.: JAI Press, 1982.

Plotkin, William B. and Schwartz, Wynn R. "A Conceptualization of Hypnosis, II: Hypnotic Induction Procedures and Manifestations of the Hypnotic State," in *Advances in Descriptive Psychology*, Vol. 4, eds. Keith E. Davis and Thomas O. Mitchell. Greenwich, Conn.: JAI Press, 1985.

*Putman, Anthony O. "Artificial Persons," in *Advances in Descriptive Psychology*, Vol. 5, eds. Keith E. Davis and Anthony O. Putman. Greenwich, Conn.: JAI Press, 1988.

Putman, Anthony O. "Communities," in *Advances in Descriptive Psychology*, Vol. 1, ed. Keith E. Davis. Greenwich, Conn.: JAI Press, 1981.

Putman, Anthony O. "Organizations," in *Advances in Descriptive Psychology*, Vol. 5, eds. Keith E. Davis and Anthony O. Putman. Greenwich, Conn.: JAI Press, 1988.

*Putman, Anthony O. and Jeffrey, H. Joel. "A New Paradigm for Software and Its Development," in *Advances in Descriptive Psychology*, Vol. 4, eds. Keith E. Davis and Thomas O. Mitchell. Greenwich, Conn.: JAI Press, 1985.

Raines, John C. "Righteous Resistance and Martin Luther King, Jr.," in *The Christian Century*, Vol. 101, No. 2, Jan. 18, 1954.

Roberts, Mary K. "I and Thou: A Study of Personal Relationships," in *Advances in Descriptive Psychology*, Vol. 4, eds. Keith E. Davis and Thomas O. Mitchell. Greenwich, Conn.: JAI Press, 1985.

Roberts, Mary K. "Men and Women: Partners, Lovers, Friends," in *Advances in Descriptive Psychology*, Vol. 2, eds. Keith E. Davis and Thomas O. Mitchell. Greenwich, Conn.: JAI Press, 1982.

Roberts, Mary K. "Worlds and World Reconstruction," in *Advances in Descriptive Psychology*, Vol. 4, eds. Keith E. Davis and Thomas O. Mitchell. Greenwich, Conn.: JAI Press, 1985.

Schwartz, Wynn R. "The Problem of Other Possible Persons: Dolphins, Primates, and Aliens," in *Advances in Descriptive Psychology*,

Vol. 2, ed. Keith E. Davis and Thomas O. Mitchell. Greenwich, Conn.: JAI Press, 1982.

Shideler, Mary McDermott. "The Creator and the Discoverer," in *Advances in Descriptive Psychology*, Vol. 2, ed. Keith E. Davis and Thomas O. Mitchell, 1982.

Shideler, Mary McDermott. "The Lover and the Logician," in *Advances in Descriptive Psychology*, Vol. 1, ed. Keith E. Davis. Greenwich, Conn.: JAI Press, 1981.

Shideler, Mary McDermott. "The Priest and the Psychotherapist," in *Advances in Descriptive Psychology*, Vol 3, eds. Keith E. Davis and Raymond M. Bergner. Greenwich, Conn.: JAI Press, 1983.

Shideler, Mary McDermott. "The Psychologist and the Theologian," in *Dialog*, Vol. 17, No. 3, Summer 1978.

Shideler, Mary McDermott. "Science, Religion, and Religions," in *Advances in Descriptive Psychology*, Vol. 4, eds. Keith E. Davis and Thomas O. Mitchell. Greenwich, Conn.: JAI Press, 1985.

Shideler, Mary McDermott. "Spirituality: The Descriptive Psychology Approach," in *Advances in Descriptive Psychology*, Vol. 5, eds. Keith E. Davis and Anthony O. Putman. Greenwich, Conn.: JAI Press, 1988.

Silva, Joseph C. "What Actually Happens to José: Cultural Displacement in a Predominantly Anglo University," in *Advances in Descriptive Psychology*, Vol. 3, eds. Keith E. Davis and Thomas O. Mitchell. Greenwich, Conn.: JAI Press, 1983.

Tolkien, J. R. R. "On Fairy-Stories," in *Essays Presented to Charles Williams*. London: Oxford University Press, 1947.

Torres, Walter J. "Puerto Rican and Anglo Conceptions of Appropriate Mental Health Services," in *Advances in Descriptive Psychology*, Vol. 3, eds. Keith E. Davis and Raymond Bergner. Greenwich, Conn.: JAI Press, 1983.

Vanderburgh, Jan. "The Positive-Health Developmental Model," in *Advances in Descriptive Psychology*, Vol. 3, eds. Keith E. Davis and Thomas O. Mitchell. Greenwich, Conn.: JAI Press, 1983.

Vanderburgh, Jan. "The Positive-Health Developmental Model of Treatment and Psychopathology," in *Advances in Descriptive Psychology*, Vol. 4, eds. Keith E. Davis and Anthony O. Putman. Greenwich, Conn.: JAI Press, 1985.

*Zeiger, H. Paul. "Human Systems Issues in Software Engineering," in *Advances in Descriptive Psychology*, Vol. 5, eds. Keith E. Davis and Anthony O. Putman. Greenwich, Conn.: JAI Press, 1988.

# INDEX

Mary McDermott Shideler is an independent scholar living in the mountains above Boulder, Colorado. She is the author of seven books and of numerous articles, most of them published in professional journals, and is a past president of the Society for Descriptive Psychology and of the American Theological Society (Midwest Division). Since 1973, she has been working closely with Peter G. Ossorio, professor of psychology at the University of Colorado in Boulder and the founder of Descriptive Psychology.